Little School by the Freeway

An Anthology of Narratives, Essays and Short Stories by
Students and Teachers at Houston Academy for
International Studies

Little School by the Freeway: An Anthology of Narratives, Essays and Short Stories by Students and Teachers at Houston Academy for International Studies

Houston Academy for International Studies
1810 Stuart Street
Houston, TX 77004

Classroom Teachers: Neelam Damani, Robbi Russey-Goldstein, Lindsay Duet

Cover Art: Savannah Tibbits, Yuliya Tkachenko

DEDICATED TO:

The Class of 2013

at Houston Academy for International Studies

ACKNOWLEDGMENTS

This publication would not have been possible without help from the following individuals:

Editors:

Kesley Rodriguez

Emma Shahriari

Cover Artists:

Savannah Tibbits

Yuliya Tkachenko

Table of Contents

11th Grade Submissions:

My Dad   **11**
By Carlos Alarcon

Moments In Life Will Always Be Treasured   **13**
By Lourdes Amaya

A Dream Not To Remember!   **16**
By Lauren Anderson

Teacher   **19**
By Angelica Arriaga

Think Before You Act   **23**
By Jazzlyn Ary

Rocks Of Power: A Re-Telling Of Adventures...   **26**
By Gabriel Bailey

Life Is Short   **29**
By Amadi Shani Barrett

Ball Game!   **32**
By Martin Bautista

Profile Narrative   **35**
By Rivan Bennevendo

Life Is A Stage, Own It   **39**
By Jazmine Borden

Mexican Christmas   **42**
By Hadie Boul

Lerconya Pelrean: Being A Mom   **45**
By Breanna' Briscoe

Never Say Never   **48**
By Valencia Brown

First Day Of School   **51**
By Paris Bullock

Isabel Marie Blanco   **54**
By Noemi Bustamante

Untitled   **57**
By Noemi Bustamante

A Bitter Memory   **59**
By Brenda Cabrera

Peter Kurtz   **62**
By Jose Cantu

The Unspoken Goodbye   **66**
By Amber Beltran

C'est La Vie   **69**
By Rea Clemons

A Sister's Life   **73**
By Israel Cordova

Unwanted   **76**
By Unique Crumby

Goal! — 79
By David Cruz

My Vacation In New York City — 82
By Carlos Davy

Dangers Of A Trail — 85
By Anibal Delgado

A Walk Down Memory Lane — 88
By James Deshazor

Six String Journey — 91
By Frank Eldreth

A Change Will Come — 94
By Logan Eythell

Relationship Blues — 97
By Calvin Fitzgerald

I See The Golden Mountaintops... — 100
By Calvin Fitzgerald

The Knowledge Giver — 102
By Ryan Garner

Our Story — 105
By Juan Granados

Fifth Grade Bully — 108
By Mikeila Grant

The Profile Of Nicole Owen — 111
By Andrew Griffin

He Promised — 114
By Erika Gudiño

Untitled — 116
By Destini Hall-Duncan

A Life In A Day   118
By James Harvey

Longing For My Father   121
By Arlette Henderson

Papa Veto   124
By Airam Hernandez

Never Give Up On What You Love   127
By Ashley Hernandez

Singing Makes A Difference Too!   131
By Markiesha Hurst

From Singapore To The Best Role Model   134
By Emily Jackson

First Day Of Kindergarten   138
By Destiny James

Different Faces, Different Places   142
By Xzavier Jelks

My Own Room   145
By Tychenellia M. Jernigan

Underneath It All   148
By Alysia Johnson

A Grandmother's Love   151
By Ashley Johnson

My Dad   155
By Altaniece Jones

Mi Abuelita   158
By Nazreen Kashani

The System   162
By Clare Legg

Untitled   **165**
By Ashondra Lewis

Untitled   **168**
By Juan Lopez

Old Friend   **172**
By Juan Lopez

First Glance   **174**
By Juan Lopez

He Is My Brother   **175**
By Marylu Lopez

A Flip Of A Coin   **178**
By David Lujan

O Bong Cua Su Cong Hien   **182**
By Joseph Mabasa

Untitled   **186**
By Lauren Macedo

The Silent Bond   **187**
By Jazmen Massie

Peace Be Still   **190**
By Denae Maxie

My Rock   **193**
By Nia Mccardell

Una Mente De La Culpa Y Rosie...   **196**
By Nia Mccardell

The Last Angel   **201**
By Kaelin Mccoppy

A Moment For Life   **206**
By Remington Mcknight

Locked Up 209
By David Mondragon

Interviewing Enriqueta Najera 212
By Lorenza Najera

Có Anh – The Personality Of A Majestic Antelope 216
By Jonathan Nguyen

I Remember 219
By Cydney O'neal

Thank You, Dad 223
By Vanessa Ordonez

A Day At The Con 226
By Nicole Owen

Perception: In A New Light 233
By Gabriel Pena

Talent Show: Rap 236
By Gabriel Pena

Untitled 238
By Hailey Phillips

Poem 242
By Filipa Ribeirinho

The Perfectly Imperfect Side Of Me 243
By Alba Rios

Interview With Batman 247
By Israel Rodriguez

Not An Option 251
By Kesley Rodriguez

Oil 256
By Maya Rueda De Leon

Temporary Situation   259
By Genevieve Sandoval

Dedication At Its Prime   263
By Angelica Scales

My Lifesaver   266
By Jonathon Schnur

Adieu   268
By Emma Shahriari

Untitled   271
By Emma Shahriari

A Plucked Flower   275
By Kamry Stewart

Grandpa Teacher   277
By Savannah Tibbits

All Is Fleeting, All Will Go...   280
By Yuliya Tkachenko

Memories   283
By Yitzel Vazquez

Profile Of A Sarcastic Girl   286
By Marianne Vina

Untitled   290
By Giavanni Walker

Take The Time   293
By Jasmine Washington

Unspoken Feelings   296
By Brittney Winston

Because It Matters   300
By Sierra Wood

A Cold Room   **304**
By Sierra Wood

Journey To Inspiration   **307**
By Janiecé York

9th Grade Submissions:

Promoting Religious Tolerance ...   **310**
By Roberto Daniel Conlon

Untitled   **312**
By Brittany Gilbert

Hello Goodbye   **313**
By Rynique Lucas

Just Give Up   **315**
By Rynique Lucas

No More   **316**
By Rynique Lucas

The Meeting   **317**
By Akhirah Muhammad

The Confessions   **319**
By Akhirah Muhammad

Timed Writing   **321**
By Angus Niziol

Script Of Biography   **322**
By Angus Niziol

Teacher Submissions:

Is War Necessary?   **325**
By Neelam Damani

The Silent Companion   **327**
By Neelam Damani

Token... Black Guy...   **329**
By Jeremy Jjemba

Discovering Africa   **331**
By Jeremy Jjemba

The Pen And The Paper   **332**
By Jeremy Jjemba

Paranoid Style Of The Rosenberg Trial   **333**
By Peter Kurtz

I Am   **339**
By Chad Meyer

Light Ray   **340**
By Ralph Polley

Pauline   **344**
By Robbi Russey-Goldstein

Table 43   **350**
By Robbi Russey-Goldstein

MY DAD
by Carlos Alarcon

Beep, beep I could hear my alarm going off, but didn't really pay attention to it. I thought to myself "five more minutes." Without notice my dad opens the door

to my room saying "their times to go were going to be late". All I could think was this I going to be a long day. It was a very cold morning down in the mid 40's. My body was begging for it to go back to bed under my warm covers, but my dad was already making his cup of coffee so we could hit the pavement.

I came staggering off from the restroom into the kitchen were my dad had two cups of coffee one for me and for him. I could see the steam coming of my cup. I grab it and hurry of to the truck where my dad had already loaded everything on and was sitting there with his hands already on the keys. I could see there was ice particles on the windshield from the freezing rain my dad had already taken off his side could see my dad was ready to go to work rain or snow to make sure we wouldn't need anything. My dad has always been a hard worker always has to have everything done in time. He has always woken up at six am to make his morning cup of coffee rain or snow everyday for the longest I can remember.

He always comes home around six or five with a dirty pair of work boots and with his worn out trusty ford hat he always carry's around. Every time I see him come off his dark green I see him tired and frustrated after the long day he has had ,but as soon as he steps up the stair leading to our house it's like he shrugs off his tiredness' and frustrations. First thing he does every time he walks in to the house is put his dusty hat on nail over the keys place and sit down to whatever meal my mom has already for him. My dad is a very caring to us whenever we need something he always tries to accomplish it for us. \

When I'm with my dad he sends out a sense of safety that makes me feel safe and protected. My dad is not very tall men he's 5,6 at the most with a beer belly sticking out his body like a sore thumb. He has greens that seem to change colored from green to blue depending on his clothes. He loves wearing cowboy boots with his old cowboy hat that makes him look like if he's going to the rodeo. My dad always takes us out to have fun as family I really enjoy spending time with him I also see the joy we bring upon him when were all together eating out playing around.

When I asked him what was he most proud off he told me it was his family? He said he was very proud to have his family together vent ought we all might have our differentness from time to time. Every Sunday he reserves it for us even if he might have pending work. . That would do anything in his power to help his family out. In his mindset the most important thing he has in his life is his family. He works v every day to bring food to our table and keep roof over our heads without wanting anything in return, but our love and gratitude.

MOMENTS IN LIFE WILL ALWAYS BE TREASURED
by Lourdes Amaya

I had been waiting my whole life, I have been saving up and wanting for this big day to come since I was a little girl; well that day was finally here. It was my big day, the day I can finally do anything and become the lady I want to be, with the ones I love, and treasure all the pleasurable moments we've had it was my day to shine and to have fun and to show everyone I was all grown up.

It was 6 a.m. supper excited ready to get my day started, ready to finally begin what I've been wanting the most in my whole life. Mom, I said; "it's time it's finally here it's the time I been wanting the most wake up wake up there's so much to do!" My mom replied;"ok its time! Call everyone so we can leave so get everything ready." We were all getting ready and went our separate ways. The guys to get a haircut and the girls did their hair and make-up. I couldn't believe I couldn't believe that I was here in hair salon lady on a chair doing my hair and make-up and everyone watching me all happy and excited also couldn't wait for me to get blessed of becoming a lady and having my day.

As soon as I got home I hurried to my room putting my beautiful dress on. Hurrying to get my pictures taken by the photographer. As Soon as we were done I heard my uncle say: "its 2 in the afternoon the limo is here time to head out to the church" While we were getting inside the limo we were getting inside the limo were already having fun. My family and I were headed to the church for my religious ceremony where I received my three most important blessed items for my Quinceanera. The Church Guadalupe was where we all met. Happy all in tears and wishing me the best, my family was proud. My grandma came up and said "Te deseo lo major en estos dias tu quince te amo mija" I felt really happy that I wanted to cry because my grandma has always been there for me since I was little girl and now I, on the stage where I'm all grown up .So now was the time for the pastor to bless me and for my godparents to give me my gifts for the mass which were the bible, the cross , and the rosary, they all symbolize a meaning of a stage of growing up to being a lady, in other words the bible means that Is that I keep the word of God in her life, the cross is a reminder that of faith that they'll hell be there for you and the rosary means a prayer and at last were given flowers that means that we offer to Virgin of Guadalupe. Church to me was the one that meant a lot because I had all my all my family next to me by my side blessing me also on that special day of mine.

Getting blessed at church was a meaning to the church and to everyone else that I will be responsible and a young lady who will continue in life as a lady. It's been times where I wasn't happy about the things I've had but it was for my good it was the time of my life for me to have fun with friends and family. It was already the night the night to shine and show how I move and show everyone what I can do in the dance since everyone knew I was shy, but most of all I was excited to have my time with my dad and cry out our memories with tears of joy and sadness because everyone knew that since I was a little girl I had always been daddy's little girl and this day was the day we actually cried it out and had our moment, even though we have rough times and go through things he will always be my dad and I will always be his little princess.

To me the day of my quince meant a lot best because it was a night to remember and will always stay with you. Especially because no matter how much times passes that love will always stay with you especially the big memories. One of the most memorable moments was when I had the traditional dance with my father. After we danced he took me aside and he told me how proud he was of me. I was happy that I had time with my dad and cry out our memories with tears of joy and sadness. Everyone knew that I had always been daddy's little girl, and this day was when we actually cried it out and had our time together. Even though sometimes we have had our rough times and went through things he will always be my dad and I will always be his little princess, and as the night ended, that is just how I felt at the end of this wonderful day. A moment in life that can be treasured forever!

A DREAM NOT TO REMEMBER!
by Lauren Anderson

I saw a dark castle with a tall, black gate, blocking me from exiting. Since I couldn't get out, I had no other choice than to go inside the horrifying castle. As I opened the gigantic, black, wooden door, it screeched extremely loud causing my ears to quiver with an enormous amount pain. I continued on my journey, walking down the hall with a light hovering over my head. Left, Right, Left, Left, Right, the light continuously followed my confusing steps not missing a beat. It seemed to know every step I took before I officially took it. THUD, THUD, THUD, the walls banged. With every step I took, I became more terrified for what awaited me at the end of the hallway. I walked for seem like hours, but just as I decided to give up I saw a door. The door contained some similarities to the one at the entrance only difference noticeable was a heart engraved in the center of it. The irregular heart splits into two pieces with a serpent tighten around it in front of my very eyes. I think it was trying to mend the hearts back together or something. I really didn't know what it was doing, but something was urging me to go through the door. It was like a supernatural force trying to pull me inside of its den or sacred ground. I reached out slowly for the knob but before my hand could even touched it, the door swung open fast. I walked inside the dark area with light over my head disappearing, but I still could see a little. Then I saw the most disgusting creature alive about to swallow YOU whole! I yelled as loud as I could 'Get off my mom, you you monster' hoping the creature would release you and come after me but nothing. The creature gazed into my eyes with his red ones. I caught his gaze trying to be strong. Then suddenly I felt a warm liquid flowing down my pants. I kept my eyes on him ready to fight as hard as I could if necessary and then the un-thinkable happened. The dreaded creature transformed into a serpent coiling around your body like it was going to suffocate you. It continued coiling your body from the body up until it reached your head, it then started to tighten its grip on your body. The snake, monster, or whatever that thing was separated his brown pulsating lips revealing two spiked teeth parallel to each other in his mouth. All I could do was stand there in the puddle of now stinky, sticky liquid that seemed to consume my feet just like the serpent was about to consume you. Out of nowhere your head pooped off your body and landed into my hands upside down! I couldn't speak or yell for nothing! The serpent looked at me and laughed saying 'Who's the monster now'. My mouth fell opened, finally, letting out a mournful yell while wet drops of pain and horror leaked from my eyes, going down my cheeks. I turned your head around so I could tell you I'm sorry for not helping, but as I turned your head around it turned into the snake's head

"AWWWWW!" I screamed at the top of my lungs opening my eyes into utter darkness, which seemed like what all my life had to offer me at the time being. I couldn't control the cacophonous noise my throat spat into the air. I seemed to have loss all premonitions of others asleep in the house. The blood in my vein seemed to oscillate from a slow, steady beat to a beat going the speed of a jackrabbit. 'Thump, Thump, Thump, Thump, Thump,' my heart sang out, it almost sang out my chest. My mother woke up to the horrendous noises coming from the black hole ,that seemed to be my mouth at the time, and ran into the darkness concerned that something happened to her little angel. Just as she stepped into the white doorway and flicked on the light switch, she noticed a puddle of clear liquid all over the bed and me crying. "Sweetie, what happened? Are you okay?" She asked with a puzzled look on her face. "I had a nightmare and got scared," I cried out. "It's okay," she said while headed to the other side of my bed to take a seat."Tell mommy what happened," she continued in a consoling tone, which made me feel a whole lot safer than I did before. I explained the whole dream to my mom, whose mouth was on the floor by the time I finished.

"My poor baby, I am so sorry you had that dream," she replied in a languishing voice "but it's over now let's go pray that God doesn't let you have this dream again or any other nightmare for that matter" she continued. "Yes ma'am," I replied monotonously. We prayed that whole night and to this day I will never forget that dreaded dream.

Angelica Arriaga [handwritten]

TEACHER
by Angelica Arriaga

I LOVE YOU (in an awkwardly creepy way) [handwritten]

My sister, Sofia, is a six-year old. Understand that at sixteen, it seems very hard to ever see eye to eye with her. We do not get along well, and we never have anything to talk about. She wants to talk about Barbie; I want to finish my homework. I never dreamed we would be able to talk about something we mutually liked, and I never dreamed I would teach her anything.

One day during the summer, I came home from my piano class. I felt tired and I felt thirsty. Although I did not want to do it, I needed to practice on the piano for a test coming up. I blew the dust off our old piano and sat on the bench. I did not feel up to this. My eyes glazed over the piano sheet music. I set my hands on the keys. My finger touched the first key. The first key was followed by an assortment of keys, each playing a note that together made this wonderful sound. As my fingers danced across the piano, Sofia listened with fascination. I could see the tunes ringing in her ear. With every note her eyes widened, her smile brightened, and her hunger for more grew. When I finished playing, I looked at her with remote curiosity.

"I... I wish I could play like that," she mumbled.

At this point, I was not sure what I wanted to say, but something compelled me to reply to her little wide-eyed face.

"Well, if you would like me to, I can teach you," I said slowly.

She smiled again and said, "Really?"

"Sit with me."

19

We sat there for a while. She started slowly playing, but she got faster. She began to understand time and rhythm. I watched her in amazement as she played the song for my parents perfectly. My parents felt surprised that I could teach her, but I felt far more astonished. I simply did not believe that I could sit with Sofia and actually teach her something. This established the first time that we had something to talk about.

My mom reached for her bag as she asked, "Angie, I'm going to the gym. Can you watch Sofia for me? Please?"

"Do I have a choice?"

She left without an answer and I stood there looking at my sister. In my head I thought "How am I supposed to do this? Isn't this like, a mommy job?"

"Alright Sofia I don't really feel like putting you to bed... so I'm going to play on the computer. You can watch TV"

Sofia did not want to watch TV. Instead of accepting her invitation to an argument, I looked for another way out.. I glanced over at a globe that sat in the corner. I walked over, picked it up, and took it to the couch and sat with it. The fact that she bugged me because she did not want to watch TV was beginning to agitate me. Despite my unwillingness, I spun the globe around faster and faster, and then stopped the globe at random times; pointing at whatever country I had stopped on.

"What are you doing," she asked as she stood in front of me.

"Finding a country to move to when I leave," I said sarcastically.

She asked, "What's a country?"

I sighed and replied, "Sit with me."

I started telling her the meaning of a country, and then I showed her the different countries around the world. She asked about people from other countries, so I told her about people from foreign lands. Then I started telling her about the funny laws that some people have to live by, like the chewing gum policy in Singapore. I told her about games people play, like rugby and soccer. I told her about how Greenland and Iceland got their names; I told her that people in Bangladesh do not get to watch TV. When my mom came home, I once again marveled at the fact that I sat with Sofia and taught her something. She hugged the huge globe with her tiny arms and waddled across the living room and put it back on the floor.

Several months later, I was once again forced with the job of watching Sofia. This time, I had to put her to bed. She was lying under her covers, cozy and warm, and so I tried to leave.

She startled me before I could leave the room. "Wait!"`

I nearly jumped out of my pajamas. I turned around and looked at her wondering what on earth she could want now.

She said, "You need to read me a bedtime story."

I replied with, "A what?"

"Read me a bedtime story," she said.

I walked over to her collection of thin paper books. These books that my mom read to her night after night looked like books for three year-olds. Some of them had only ten pages and others may have been longer, but the font on the pages seemed large enough to be only worth four pages.

I raised an eyebrow as I stared at the books and said, "What is Mother reading to you? This stuff is junk. I'll be back."

I walked into my room and went into my closet. I have a miniature library in my closet with books that I have had since childhood. I quickly made my selection and returned to Sofia's room. I held up "The Boxcar

Children" in front of me and conjured up a cheesy smile. The book, a withered paperback, looked huge in her eyes.

"That book looks big," she said.

"Well, we probably won't finish it tonight, but we can start by reading the first chapter now, and then read the rest of it night by night" I replied.

She agreed, and I sat on the bed with her and opened the book. As I read the words, I could smell that old book smell that can sometimes be found in dictionaries in big libraries. The dry pages came to life as I changed from voice to voice trying to portray the four children of the book. When I came to the end of the chapter, I closed the book. Sofia did not want to stop, and I knew that she loved it.

I felt victorious. I once again gave her knowledge. I gave her something that we both loved. Even though we still do not have a lot in common, I realized that teaching her new things made us both happy. I felt the magic of the moment. I love my sister, and I love teaching her.

THINK BEFORE YOU ACT
by Jazzlyn Ary

It's five in the morning. I am instructed by the juvenile correctional officer to remove my clothes, and place them in the plastic bag. "When you are done taking a shower, you must wipe down the shower walls and floor; wash your hair thoroughly and redress in your blue jumper." I followed the instructions of the over masculine female with a very deep man like voice and a very low hair cut. I questioned the authenticity of this really being a woman, to myself of course. However I followed instructions. As I stepped into the steaming seemingly refreshing shower, my tired, besieged, overwhelmed feeling went down the drain along with the suds from the correctional facilities cheat soap and shampoo. I still felt exhausted. I had been awake for twenty two hours. I finished my shower, wiped down the walls of the small square shaped cubicle that I took my shower in, and redressed in the oversized blue jumper. I was lead to my cell. A rectangular shaped room with a door that clinked and sealed shut when I walked into the it. A hard cement block protruded from the wall as to be a bed of some sort and was covered with a thick cotton pallet. The mirrors were not very reflective; they looked very dull and seemed to be covered in a dust that could not be wiped away. The toilet was clean, spotless even, and connected to the sink. I laid out the sheets and covers that I was given earlier on the cement block, and laid down. The covers were thick, itchy, and very uncomfortable. So I decided to just use the sheet to cover up with. I attempted to go to sleep. However, the sun was rising in the small window at the foot of my bed and seemed to glare directly into my eyes. So I lay on my back staring to the ceiling, contemplating how in the world did such an intelligent, strong minded girl like me end up in a place like this?

Only a few hours before I found myself in these four cement walls, I was laying out my clothes for church the next morning. One phone call I received changed my track of mind and fast. "There's a hotel party downtown" my very excited friend shouted through the phone! I knew that my Godmother was a very hard sleeper and would not hear the car start, so I began to get ready to have a night on the town. I emptied my backpack and put my cute clingy white mini dress and a pair of my favorite tan lace pumps in it. I took piles of clothes and put them under my cover as to show the outline of a body, my body. With keys in hand, I snuck out the back door. When I opened the door my neighbor's dogs went into a barking frenzy. They always do that to the slightest of things, so I ignored it and walked around to the front yard. My Godmothers truck was in the driveway behind my mother's car. So I used my awesome driving skills and shimmied my way out of the tight spot. I loved driving that car. 2006 Impala LT that drove as smooth as silk. With much anticipation I reached my cousins house to pick her up. She dressed and we headed for the car. Seconds later I get a call. I open the little blue device to see who it was. A small chill went down my back as the word Mother went across my screen. At first I was thinking she doesn't know about the car, she's way in Florida, she probably just wants to say goodnight or something, Right? NOT! I answer, "Yes Mother?" "Where is my car Keisha!?" I give some bogus answer and she goes into an intrusive very angry rage and ultimately tells me to get back home at once. My magnificent rebellious mind decides not to listen and to go have fun. She's way on the east coast, Ill just deal with the consequences when she gets home. So I take of down I45 towards downtown. I exit the freeway, and to my surprise I had missed a call on my phone. It was from my mother and she left a voice mail. So I listen to the voice message and basically she said that she was calling the police since I didn't answer the phone. I made a right unto a street that about a block ahead had a black BMW waiting at a stop light. Trying to call my mother back and not paying attention, I gently bumped the BMW's bumper. Anxious and scared out of my mind for not even having an ID, and about being in my mother's car, I decided to drive around the car I hit and make a run for it. He chased me until I stopped. The cops came and I was immediately incarcerated.

I replayed these events over and over as I lay there. Wondering what would've happened if I could go back and change things. Like what if I would've just stopped when I hit the car? Or what if I just would've went back home. Or what if I would've stayed home and not took the car. All of that didn't matter anymore, because now I was lying in a juvenile jail left alone with my haunting guilty thoughts. No thoughts of changing the past would get me out of the whole I had already dug myself into.

ROCKS OF POWER: A RE-TELLING OF ADVENTURES IN VIDEO GAME EUPHORIA
by Gabriel Bailey

This story is a frame-by-frame review of events that took place in the year 1999. The child, Gabriel Bailey, has been exposed to some... new and foreign object by the name of "video games". This story comes straight from the mind of said child and tells his initial reactions and feelings towards this new form of "entertainment". The ideas and statements may seem convoluted to us, but to Gabriel, this all makes sense. You have been for warned.

What is this? It looks a little like a fancy VHS tape player or something. Why does it have all these extra cords and stuff attached to it? Well, it at least it hooks up to the TV like a VHS. That means it's got to be some kind of technology, and some is always better than none.

That's good, last time Terry tired to trick us, it involved a stick, a window and a blindfold. I still can't sit down without flinching. So, Terry thinks that this so-called "game system" is going to be another thing that I'm just going to take a face value? I think not Sir. However, this is my grandmother's house and, last I checked, doing anything related to technology is better than going outside and helping her in the lawn. I swear that woman is a slave driver!

Terry, the eleven year-old liar extraordinaire, says that, "We all can sit down and play a game on the TV." Sure, like that's even possible. This guy must not realize that I'm five years old. I'm smart enough to know that's not possible. I hate when he does this stuff. Trying to trick me. Well, this time I got him figured out! He's not getting me with this gag!

Looks like he's done hooking up the crazy thing and... what's he doing? He pressed some button on the crazy thing and now it won't stop flashing and making weird noises. The idiot still hasn't turned on th- never mind, he just turned on the TV. If he plans on tricking me, he might want to get the "punch line" right. Trying to trick a fella using television technology and not have the TV on? Jeez, how dumb does he think I am?

Now what the heck is this on the TV? If this is some tape, I sure as crud haven't seen it before, and I've seen every tape in the planet. What the heck am I supposed to do with these remote things he just plugged into the tape player and handed me? Wow. Whatever is on the TV, it's extremely... different. With all these flashing colors and stuff. Well, this is pretty interesting. These guys on the tube are beating the snot out of each other with punches, kicks, boxes, pipes, and all types of other stuff I don't even know how to describe! From the looks of it, they all seem to be trying to grab these floating stones. I wonder why? I mean, it's not like there's a lot of them. There's only like three of them. Looks like one of the people has finally managed to get all of the stones and... oh my.

WHAT THE HECK IS THIS!? Why did the guy just up and transform? Look at him! This started off as a fair fight but now... Good Lord, man! Did he just shoot a beam from his hands? Why is he so much stronger than the other guys? Of course he won! Hey! I was watching that! Where did the people go? What is this? The heck is a "pause button"? Look, VHS player, all I want is those guys back on the screen. Alright, so now Terry's pressing some buttons and some stuff is happening.

Now the game wants us to choose a person to play as. I guess I'll be this green guy with the swords and the bandages. He looks pretty cool. Another menu of stuff for me to look through? I don't care about this stuff game, just get me to the action please. Pick a stupid level Terry, gosh! Finally, took him long enough. Now then, what am I supposed to be doing? Oh, you're gonna give me sometime to figure out the locations of the buttons on this thing? Fatal mistake, cousin, fatal mistake! Ok, I'm ready, let's do thi- hey, what's he doing? I said kick, man, kick! Why is he jumping? Oh, finger was on the wrong button. Alright, now let's see here... punch... punch... kick... jump... Wait. Crud. Stop hitting me jerk! Let me hit you first! Stand still! Quit cheating! What? I lost? How? The game just got started! Rematch... rematch, I say!

I was only five when it happened, and I didn't know what to do.

Unfortunately, that's all of the story. Apparently, Gabriel continued to ask for rematch after rematch after rematch. It's said that he still attempts to play these "video games" to this day. The only thing this child's point of view has proven, is that these "games" are just as addictive as we expected them to be. However, they also seem to keep the child preoccupied. Keep this product in circulation, but keep a careful eye on it.

From,

P.A.R.E.N.T.S.

(Pesky Adults Running Everything, Never Trying Stuff)

LIFE IS SHORT
by Amadi Shani Barrett

Life is short. That's what I hear almost every day of my life. Hearing this, I try to just live my life day by day. I have many problems from school, work, to financial problems. Sometimes, they collide together to make one HUGE problem. Wbhen events come around I like to forget about these problems and party, look beautiful, and stunt. Partying is a very fun thing for me to do when life seems to take a toll. It helps me make the most of being with my friends, listening to music, and dancing. Looking beautiful is not really hard for me. I just put on outfits that fit my character for that night and I rock it. I put on makeup too. I do this to enhance my beauty. Stunting is simply making your haters wish they were running with you, instead of running against you.

It was December 19, 2010, three days after my sixteenth birthday. I decided that I wouldn't let the fact that I couldn't have a Sweet Sixteen birthday party stop me from celebrating. Everybody was going to a teen club called Isis located downtown. It was a Sunday night. I made the choice to go out and party, look beautiful, and stunt like it would be the last time I could. Alysia, Breana, Carletta, Nia, Carletta's friend, and I went to Isis and had the night of our lives. I wore a gray long sleeved lace shirt, some blue high-waist shorts, and gold sandals. I knew I was all that in a bag of hot chips. My friends and I danced until we couldn't dance anymore. It felt so good to finally be sixteen.

The only regret I have about that night was that my friend Ashley couldn't spend this wonderful night with us, because I was "beefing" with her over something so stupid. Now, as I look back on that night without her, I wish we could've resolved our problems so we could have had the times of our lives together. "They" always say, "Live your life with no regrets." I'm disappointed that I haven't.

Ashley called me on March 26, 2011 and asked, "Amadi, What are you wearing to the Jungle tonight?" I said, "Girl, I don't really know yet." Ashley's birthday was on March 25, 2011. She was turning sixteen just like I was in December. The Jungle is another teen club where parties are held. On March 26th Sissy Nobby was performing. Sissy Nobby is a New Orleans bounce singer who everyone loves. Anyways, before the big party Alysia and I went to Ashley's house. We went over there so we could pull up to the Jungle together, then we could spend the whole night together with no complications.

While at Ashley's house, I realized that I didn't want to wear what I packed to wear to the Jungle. Ashley handed me this beautiful jean and gold romper out of her closet. I yelled, "I'm definitely gone look good in this." In my mind I knew I was going to party, look beautiful, and stunt. Alysia, Ashley, and I lived that night up like it was our last. We had so much fun. We danced to every one of our favorite songs by Sissy Nobby. That night I had no regrets at all. I forgot to mention that Nia and Ashley's best friend DeNae showed up too. We lived it up for Ashley's birthday.

Almeda Skating Rink to us as children was a place where we went to skate and socialize. Just recently they changed Almeda Skating Rink. They kept the same concept of skating and socializing, but they turned it into a place where you party, skate, and socialize. On April 21, 2011 a promoter by the name of J Smoove threw a party at the Almeda

Skating Rink. In preparation for the night, Calvin and Alysia came to my house so my mother would drop us off at the party. We all got dressed at my house. I was ready to party, look beautiful, and stunt. Calvin asked, "Madi, you ready to South Dallas Swag?" I said, "Heck yeah!"

I wore a green vest, a floral shirt, and some blue shorts to this event. This night was one of the best in myhad to b the best event of my high school life. All of my friends came to Almeda Skating Rink that night. Alysia, Calvin, Ashley, Markisha, Tiara, Jayln, Greg, and Vinlencia showed up that night. Everything went right. It was all laughter and smiles while everybody partied, looked beautiful, and stunted. After the party, Ashley, Calvin, and I spent the night at Alysia's house. We had so much fun. We talked about Calvin all night and laughed until we couldn't laugh anymore.

I am happy to say I am still alive. When problems come along I can't just cry and complain. All I can do is live my life the way I'm supposed to, and leave my problems where they came from. I will always remember what "they" say, "Live your life without regrets."

BALL GAME!
by Martin Bautista

The thought of pitching a no hitter never crossed my mind. The urge and anxiety building inside you to get the last three batters out of the game is enormous. However as a pitcher you have to remain calm and ignore all noises from your surroundings. This is important because you have to locate your pitches to be successful in the outing.

The day was June 22nd, 2004. The sun was long gone and the moon was shining brighter than ever. It was the bottom of the 6th inning and my team was batting. I was sitting at the very end of the bench where I could get away from everybody. The main highlight of the game was that a young boy called Martin Bautista. In which he had a no hitter bid through 6 innings. As I sat by myself I tried to remain calm, but it wasn't working. All the hype from the people from the stands was getting to me. My head was spinning from excitement that I might have a chance to actually pitch a no hitter. Through the entire time that I was trying to calm down and focus on what pitches I should pitch to the next three batters. My teammates came and patted my on my shoulder all exited that I had the no hitter bid. I looked up and smiled to them, but deep inside I wished they would leave me alone, so I could concentrate and get myself together.

"Strike three you are out," the umpire scolded. It was the third out and my team was heading on to the field with a 1-0 lead. "Let's go Colts, let's go Colts," the spectators screamed as we went onto the field. The walk that I took towards the pitching mound was the slowest one I had ever taken. Maybe it was because I had butterflies in my stomach from all the anxiety that I built in the dugout. The walk toward the mound I held my head down. Just thinking, What if I let my team down and make an error. Leave a hanging curveball over the plate, or throw a slider that doesn't spin out, or leave a fastball right over the plate that the batter can hit over the park. All this what if's filled my head. "Common man you got this, loosen up only three more batters and we go to Kansa City for the Little League World Series," my teammate told me with excitement as he jogged pass me towards his position. I remember as I took the mound I turned over to look at my dad that was standing up against the cage with my mom. The look he gave me was a look that I wasn't expecting. His face expression was blank. This made me even more nervous. I had pitched 6 straight innings and retired every single batter none of them reached base. I bent over to pick up the baseball from the mound. I gripped the baseball inside my glove and awaited the signal from the catcher. "Play ball," the umpire scolded. The laid down three fingers and tapped his left leg. I quickly nodded. A curveball low and away. I proceeded with the pitch. "Bang!" the batter made contact with the pitch. At that moment my heart sank to my feet. I kept looking straight towards home plate and didn't look back to see whether or not the hit ball was a hit. I stood still midway from home plate and the pitcher's mound motionless. Inside my head I was thinking, "oh my god I just lost my no hitter!" I suddenly feel someone touch me on my left shoulder it was my first basemen Alex. He handed me the ball and said, "Only two more outs Martin and you will make history." I was confused on what had happened. I was sure that was a base hit. I walked towards my pitcher's mound to face the next batter.

It was the top of the 7th inning with one out. I gripped baseball nice and firm and looked at the catcher. The fingers were; one tap to the right; Fastball inside. I proceeded with the pitch. "Bang," the batter made contact with the ball, but this time I quickly look back because it was a pop-up. As I knew he would my left fielder caught it. The last and only batter was coming up. Chills went through my spine. The catcher gave the signal and I quickly nodded. "Strike one," the umpire screamed. The catcher gave the same signal. "Strike two," the umpire yelled. The third signal from the catcher was a curveball. I gripped the ball with all the strength I had and I proceeded with the pitch. "Strike three," scolded the umpire. That was game. I had just pitch my first ever no hitter. Every single of my teammates ran towards me all happy. I quickly fell to the ground, and everybody just started jumping on top of me.

Never in my mind I would of came to think that I was going to pitch a no hitter. I had to calm myself down several times for me to accomplish this historic outing. This was important because I was able to locate my pitches and finish the game strong and without a hit.

PROFILE NARRATIVE
by Rivan Bennevendo

I walk out of my room, away from that sensation of blaring Dubstep music in my ears, away from that cool breeze from the fan, away from Spongebob Squarepants. The carpet's just been pulled up in the living room and the hard, wood floors are cold on my bare feet. The lights in here are dimmed but the energy-saving bulbs in the dining room are piercing through the air. I see my dad to my left, wearing his usual blinding white t-shirt and basketball shorts, staring dazedly at the hypnotic computer screen as he types away. He's in his notorious half-hunched position, probably working on some kind of document for work. He works on the computer all day at his job. He's some kind of data organizer at the plant.

My dad is probably a little shorter than the average man and a little more round too. Despite his thick brown and gray, Russian-looking mustache and puffy cheeks, he's got wonderful light brown eyes and a warm, welcoming smile. His jet black hair, absent of any grays, stays combed back revealing its slow but sure recession. His big, strong back takes up more room than the chair provides. While still staring at the screen he relieves his left hand from typing for a few seconds to take a swig of his Coors Light.

"Quick, Rivan! He's lost focus. Now's your chance." I tell myself.

"Hey Da…"

It's too late. He's set down his drink and is now typing again. I continue to walk toward him and eventually make it to the seat right beside him. I glance at him. I glance at his screen. I'm prepared to call him more than once.

"Dad" I say.

No answer.

"Dad!" I repeat more sternly.

"Huh? Yes? What?" he asks, as he awakes from his trance.

"Well, are you ready?"

"For what…? Oh right! Okay do you have one picked?"

Tonight is movie night so we usually like to start one up at eight or nine. Unfortunately I don't have one picked out yet but this shouldn't be hard. Dad likes action; I like action. Dad like mystery; I like mystery. Bourne it is.

"How about Bourne?" I ask him.

"It's like you read my mind!" he exclaims.

"Popcorn?"

"Yep."

"Peanuts?"

"Mhm"

"Cheese-its and a drink?"

"Sounds good."

Okay. So now it's time to get started. I put in the movie and let the previews play while I get the snacks ready. Dad slowly starts to log off of his computer and eventually closes it. My dad is indeed a very busy man but I think at the end of the day one of his favorite things to do is spend time with his kids, me and my brother, Reuben. Once were finally set, we watch the movie. Although the snacks are completely finished after the first thirty minutes of the movie, we still enjoy it. Afterward, dad sends me and Reuben to the restroom to brush our teeth and tells us to get ready for bed. Finally we make it to bed and dad always makes sure to visit us before we go to sleep to say prayers and to remind of things we'll need for next day. It's been a long day but after a fun night with my dad and brother, I sleep comfortably in my bed.

I unwillingly wake up to my morning alarm and dad walks in to tell me it's time to get up.

"Get up son. Throw some water on your face." He says.

"Ugh. Okay." I grumble back.

We're running a little late so we have to stop at Mc Donald's on the way to school. To dad it's a downgrade from breakfast at home but Reuben and I love it. We order our usual pancakes and sit by the flat-screen to watch the news. Politics are so chaotic these days but dad keeps up with it all. He tries to ignore all the mumbo jumbo that the press so vividly emphasizes. When it comes to election time though, he's all about his ethics. He'll stand behind a pro-life candidate over a pro-choice candidate any day.

Now we're on our way to school. Reuben always gets dropped off first since his school is right by the house. I don't really mind it though because it gives me and dad more time to chat. We finally pull up to the school and say our goodbyes.

"See you later." I say.

"Bye Rivan. Don't forget your guitar." He replies.

"I won't."

"Call me after school."

"Okay."

"Remember to work hard."

"I will."

Although dad supports me in most of my endeavors like guitar and basketball I think one of his number one goals for me is to grow up to be the most well-educated, responsible, God-like man I can be. I try hard not to disappoint him.

It's been a long day at school and I take the bus home. I usually get home about an hour before dad and knockout my homework. When he makes it home, he's sure to greet the family before sitting down to eat. After a delicious meal he resigns to his chair in the dining room to finish up some work. After about half-an-hour though, he stops and takes a glance at me.

"Finish your homework?" he asks.

"Yes sir." I say confidently.

"Movie time?" he asks with a sly look on his face.

With a smile on my face I reply with, "I'll get the snacks."

LIFE IS A STAGE, OWN IT
by Jazmine Borden

As I stand next to the stage waiting for the judges to call my name for my audition in the school's production of Romeo and Juliet. I begin to get that weird, butterfly in my stomach feeling, that people get when they do something exciting or nerve racking. Thoughts begin to fill my already cluttered brain with vivid images of all the things that could go wrong if I don't get up and walk away right now. I begin sorting through my competition to find that half of them are very good actors but only a few have a chance at beating me in getting this part.

The judges call my name and as I walk onto the stage an anticipated hush falls over the audience that has come to watch the auditions. I take a quick bow, state the character I'm auditioning for, which is Juliet, and the scene I will be using. I can hear a collective gasp go through the crowd because I did not tell anyone what part I was going to try out for, fearing that someone would say I was not good enough. As I'm getting into character someone in the audience, probably one of my friends yells, "Come on Jaz, you've been here before. Don't let them get to you." These words, although meaning to help me get into character, take me back to a time when I was living as part of the background dominated my life.

"Mom, did you have to switch my schools in the middle of the year?" I say as we drive toward my new elementary school, "It's going to be hard enough being the new girl, especially since everybody already made friends."

My mom laughs at my desperate attempt to get out of the first day at a new school. I'm the only one in the family who has issues with making friends or being in large groups for that matter. Once I get to the school I find out that going through the day unnoticed isn't going to work. So I tried to be as indifferent as possible in what was happening. I guess this approach was a failed attempt because Sara, who later became one of my closet friends throughout school, came up to me a said, "Geez Jazmine, why you look so serious. Lighten up; you need to have more fun."

These thoughts flood my mind as I try to remain in character. As my audition progresses I begin to waver in the mini monologue that the scene I'm performance requires. I look around the crowd to see that they aren't paying attention and by the expressions on their faces they could care less too. My mom once told me that the only way to get a crowd's attention is to demand it. "Become the center of attention and own it and no one will be able to take that away from you," my mom said to me. As I reminisce over my mother's wise words a memory of the State Cheer Competition takes center stage in my mind, cursing me a momentary lapse in concentration.

"Ok girls, this is it, we came this far and I'm not leaving here without winning", exclaimed the coach as all the girls on the squad nod in agreement. We came all the way to Austin placing first in the city and as captain I refused to go home without the winning check.

"Jazmine, you have to get up there and perform like you own the stage and everything on it", the coach says to me with such intensity, "Make the judges believe you've been doing this your entire life, and you're just giving them a taste."

Once our names were called we got onto the platform to perform our routine. The crowd was going insane when we started doing out stunts and the rest of the squad responded by giving it all we had. At the end of our routine there's a stunt where they picked me up and throw me in the air. It would be an easy stunt but while in the air I have to do a toe touch, then on the way down, curl up in a ball. At the last second I have to straighten out so they can catch me. This stunt has never been done in the competition before and we have been practicing for so long I knew were going to nail it.

Once we finish our routine the crowd and the judges are on their feet, screaming and clapping. After a few dreadful minutes of waiting, the judges announce that, my team won the competition. After we took pictures with the check and got congratulations from the judges, my coach came up to me. She said, "See, if you act like you own it and give it you're all, then it will be yours in the end."

These thoughts cloud my mind as I try to regain the audience's attention. I focused on my coach and my mother's word and realized that the only way to get the crowd to listen is to claim this role as mine. Taking this I deliver them with such intensity that as my audition comes to an end, the crowd burst in to applause. I take a bow and wait for the judges to give me their commentary. After a couple of minutes of waiting for the judges to collect their thoughts, they finally decide to tell me what they thought. The judge in the middle, a short lady with round glasses, spoke up ,saying, "young lady you are the perfect example of fire and ice and that is why you will be lead in our production of Romeo and Juliet," with a slight smirk like she knew I had it in me all along. Well technically I had it but finding a balance is the hard parts because no matter how hard you try some things just never change about any person.

MEXICAN CHRISTMAS
by Hadie Boul

On the way to my grandma's house in Baytown, my mom decided to blast a CD with Christmas carols on it, so everyone would get into the Christmas spirit. My step-dad and brother sat back rolling their eyes while my three year old brother wiggled around in his seat. I was sitting in the very back seat, by myself, thinking about all the delicious food that would be at my grandparent's house. After all, I knew my grandma loved to go overboard with cooking on holidays. Waiting in the car I looked at all the Christmas lights on people's houses. Since it was already the evening, the lights were very visible, as they lit up the whole street.

Thirty minutes later, we pulled up in my grandparents drive way. The smell of sweet sugar cookies, hot chocolate, and fire wood seeped in through my nose. I closed my eyes for a few seconds as I enjoyed the warm feeling and got, with my tongue tingling to the smell. The door flew open while my grandpa came out with a big smile on his face. My youngest brother, Sammy, ran up to the door yelling, "Grandpa! Grandpa! Where's Wella?"

"She's in the kitchen mijo", my grandpa relied.

"What is that, grandpa? Is that hot chocolate?" My brother started giggling.

I looked up to see my grandpa making crazy faces at my brother just to get him to laugh. Who doesn't love the way a three year old laughs so innocently? My parents and I followed behind my other brother while my grandma came down the hallway with the hot chocolate and cookies that filled my nose.

"I knew it! Yessss. Hi grandma, we miss you", I said while shoving a cookie into my mouth.

"Your welcome. Now come to the kitchen, dinner is almost ready", she replied.

"Dinner! Exactly what I need! I've been thinking about food the whole way here", I yelled with a big smile on my face.

Somehow my nose didn't catch the smell of the amazing looking enchiladas, tacos, beans, rice, menudo, potatoes, fajita, and dessert. Before I even got to see what else there was, I was already in my seat; mouth watering. We sat at the table saying what we were thankful for, what we thought we were getting for Christmas, and joked around about random things. By the time we were done, my mom told my brothers it was time to sleep so Santa Claus could bring the presents. My mom let them open up the one gift she knew were their pajamas, and took them upstairs to sleep. I sat by the fire, staring at the flames and drinking my hot coco. Finally, my mom came back downstairs and brought me a bag of all kinds of little objects to put in stockings. I filled up my brothers stockings after I filled mine with all of the stuff my mom let me pick out the week before. There were two hours left until midnight and my family was in the kitchen drinking and playing card games. I went into the living room and sat on the floor, shaking my presents, trying to figure out what was inside of each one.

Hours passed and finally it was midnight. The cookies that my brothers left out for Santa Claus were eaten (by me) and the hot chocolate was also gone. My brother came walking down the stairs with half opened eyes and half-smiles on their faces. Since they were still sleepy, it took them a few minutes to get excited. Once the presents started getting passed around, everyone was wide awake.

"Oooh oooh I know what you got!" My brother said.

"Well shh, don't tell me, silly. I'm about to open it", I whispered.

"Okay meanie, pass me mine", He said with a huge smile on his face.

I passed him his present, which was a NERF gun that I happened to wrap. The tag on it said 'From: Santa Claus." Oh how I loved being secret Santa Claus. The smiles on everyone's faces grew wider and many thank you's were passed around. The expressions on everyone's faces were priceless and I sat there for a moment; thinking about how cool it would be if every day was like this. There was nothing but silly smiles, happy faces, and laughter. Around two o'clock in the morning, I was in such a good mood, with my heart still bouncing, that I didn't want to sleep. My brothers and I stayed up all night while they played with all the new toys they got. The adults stayed awake playing all kinds of card games while laughing all night long. We were all exhausted by the time the sun came out.

The next morning, when I woke up from a short nap, I woke up to pancakes, bacon, eggs, potatoes, bread, tortillas, and left over's from the day before. I ate so much that I felt like I couldn't even walk. I walked out onto the porch to see what the weather was like. The sun and wind felt amazing! Remembering that I had to go to my step-dad's sister's house and my dad's sister's house, I went inside to take a nap, realizing that I had a big day ahead of me, with two more Christmas's to come.

LERCONYA PELREAN: BEING A MOM
by Breanna' Briscoe

I have always known my mom to be three things: loving, a big kid, and strong. She never candy-coated things for my sisters and I, and she didn't plan on starting either. I've always felt that she was an amazing mom, but I never knew exactly how she stayed so strong and happy. I was excited about doing this interview with my mom, because I would be able to get answers to questions that I have wanted answered for a long time. My mom wasn't exactly excited about the idea of the interview. When I asked her to do it with me she replied by saying, "Tell Mrs. Damani I will just take the zero. Better yet tell her I was on vacation!" so in order to get these answers out of her, I would have to trick her into it later on that day. My plan was to walk into her room and sneak a question in every few minutes during one of her conversations. I just knew it would work.

As I walked into my mom's room later that day, I had a sense of fear yet goofiness just because I knew I had to trick my mom into doing this interview. My mom was talking to my little sister and I tried to blend in as well as possible so that I could sneak my first question into the conversation. Once I had the courage to ask my mom the first question, with a serious face so she wouldn't figure out my plan, I curiously asked her, "How did you become so strong?" She answered, "Going through things good and bad, people using me, and messing up in life. Also being taught at home that no matter how bad someone has hurt you that you don't retaliate, and do what they have done to you, and to always stay being the bigger person." After she answered, I knew I had her tricked and I could continue the interview without her knowing. I was pretty confident in my plan until she asked me, "Bre, are you interviewing me?!"All I could do was answer with a sarcastic "No!", but I didn't give up.

I continued to bob and weave in and out of the conversation until she finally let her guard down and happily answered all my questions. I started to ask my mom questions about her experience of being a mom. For the longest time I thought my mom was the "Human Handbook to Parenting" because it seemed like every time a relative or friend asked a question along the lines of parenting, she always had an answer. She told me how the hardest part of being a mom was "doing it by herself". She also told me how although being a mom could be fun it could also be difficult. Especially, when it comes to making sure everyone is okay and has what they need. She also told me how it was important that she remembered to take care of and treat herself.

As we got deeper into the interview, I started to appreciate my mother and the things she does for my sisters and I. I finally understood what she did to keep my sisters and I healthy, happy, and alive. I learned more about my mom's ambitions and dreams; like how she would like to go to France to be a pastry chef. I already knew what many of her dreams were from daily conversations with her, but I wasn't fully aware of the sacrifices she had made in order to have us.

Of course, like any other young mother, my mom would love to go back in time and redo some things in her life. Some of those things would have been to finish school, get a career, and get married before she had kids. She wouldn't take any of the life she already has back. My mom told me, in so many words, that she would rather be successful with us than successful without us.

The final and, in my opinion, the most important question I asked my mom was, "Have you raised us the way you admired raising your children when you were younger?" and her answer was "Yes." This was the most important question for me, because as long as I knew that I came out the way that my mom aspired me to come out, then I was okay.

I felt like I could sit for hours and talk to my mom about life and being strong but after about an hour she told my little sister and I to go ahead and get ready for school tomorrow. I felt like after the interview with my mom that I had a better and clearer understanding of her and how she functions while raising us. I now appreciate my mom so much more than I did before the interview; and I thank God everyday for bringing me such an amazing person to have as a mother.

NEVER SAY NEVER
by Valencia Brown

It's hard growing up with a sister that's ten years older than you when you have a mother on drugs. I was six and my sister was 15 going on 16. I had a mother who was on drugs so she made my sister take me everywhere. My sister hated having to take me everywhere she went. When she went out with friends my mother would tell her to take me. When she went to spend the night at friends houses my mother would make her take me. My sister played my mother growing up. Even though my sister hated taking me everywhere she still treated me right. Sometimes she would say things that would hurt my feelings but I didn't show it. All I heard when she and her friends hung out wasn't how she was never having kids. I would laugh because at a young age I knew a person couldn't tell the future. My aunt had come to stay with us and her and my mother got into so she called CPS on my mother and had us taking away. So my sister had to become even a bigger mother figure in my life. After a while my mother got her act together and got us back. Since my sister had to play that mother figure in my life she was started saying she wasn't having kids.

"Push! Push!" was all I heard sitting in the hospital room. It was April 8, 2002. My 16 year old sister who played mommy to me was really about to be a mommy and had just gone into labor and was having my niece. As I sat there looking at my sister frown in pain it made me sad. She was 16 years old and about to be a mother. She wouldn't have a teen hood because my mother told her that she had to take her baby everywhere with her. After she pushed my niece out I remember seeing the alien looking thing cry. They had to take her to NICU because she didn't want to breathe and was holding her breath. She was a stubborn baby and didn't want to breathe. She finally cried after the doctor popped her on the butt. After they took her to NICU we went down to see her. They had her stable but they had her on a breathing machine When we made it back to my sister's hospital room she s slept peacefully but woke up and told my mom she's not having any more kids for awhile. When it was time for her and my niece to come home I had a healthy and pretty niece. Once we arrived home it's like everything changed and my mother didn't trust my sister. When my sister would be up late at night with my niece crying she would tell my sister to bring her here and my niece would go to sleep instantly.

9 years later I'm sitting on my bed and I got a phone call. My sister called me and asked me if I had gotten her picture and I told her no I didn't so she told me to wait for her picture message to come through. When we hung up I received a picture message from sister. It was a positive pregnancy test. My sister is pregnant and I'm so happy. Her boyfriend of 12 years has come home from overseas and I've been begging for another niece or nephew. My niece had just turned 9 and my sister was finally pregnant. I was so happy I didn't know what to do. I told my mother and she was happy as well. My sister is 7 months pregnant and is due December 30, 2011. As I think about all the time my sister use to say she was never having kids and she got pregnant. Than how she would never space her kids out how my mother did us. Now just like us her kids are going to be 10 years apart and she's having two girls. All I can think about is never say the word never.

I've looked back at my childhood and see that everything you say and do can affect your future. People always say never say ever and in my sister's case I see that's true. I see how having a child young can affect you and I do not want to have to go through that. It's tough being a teenage parent. Seeing how everything has happened I'm happy it did because it made me who I am. Many people may not understand me but I love being misunderstood. I may say never but I do know I'm not having kids until I'm older.

FIRST DAY OF SCHOOL
by Paris Bullock

"Paris, wake up!" My mom said waking me up from a good night sleep. The day was finally here. I was about to go to school for the first time. That night before, I was very excited that I could barely sleep thinking of how my day would go. My mother had relaxed my hair, twisted it, and curled it at the end. I had new outfits and colorful berets to match my clothes. My new backpack was pink with Barbie logo across the front. My socks and shoes were set out to be worn.

It was about to be my first day in kindergarten at a Catholic School. I always wondered what school would be like because all my cousins and uncles attended school. My cousins and uncles were a few years older than me. They brought home cool projects and activities. I walked to their school every day with my grandmother to pick them up, but on a few occasions I went into their classrooms. Whenever, I went to their school I wanted to stay because their classrooms seemed very interesting. On this day, it would be a beginning to something that will help shape my future.

I woke up with a smile that could never go into a frown. I got up, got dressed and brushed my teeth. I had a little trouble getting dressed, because my head got stuck in the neck part of my shirt. That caused my hair to mess up a little, but that was not going to ruin my day. When I got into the truck, I kept asking my mother questions about school. "Mama, what kind of things will I do? Will I make new friends? Is it going to be fun?" The questions just kept coming. My mother answered a few of my questions, but I knew I was getting on her nerves. She replied, "You will see when you get there." We arrived and my hands became sweaty, and I was shaking a little. "Paris, are u ready?" my mother asked. "Yes, mama I am a big girl." Deep down this was scary and I wanted to go back home.

My mother and I walked inside the school cafeteria seeing a lot of nuns in long black dresses, and a lot of students in the cafeteria. I began to become very shy. I did not want to let my mother hand go. My mother had to leave for work. My mother was leaving me at school to go to work; she gave me a hug and a kiss on the forehead. This was a strange place and I did not know anybody. My uncles and cousins went to the school down the street. I didn't know what to say to people. I didn't want people to not like me because of what I said. I just sat at the end of the table by myself. "What is your name?" Sister Mary Castalo asked. I was very nervous to talk to her because my mother always told me not to talk to strangers. Then I finally replied, "My name is Paris." Sister Mary Castalo told me the name of my teacher and the location of my class.

"Ding, Ding, Ding!" The bell had rung for the students to go to their teachers. The kindergarten teachers were standing at the cafeteria door with their student list. I waited until I heard my name being called to get up from the table. I heard a tall bright lady with a wooden cross on her neck call my name. I wasn't sure it was me at first, until she called "Paris Bullock." I got into her line with the other children. My room number was 108 with 15 students. The classroom was huge. It had alphabets, numbers, and drawings on the wall. The wall was like nothing I had ever seen before. As we walked inside, the teacher told us to put our backpacks in the cubby's with our name on. The cubby I was assigned to was blue and rectangular. After we put our stuff up, all the students stood in a circle. We wrote our name on a sheet of construction paper so that we could introduce ourselves. It started with the teacher introduced herself, picked a student to introduce their self, and the student had to pick another student to introduce themselves. After we wrote our name, we colored on our paper about anything we liked. Later that day I went to recess, and I had naptime. At recess, I played dodge ball and tag with my peers. That is when I started making friends. I was happy I made a lot of new friends that day. My first day of school was exhausting but I wanted to do it all over again.

ISABEL MARIE BLANCO
by Noemi Bustamante

Sitting there, listening to La Vie en Rose, waiting for the phone to dial. I imagined what Isabel would be doing. I hear the line click, her voice sounded anxious, that moment I realized she seemed nervous. The way her voice always goes high pitch when she gets nervous. The lamp in my room illuminated the questions that laid there in front of me. I asked Isabel to give me a second, while I would look for a pen. I placed the phone down and headed towards my bed to look for a pen, but instead I found myself staring at a photo that was taken a little over a year ago.

In the picture Isabel and I had huge smiles across our faces, while her arm inner locked with mine. With the sun illuminating at the left corner of the picture, it allowed the camera to see Isabel's beautiful structure, giving her a look younger than her actual age, 43. Her highlighted blonde, brown hair, only reaching her shoulders, gave her round face a warm look, allowing you to know she was friendly, and kind. The dimples that helped cover up her round cheeks that hid her freckles, giving her skin tone a honey yet pale look. Her round, light brown eyes are carefully hidden safely behind her glasses, which bring out her contagious smile.

I can still remember her scent that day. She smelled like Japanese cherry blossom, the scent is neither strong nor light; it is just evened out to the point that the smell does not bother anyone. I suddenly hear Isabel say, "Noemi? Are you there?" I responded immediately, "Oh yes, sorry I got distracted." Once I grabbed the pen, I adjust the lamp and prepared myself to write down her answers, on the other line I heard my friend Joseph, her son, ask, "Mom, who are you talking to?" Isabel laughed, and responded, "Mimi, silly!" I pictured Isabel saying it with a huge smile on her face.

Once I started asking her the first couple of question, it seemed as if she felt more relaxed. But when I asked more serious questions, that were personal, she seemed to have a more difficult time answering. One of the personal questions that I asked that I felt made her act more tense was, "Who do you look up to? Why?" Shortly, after I asked the question she stayed quiet for about a minute. I could hear the television playing in the background, that's how I knew she was still on the phone. After a minute or so she responded slowly, "The main person I really looked up to was my grandmother. She would always tell me stories that would teach me a life lesson. She would just be there for me, whenever I would get into some type of trouble, as a teenager. She always made me feel as if I could tell her anything, without being judged, or misunderstood. Even now I still remember her lessons, but yeah, my grandmother was the main person I admired next to my parents."

The following question that I asked made her react calmer. "What impacted your life the most?" Shortly after asking the question Isabel remained silent. Her silence made me realize, that maybe what I had asked seemed too personal. All of a sudden I hear her take in a deep breath, then she responds, "I would have to go with my oldest brother passing away." She paused and inhaled deeply again. "He meant a lot to me, and I had admired him for stepping up to my dad's place when my father couldn't be there. My life changed after that, I felt as if a new window had opened and it had opened up my eyes at that moment. It really changed my life in a lot of things. That eye opener helped me realize that I had to fix my life, at that moment. So it got me more involved with the church, spending more time with my family, and finished what I started." Hearing Isabel open up to me made me feel so special, especially since I never really knew any of their family history until that day. I admired her for her courage to speak of such an event in her life. It just added another reason as to why I look up to her.

Interviewing Isabel made me learn so much about her, a lot of things that I was not aware of. I feel as if the whole interview made me open my eyes and realize how certain people can really help form your personality. The interview not only made me realize certain things, but it also made me look at Isabel differently. The way Isabel stayed strong through personal questions helped me view her more as a strong person. I now see Isabel as a strong, courageous, kind, woman, who is not afraid to face up to neither reality nor the past. This is what makes Isabel Marie Blanco, Isabel, the mother of 2 children and a stay at home mother.

UNTITLED
by Noemi Bustamante

Amanda, to my family, was just a dog, an animal, but to me she was more than that; she was my companion, a best friend, a family member. Even though she was not human she still attained the human qualities that made me feel comfort in her embrace, secure with her round brown eyes, and safe with her feisty, white, teeth. The day I confessed how much I loved her, was the day I knew she was no longer my companion but rather the loved one I had lost. Sadly, cancer had taken her away from me, I was angered after that day; I saw no point in growing attachments with a dog or a human. I thought there was no point into creating strong relationships with something or someone that wouldn't be with me forever. I remained hidden within my four walls, refusing to get hurt again, refusing to forget. Until, I decided to visit her grave, for the first time in 5 months. Sitting there I noticed the flowers that were growing on top of her grave. At that moment I came to realization that when something dies, something new is born. Amanda's death helped me see that, that love does not stop, it continues. She helped me understand that love can be upheld eternally, and it shouldn't be something that should not bring pain, but rather peace, and strength. Through which, I can say I have opened up my heart to a new pet, and have become stronger in the aspect of being able to be more open minded about life. The difference between me back then and me now, is how I have carved myself into a stick that can withstand any obstacle, and can overcome it.

Blue Print of a Heart
by Israel Rodriguez

A BITTER MEMORY
by Brenda Cabrera

My pueblo, or town, is not a big place. It does not have a lot of luxuries or commodities. It does not even have an adequate hospital, just a clinic for minor health treatment, like flu's and shots. The road is not even paved; it is just dirt and a lot of little rocks. However, none of this matters to me because I am happy to be with the people there. I live with my mom and sister but besides them, I have my grandparents, Domingo and Luisa, who live just next door to my house.

At school, it had been just another day like any other. I was walking home from school on that rocky road in which I had walked for the past 3 years of my school career. It was a beautiful afternoon; the sun was low on the distant horizon, like a giant ball of fire whose light was extinguishing in the west. A soft breeze swayed the branches of the trees, as if to make them dance to the rhythm of the wind. I walked the short way to my home with my mind full of thoughts about spending the last two hours of daylight playing with my sister and cousins in the little hill behind my abuelita's house; however, little did I know that destiny had made totally different plans for me.

As I approached my house, I realized that something was wrong because the street was quiet, too quiet. We were nearing Easter and we used to prepare for it by doing little discussions, or platicas, and sermons with our neighbors and this was about the time everyone got out of these little gatherings but no one was on the streets. I kept walking barely paying attention to this fact when a man approached me. I do not recall who he was but I do remember clearly the message he had for me.

"They took your abuelita to the hospital. She was in a serious condition. Go look for your aunts and tell them," he said in a calm but serious tone and then continued on his way on his horse leaving me there, stunned. What had I just heard? My grandmother? In the hospital? This couldn't be true. There had to be a mistake. Suddenly, that gentle breeze had just turned into a violent gust of wind that was choking me and wanted to tumble me to the ground; in one instant my life had been turned upside down. I furiously ran to my house only to find it locked. I then ran to my grandmother's house only to find it dark and deserted. I was starting to feel dizzy.

My 9-year old mind could not process all of these facts. I started crying, I felt lost so I headed outside to the street not knowing what else to do. Then, on the distance, I saw my cousin Zayra running towards me; she seemed scared and like she was on the verge of crying too. "Your mom just called my house to let us know that our abuelita Luisa is in the Santa Catarina Hospital. We need to let my mom and tia Amanda know," she said struggling to catch her breath.

So we ran from place to place, first down the road and when they weren't there we hurried up the road looking for my tias to inform them of what was happening. However, we didn't know where they were because they too were supposed to be at a gathering. When we finally figured out where they were we busted into the house finding it hard to recover our breath and interrupted their meeting. We spotted my aunts seated at the very front and saw their expression of surprise to see us there. I was the one who broke the bad news to them. "We have to go! We have to go!" I pleaded them, feeling the warm tears starting to gather in my eyes. "Calm down Brendita. What's wrong?" questioned my tia Amanda. "Mama (grandma) Luisa is in the hospital at Rio Verde," explained Zayra, hugging her mom for comfort.

Tia Amanda reacted quickly and hurried us to her house where we found her husband, my tio Polo, and the last thing I know I'm at the back of his truck on our way to the hospital. We flew past bumpy rocks leaving particles of dust behind and trees and houses blurring past us. While we raced past houses, my mind raced with thoughts about what had happened the last 30 minutes of my life and tried to make sense of them hoping all of this was only a nightmare.

It seemed like it took us forever to get to the hospital, however, it only took us half the usual time due to the rush we all had to get there. As soon as I entered the emergency room the smell of medicine, sickness, sadness and hope greeted me. I looked around and then there at the end of the hallway were my mom and sister. Even from far away I could see the fear and anguish written in their faces. As we neared, I noticed my sister had one of my grandma's black shoe and blue shawl in her hands. "She had a stroke. When we got here, it was too late already. The doctor says she doesn't have much hope," my mother said in a somber voice. We all hugged each other and cried.

Moments later, I went to see my grandmother but I was shocked when I saw her; this was not her, this was someone else. She was a different person, someone connected to many machines and tubes and then I noticed she still had on her other shoe. Three days later, we brought her home from the hospital; however, she was lifeless. She did not move, eat, or speak anymore. After a week, my dad and his siblings decided to take her off the artificial support system and that was the last time she was with me. It is incredible how life can be changed and how easy it is to lose a loved one. I miss her advice and affection. I wished I still had my grandmother with me, but I know that is not possible. Now I try to spend as much time as I can with my remaining grandparents because I learned that you never know what the future might hold for you.

PETER KURTZ
by Jose Cantu

The weather was nice that Thursday afternoon at school. The sun shone majestically as its rays warmed the cool, autumn, Houston air. I hastily walked up the outdoor stairs to room 206 to fetch one of the best instructors that I have had. We walked slowly through the open air hallway-balcony of the second floor. My interview subject walked down the stairs with purpose while I hurried trying to keep up. We passed the outdoor courtyard of HAIS, as we ambled to the teacher's lounge.

The feeling in the room was relaxed and calm as Peter and I walked into the teacher's lounge. Out of respect, I never called the man I was about to interview by his first name. He is the typical small town boy with big aspirations. The difference is that he achieved his goals which made him wise and intelligent and also a great teacher.

"So what is your favorite color?" I began.

"Purple," he responded, with little hesitation.

According to Peter, the color purple represented royalty in ancient times because purple dye was so difficult to obtain that only the emperor could wear it. Peter's interest in ancient Rome however, was a longer anecdote and more interesting than his favorite color.

"So you seem to have interest in ancient Rome. Why is that?" I asked him.

"It started because my mentor was a specialist in Roman history," he answered. After attending school his entire life, Peter had vast knowledge of U.S. history, but fell short when it came to the classical period. He became infatuated with this subject and began translating ancient works. He even went all out and learned Latin.

Peter's work paid off a few years later when he completed his Master's degree in Roman studies in the city of Manchester. He was then accepted into the British School at Rome, which was a very prestigious achievement. "While there I was given over 45 permits to go into different archaeological sites, and I got to work with a lot of world renowned historians. I got to go into all of these archaeological sites and I got to do research at the top level of three different countries including the US, UK and Italy. It was amazing working on this and being at the heart of all of this research," he told me.

"So let's backtrack a little," I stated. "How was your education before you met your mentor?"

"Oh, it was poor!" he exclaimed. I grew up in Boise, Idaho. You don't even need a degree in Idaho to teach." Peter did well as a student whenever he had a good teacher. Conversely, when he had a bad teacher, he did poorly as a student. It was an extremely bad education. "I actually learned math and how to use proper English in history class."

Even though Peter's teachers were not necessarily qualified to teach, Peter prevailed.

"So how did you transition from having a really poor education to being a professor?" I inquired.

"Late nights. A lot of late, late nights," he answered humorously. The teachers, because of their under qualification, did not know the subject that they were teaching, therefore, Peter spent his evenings in the library reading about what he supposedly learned in class. ". Teachers in high school would say the truth is this, but I would come back and say 'well this book says this' and the teachers wouldn't know anything about it. So it was always of argument so my teachers always ended up putting me outside the class room so I would get my C." When he got to college though, he realized that he had not learned much in school, so it was back to the library.

"How did you go from Boise to England?" I asked him.

"... I got my degree in Boise so what I did was I felt that I needed to know more..." Peter wanted to go and study in England, but nobody beside his wife and mother believed he could succeed. He did though and in a major way. "My master's was first class from Oxford and Manchester," he said proudly.

After he achieved such a high honor, people back in Boise showered Peter with praise. He realized then how "cheap" people's approval was. "I was only gone for 2 years and everyone was like, 'Well we need to know what Peter's opinion is on this? What's Peter think?'" He was not happy with his situation in Idaho. When his wife asked him where he wanted to go, Peter answered, "Wherever you want. Throw a dart on the map and let's go."

Peter and his wife came to Houston because of his wife's job. However, "I was offered a job as a professor at Cyfair. I said no though because I wanted to teach in the city."

"So is that how you ended up here at HAIS?"

"No, how I got here was because I got sick in 2007. We were planning on not staying here very long. I didn't like Houston at all. When I got sick in December 10, 2007, I passed out and I woke up 15 days later in a hospital with them taking equipment off of me." He had fallen sick with acute respiratory syndrome. "I worked myself to the ground trying to get out of here and I nearly died because of it." When he got out of the comma, Peter had to relearn everything from walking to shaving. "What I found was that Houstonians are very kind. The school put a fundraiser for me and raised thousands of dollars. I was able to keep my house. That changed my perspective on Houston and on life."

After recovering from his illness, Peter Kurtz began working at the Houston Academy for International Studies where he has been ever since as a history professor and as my inspiration.

THE UNSPOKEN GOODBYE
by Amber Beltran

"Amber, I don't have the courage to tell you one last goodbye. You were my reason to keep holding on, but I can't do this on my own anymore.. I feel so alone. One day, we will be able to walk, holding hands, roaming this big blue world of ours. I love you, forever and always is not far from me, but wait for me, like I will be waiting for you wherever death takes me. Please, promise me, that you will always remember me with smiles and, never harmed. I am so sorry. Please forgive me. Please don't blame yourself. Your beloved friend, Michael." (November 24, 2009)

Receiving that letter was the end of me. The beginning said all of my worst fears; you said you couldn't take the hurt anymore, said the hurt was no longer bearable; what hurt?. I felt lost at a sea of emotions, I had no idea what was going on. I always hoped I could be the one to erase all your pain but I guess I was proved completely wrong. At that very moment, all of our times we had together flashed through my mind; moments that used to bring a bright smile to my face, now brought nothing but tears and a rush of sudden betrayal. I continued asking myself, why? You never gave a cry for help, or was I too blind to see the hurt you truly felt? Could I have stopped you with a simple kiss? If only you knew how I felt for you.

Everything hit me so quickly. I was full of anger, remorse, uselessness, and pain. I just felt myself spiral into a state of insanity, that no one could get me out of. I kept thinking, Michael would know just what to do, then I would remember he's the reason I'm in this. Could I have saved you from yourself? What can I do to save myself now? My legs soon gave out from under me, I felt myself fall to my knees and as I looked up to the cloudy sky, I whispered "Michael. How could you do this to me? You said you would never leave. Talk to me, please." I wasn't expecting any great direct responses, but I prayed for a simple rush of wind or a whiff of his favorite cologne. Nothing. Did you not care anymore?

My heart continued calling your name. I felt my body get taken over, trying to reach into your imaginary arms. I knew you were no longer there, but I couldn't accept losing you. I needed you, I longed for your presence. You said I was your reason of holding on; I no longer felt the closeness I thought we had. I felt like I was lied to all those years, I needed you more than you ever needed me, and that was finally proven. Michael, you had my heart in your hands, and it died with you.

In the depths of my imagination, your state of mind was so perfect, so unexpected. Could I have ever guessed this would be the end? Could I ever imagine life without you? No, I couldn't, but I had to. What hurt the most was that you lied right to my face when I asked "Are you okay?" I felt that we could speak about anything in this world , that was untrue. You kept the most important things to yourself, all your hurt and fears. Did you feel I couldn't handle the truth? Did you feel it was safer to hold things in?

I imagined In a dream I saw your lifeless body, hanging there, silenced. Your bright brown eyes seemed so dull and full of agony were so dull and blood shot red. The scars on your arms looked re-opened and so fresh, with blood running down the open wounds; but in this image the blood wasn't red, it was black as coal.. A very distinctive bruising was imprinted on your neck, and that wrapped around your throat line; with the rope torn at the ends. Your lips were purple as violets in the summer nights. I tried to grasp for your lifeless hand, to feel your touch once more before it was taken from me forever; but you kept slipping away from my grasp. You were really gone. You then opened your eyes, your devilish crooked mouth; looked at me and said "This is where I want to be. Be happy."

I responded in a furious yell, "Be happy? How do you expect that Michael? You betrayed me!" Tears running down my face, gasping for air, "I hate you." How could a love so strong for someone be ruined with a simple contemplated death? I was locked in a thought I wanted to leave so badly. Deep down, I knew I felt some sort of hate for Michael; , but I didn't want to hate him. How could a love so strong for someone be ruined with a simple contemplated death? I needed closure, I needed my unspoken goodbye.

C'EST LA VIE
by Rea Clemons

The Beginning:

This past year of my life up until my vacation depicted everything that haunted me. I went from what I thought was a low point of my life and finally healed to have everything stripped away from me, again. Last year was different. The year seemed like it only left me with enough to start my life over again. This journey started when my dad left which for me was difficult, being a daddy's girl, and is something that I am reminded of everyday. My first birthday without him proved to be the most difficult.

The Party:

It was a Friday and I was so happy because I was going to spend the weekend with my best friends and I felt like my week had been great; during French class all that was on my mind was the crazy conversations waiting to be had and the things we had to tell each other. I could not wait because to tell them about my week and what had made this week memorable. I rushed out of the building as soon as my mother called to tell me that she was waiting for me, ready to pick up my friends and begin the perfect end to my week. When my mom picked up my friends and we celebrated my birthday and it was everything I could have ever imagined.

The Dinner:

It was about a week later, my Sweet Sixteen dinner with three of the most important people that have always been in my life, my mom, aunt (whom I all Tía), and cousin Yasmine (who is like the sister I never had). We were all on the way to eat some of my favorite food of all time, seafood, at Joe's Crab Shack. I couldn't wait because this was going to be the last day I would see my Tía and Yasmine, because I would be in Louisiana for the rest of the summer. visiting family I loved this dinner so much but with each bite of food and laughter that came from the reminiscing of times when I was younger. I couldn't help but think of my dad and the way he would react to each of these stories. This entire was truly my emotional rollercoaster because it only made it even more obvious to me of yet another event that I could share with my father.

The Gifts:

After my amazing dinner all I wanted to do was run home and see what gifts were awaiting me as soon as walked into the front door. To help my mom feel like I was truly happy that night I talked to her the whole ride home and fought the urge to tell her the thoughts that were running through my mind. I unlocked the front door and proceeded to the location of all of my cards. I had one card from my aunt and two from my father. When I realized that these were my only gifts I immediately was more and more depressed by this "special" birthday of mine. Nervous I opened the card from my aunt and was happy to see a gift card to Target, one of my favorite stores by far. After opening this card I became extremely nervous between my mom breathing down my neck insisting on knowing what my dad and his sister had to tell me, and the cards my dad had sent me.

I opened the card that was lighter of the two nervous to see what he had to say after the multiple emails I had forced myself to ignore. The card was simple and only had the heartfelt message a Hallmark card author had written to their daughter with a scribbled "Love Daddy" on it. It hurt to see that he had put no effort into my plain gift, but kept in mind that I still hadn't opened the second card. I picked up, shook it, and immediately knew its contents, a necklace, and couldn't help to see what this piece of jewelry looked like. As I broke the seal of the envelope, I felt the chain of the necklace and the imprint in had left due to the shipment from Kentucky. When I opened the card I felt a sort of ping in my heart, the necklace a simple gold crucifix on a simple chain. It wasn't the cost of the 24-karat necklace that caused me to feel a strong attachment to it. This necklace's symbolized the many times I found comfort in him as a child from all of my troubles. I fought to hold back my tears until I was in the comfort of my pillow and away from my mom because the last thing I wanted to do was to talk about what I felt. I waited until I got to the comfort of my pillow, I fought back my tears so that I didn't have to explain how I felt.

The fight to keep my emotions from exploding and displaying to my mother how I truly felt about the past year of my life only added to my motivation to get to my room. I quickly told my mom thanks for everything and gave her a hug as she gave me my last birthday wish of the night. I could barely get comfortable in my bed before all of the greatest troubles that I had of the year could pass. That moment felt like the lowest moment of my entire year.

My Understanding:

The next day I held on to that necklace with all my might and thought about putting it on before I went to sleep that night. That afternoon, before I could even eat my lunch I lost my gift, right next to a computer in the lab. When I finally realized it I left the necklace, it was too late. This simple event made everything about that year clear to me. After mourning what felt like losing him again I had an "Aha Moment!" I realized that the only way for me to truly repair my wounds is to understand that no object can replace what you need, which for me is closure. This experience helped teach me that even if my mom and dad were breaking up and my dad had moved, that I still had him close by no matter what in my heart. It also taught me that you cannot change the past and to realize that it was just life, or simply "C'est La Vie," as the French put it.

A SISTER'S LIFE
by Israel Cordova

The day was very warm, and the night was even worse. The heat was unbearable, and seemed to cling onto your skin as you walked. It was one of those days where you just wanted to not do anything because it was just so hot. I was getting everything ready for the interview, which consisted mostly of just a couple chairs and a "some-what" clean room. I heard the knock at the door and I rushed to greet my interviewee. My sister walked in the door and greets everyone with a smile as wide as the moon. She seemed ready to start and was full of joy and excitement. I told her that I wasn't so sure the questions were "stellar" but she just gave me a reassuring smile and told me I would do great. I showed her to the room where the interview was going to be conducted in, and took a quick glance inside for any misplaced items. I placed the recorder on the table and closed the door. I hit the record button. "Let's get started shall we?"

My sister was born in Houston, Texas into a stable divorced home. Her parents were very, as she said, "Unified", and didn't have problems perhaps a normal divorced family had. She went to many different schools during her childhood mainly because she kept moving around. She attended 5 elementary schools, 1 intermediate school and 2 high schools. Along the way she attained an interest in music by learning to play the cello and starting on a vocal musical path. This path would eventually lead to a tough decision she would have to make in her future.

One of her most prominent memories is her *Quincenera* which she had at 15. Along with her *Quincenera,* she also remembers her high school prom which she considers one of those things that "every girl remembers". Of course she has also had some sad memories which she still remembers to this day. When her grandmother passed away, it affected her very deeply due to the fact that she could not be there. It took her a while to get back on her feet but she did, and saw another shocking surprise in her life. The birth of her 2 brothers and sister, after close to twenty years of just being the only 2 siblings in the family, shocked her and her brother. She considers this event as something "wonderful".

As a child and young adult my sister had many goals. Most children have the dream of being an astronaut, artist, doctor, and more. My sister at a young age wanted to be a lawyer, and she kept this aspiration later on throughout her life. Another notion my sister had was a possible future in music. My sister at the time was a very good singer (and still is) and when she studied in college she had to make a tough decision. She could either go down the path of music, or choose another career. She in the end chose another career, because she wanted to make sure that she was in a career that could provide her financially. She chose accounting because she wanted something that could "get her foot in the door".

She to this day continues studying in hopes of pursuing her accounting career. She currently studies at the University of Houston at Clearlake and is trying to decide in getting a MBA or CMA. She currently works as an accountant for a construction engineering company. When asked if she had any what ifs, she responded that her choice in a musical career would be her lifelong "what if".

Her inspirations are both of her parents. She said that her mother has been a great inspiration for her because she has seen her mom striving to demonstrate the importance of education. Even as an example when her mother went back to school and opened up a business. Her father was also an example to her because he was always trying to provide the best for them when he could. They didn't have much but what her father could give, he did. To my sister those were her two main inspirations.

My sister's only regret: "What if I had pursued a musical career instead of an accounting career?" As for hobbies, my sister has a great voice and often sings whenever she can. She is an avid reader and enjoys any good book any time. She has always wanted to travel. She absolutely loves art and wants to travel to the world's museums to see these masterpieces. When I asked her if she had any advice for students in high school to prepare them for college she said, "I would say to take a deep breath because college is absolutely nothing like high school."

To end, I believe my sister is a person who has gone through struggles, triumphs and challenges. These struggles along with her triumphs have shaped the person I stood talking to on the day of the interview. With great role models and inspirations, she has had help on her way to success. My sister is somebody I would choose as a role model in a heartbeat because of her constant determination to advance and progress, and her positive outlook on life.

UNWANTED
by Unique Crumby

"Hey I'm going to be home late." I spoke into the phone, "Just calling to remind you."

I left my stepdad a message on his phone since he didn't answer. I was only reminding him that today I had to stay after school late for my after school program. It's the first day of it and I was making sure that my stepfather remembered. I told him earlier but he has work so I'm sure he forgot. 21st Century, the program, is just something for us to do after school to either learn something new or be in clubs and such.

"Unique come on they have new stuff to try." my friend called out to me.

I smiled and left the main office of the school. She's right there are a lot of new things. Drama, baton twirling, even diabolo. Diabolo seems interesting most likely because I have no idea what it is.

"What are you going to do?" I asked my friends.

"Not sure." replied one of them, "Drama sound fun."

"Yeah I think so too." added another of my friends.

I nodded in agreement but told them I was going to check out the diabolo. The teacher introduced herself. She was from Korea and had practiced Diabolo for awhile. She explained that it's actually like a yo-yo. If fact it is a form of yo-yo from China They are usually made of either rubber or plastic but ours were made of both. The diabolo itself is very interesting to look at. It resembles a larger version of an empty spool of thread. The differences lie in the creation and what they're used for obviously.

"Okay first you place the diabolo spool on the string." she instructed, "Move it along the floor. Then use your dominate hand to wrap the string around the middle while lifting it up off the floor."

I was learning so much. Basic tricks for the diabolo Even so I left early because I felt like something was wrong. Something is drawing me in to the place I call home. I'm not sure what but something is telling me. It had become dark. Day lights saving time had already passed and the clocks moved backwards an hour it was only five, thirty minutes before it was over, and school had let out at three o'clock.

"Where have you been?" my stepdad inquires as I enter the house, his voice hard and unwavering.

"At school." I replied uneasily.

"Why didn't you tell anybody?"

"I did." I retaliated shakily, "And I called after school was over."

"I didn't get it!" he yelled his voice reverberated throughout the room.

I flinched back. Even though I was used to the screaming, it happens so often here, I didn't know how else I should react. Normally when I do something wrong I would have been hit by now. Yet nothing has happened so I don't know.

"Go get your things and call your mom." he barked, "You can't stay here."

I feel like that's worse than being hit. I'm not supposed to live with my mother and he knows this. He's the one who called Child Protective Services on her in the first place claiming she was an unfit mother. But there's nothing I can do, there's nothing anyone can do. I have no other place to go besides an orphanage. No other relatives can take me in because they live in a different state. I may not technically be able to live with my mother but she does still have custody of me. If she says I can't leave the state than I can't.

I left to the room my sister and I shared. I begin to pack my things trying my hardest not to cry before my sibling. My little sister helps silent as well. My little brother is off doing god knows what. As heartbroken as I am I won't appear weak in front of my younger sister. I'll stay strong and confident for my siblings and others out of love. Always love because without it there is nothing else. My mother wouldn't be here to the next morning so I stayed in the bedroom not wanting to cause any more trouble. While my sister was out of the room I silently let the tears I had been holding back fall as I drifted off to sleep.

GOAL!
by David Cruz

When I looked at the clock I almost had a heart attack because the game was going to start in less than 25 minutes. So I showered, got dressed and gathered my stuff and was out the door in less than 10 minutes. My mom was staring at me the whole time and told me that I had gotten ready so fast like if someone was coming to get me and that I had hurried up so fast so that I could get away. I just told her that I was in a hurry to get to the game because I didn't want my teammates to be mad at me for arriving late. So it was a 10 minutes drive to the park and I arrived just in time with 5 minutes to spare.

When I arrived we had 5 minutes to warm up before the game started. So we all got into a circle and started stretching so that we wouldn't pull a muscle once inside the field playing. One of my friends was shaking like if he was cold but it was actually from nervousness which we are were because this was a really important match to decide the last team to go to the league quarterfinals. No one knew what would happen once inside the field but we were determined to win and you could see in the face of the other team as well and just looking at them give us the creeps because they meant business. So when the referee blew the whistle to start the game we got in line and marched into the field like warriors entering the battlefield and only the best would come out victorious.

The other team started with the ball and with the whistle the game began and we quickly gained possession of the ball. We where charging them like bulls, but they weren't quick to counter, they didn't expect us to play fast in the beginning. We got a couple of times into the goal area but weren't able to connect in making a goal. I was playing defender and was getting pretty bored because the ball never came to where I was because it was mostly in the middle like it that was the only area that we were playing in.

So our team had the ball and we were making our way to the goal and one of my friends was wide open just outside the area and they passed him the ball and he kicked it. It was like I could sense that it was going in because he kicked it with such force like a cannon shot (or as we Hispanic people like to call it "CAÑONASO") and you could just hear the impact his foot made with the ball and it was too high for the goalie because it went right in the angle.

We celebrate the goal but the coach told us not to get confident because there was still time. Too bad we didn't listen because the other team caught us off guard on our right side and was at our goal I tried to get to the goal from the left side but I was too late the ball had already gone in. So the game was tied with 10 minutes remaining. We were all disappointed because they scored on us. All we heard was the coach on the side saying

"Keep your heads up it isn't over until it's over." Somehow that gave us courage and we started dominating the field and our best player made his way to the goal but then out of nowhere a player from the other team tackled him and all you see is him falling to the ground with pain in his eyes. When we go over to check him out he told us his ankle snapped like a twig and that it really hurt. We were all sad because he was our best player and we couldn't win without him. He said that he believed in us that we would win. We had to make a substation for him and it was a foul so we had got a free kick and they had put me to kick it. I was really nervous because this could decide it all that if I make it and we win or we stay tied and go to penalties.

When the whistle blew, I took a deep breath and kicked the ball and I could just see the ball swerve right over the defenders and into the goal the goalie was too far from it and with that the ref blew the whistle to end the game and my teammates ran to me all excited because we won and were going to the playoffs.

MY VACATION IN NEW YORK CITY
by Carlos Davy

It was a bright sunny and clear day in the middle of summer of 2009 when after a grueling whole day of car traveling my family and I reached the amazing city of New York. I had been visualizing my experiences in this city weeks prior to my visit there, and was very excited once I got there; I just knew that all my dreams were going to be made true. One of the things that made this trip unique and more enjoyable was that I wasn't going with my parents but with my uncle and his family, so I felt very free and much more relaxed without my parents.

It was very close to noon after we made it through the vehicle booth station and were driving from the state of New Jersey to the great island of Manhattan. At this moment I immediately took my eyes off something I cannot quite remember I was doing and look out the window. I got extremely excited and felt great that I had finally gotten to my destination once I saw it… and what I saw was a humongous wall of high rise buildings stretching at least a few miles long, or so I thought, in a way that the closer I got, it just made me feel more small and unheard, since it was pretty loud in the city. Never before had I ever seen such an incredible skyline made of an average, I would say, of 700-800 feet tall buildings covering an immense area, and what make it more fascinating was that the architecture was so diverse in each and every one of the buildings' designs that it was as if each building had its own different story of why it was made.

We were crossing the widely-notorious George Washington Bridge constructed entirely of stainless steel painted with a light bluish color. As we slowly approached the city I decided to scroll down the window to have a better sight of the scenery. As soon as the window was lowering, I could already hear the loud rumble that the city generated. It immediately started to smell a little like smoke from the pollution from the cars and the buildings. "I am finally here," I told myself with excitement.

We went into Uptown Manhattan and saw mostly small refineries and a few small buildings here and there. Before I knew we were in the borough of the Bronx and were going to park our SUV in a parking garage. Just to do that took us about half an hour to find a parking space and pay up the manager.

After that, the first place we decided to go was a McDonald's, as we were very hungry. There, we met with my older cousin, Alan, who lives in Bronx and knows very well the city. At first we thought that as being in the most culturally diverse city in the world, we should go to some original Chinese food restaurant or some traditional Italian cuisine, but we were so hungry that we just went to the nearby McDonald's. To our surprise, it wasn't crowded at all and so we ate our Big Macs excitedly, thinking of all the discoveries that we still had to uncover in this great city. That was perhaps the best Big Mac I ever had.

When we finished eating, we were so anxious to visit all the magical places that made New York City the capital city of the world. I still couldn't get over the thought that I was finally in New York and I had to wait no longer. It took us a while to decide on where we were going to go. The World Trade Center (WTC), we decided. Ever since the September 11 attacks, we had been curious about how the WTC looks like. We realized that our journey there was going to be a little more difficult than we had expected. We had to buy our subway train tickets, which took quite some while, and then wait for the train to come, which was actually pretty fast.

When I was about to step onto the train, I got a little scared because I knew that the New York subway system was no joke and the trains went quite fast; not even close to Houston's metro rail . And before I knew, I was right. The train accelerated unexpectedly fast and I abruptly slid sideways. I think this was the part when I went into some form of momentary paralysis as my head was spinning full of thoughts and strong feelings of where I was and where I was going. It was a very dark tunnel that you couldn't see anything and kept like that for just a minute, and in that minute I felt like I had gone through a whole lot all inside my head. This was the only time when I felt somewhat weird, not happiness nor harm, but some weird feeling, perhaps some mental distortion that to this day I keep wondering if it will ever repeat itself again.

DANGERS OF A TRAIL
by Anibal Delgado

A couple of years ago, me, my mom, and 2 friends went camping high in the mountains and swam in a lake that's up there. We started hiking up the trail towards the lake at almost dusk, so by the time we got to the lake, the sun was setting. As soon as we got there, I found out that I had dropped my shorts somewhere on the trail. I figured they couldn't be too far away, so I'd just walk back and find them. My friends didn't want to go back down the trail, so they made a fire and set up the tent while I went back with a flashlight to find my shorts. I walked down the trail and lost track of time and how far I was from the lake.

Eventually, I got to the beginning of the trail and by my friend's van with no shorts in hand. I searched the car and they weren't there, so I decided to go back to the lake trail so the rest of the people wouldn't worry about me and the next day I'd just miss swimming. After a while of walking down the trail, I saw something blue in the dirt. It was the shorts! So I headed towards the lake. However, I had barely started walking when I heard creepy sound just ahead and got scared. I stopped and listened. I kept telling myself it was just my imagination. The sound faded out a bit so I started walking again. My flashlight had very little battery left so I had to look hard to know where I was going. But as I strained to see in the darkness I noticed a few stars blacked out ahead. At first I thought it was a tree. Then I heard a loud grunt and got even more scared than before. I raised the extremely dim flashlight and could see two little reflections glinting off the eyes of a giant moose that was standing right in the middle of the trail. I didn't know what to do. I got the dumb idea in my head of running past him. Then I thought of what might happen if the moose attacked, so I decided to run back the other way. I took off back to the bottom of the trail. There was a ski lodge there with a phone in it so I called my friends at the top of the trail to try and tell them what was going on. I called both phones, but there was no answer, just message machines. I left them both a message saying I was stuck at the start of the trail, running from a moose, I was going to stay in the car and they could come get me in the morning. After trying to talk them some more, I got in my friend's van and decided that instead of sleeping; I would go home, get a gun, then come back and walk past the moose. So I drove all the way down the canyon, got to our lodging house, went inside, got the gun, and got some water. Then the phone rang. It was the police. They asked me if I had stolen my friend's car, and I said, "I didn't steal it but I did take it." They told me they were with him at the start of the trail and that he wanted his car back, so I went out of the house, jumped in the car, went back to the canyon, and found him with some cops at the start of the trail. The cops were really laid back and unconcerned, so that was really no problem. They just told me to be good and left. My friend was mad at me and scolded me the whole way down the trail. He kept asking me why I was scared of a moose.

Then, halfway up the trail, we ran into the same moose. We walked past him and he didn't do anything. My friend laughed, "See, it's not dangerous." When we arrived at the lake we found our other friend cowering in a tent. My friend with the car tried to get him to tease me too about how moose aren't scary, but it he was scared and said, "I don't blame you. A moose was up here walking around the tent and I was freaking out!" So he teased the both of us, we went to bed, and swam the next day.

I found out that the reason I never answered earlier was not because they had no service but they were too lazy to answer a phone call from an unknown number. I was pissed off! If they had answered the phone, I wouldn't have taken the car home, the cops wouldn't have been involved, and I would get to hike to the lake with everyone without getting teased the whole time!

A WALK DOWN MEMORY LANE
by James DeShazor

We had finally arrived to her mansion of a house after a lengthy drive. We were one of the first ones to get there, we were usually late for events but this time we showed up on time. Bryant, Mrs. Frieda's son, happily greeted us at her glass front door and we entered the well-decorated house. Mrs. Frieda always decorated for the holidays and she always does an immaculate job. After we exchanged greetings and salutations with everyone, my two god brother's Josh, Caleb, and I made our way up stairs with Bryant to his room. We could not eat yet because not everyone was present and we were all going to pray together. To pass the time Bryant plugged in the Wii and we played Super Smash Bros.: Brawl. It was the new version of the game and we had never played before. I was so excited to play; my favorite character to use is Yoshi. It was similar to the old version, Super Smash Bros.: Melee so we caught on quickly. We played round after round after round until the remaining guest had arrived. My godmother called us down, "Boys c'mon down its time to say grace!" We made our way down stairs, we joined the circle and we bowed our heads. Mr. Kim, Bryant's dad had led the prayer. When he was done, we all said, "Amen" sat down, and ate.

The year we spent Christmas at my godmother's house is one I will never forget. The day had flown by so quickly, and nightfall had arrived, and I have not gotten one gift: not even one all day. Just one gift is all I wanted, just one; it was not even that expensive. I was not like most kids that asked their parents for the world I just wanted one gift. My Godmother had invited us to her house for Christmas Eve; we usually spend it there any way. When we got there, we exchanged gifts. I got a gift my parents were hiding but it was just a tiny box; seriously it was tiny enough to fit in my pocket I couldn't tell what was inside "Maybe it's a gift card" I thought. I did not care to open it and stuck it in my pocket. Then down stairs, I heard a loud scream. I hurried to see what all the commotion was. It was my God brother Caleb; he had been all worked up over his gift. My God brother was excited about his new Nintendo 64 and a fresh copy of Diddy Kong Racing. He quickly tore the box open, ignoring the instructions and plugged it into the TV. We played together for a while and I got beat every time, we played so much I even decided who my favorite character was. I wasn't very good at games but I thought they were still fun and they sparked my interest. My mom called me down stairs and told me my godmother had a gift for me. "Why don't you take a look under the tree it's the box way in the back", Said my godmother. My heart began to race, I ran to the tree at a breakneck speed. Keeping my composure I carefully moved the bigger boxes out of the way carful so I didn't break anything that's wasn't mine, until I saw another box. This one was quite bigger than the first one wrapped in gold wrapping paper with a big sticker on it that read "To: James!" It was wrapped so perfectly I did not want to rip it open. Captured by its hypnotic glow I picked it up. There was a card attached to it that read "Big things can come in small packages, Merry Christmas and happy birthday." I picked it up and took it to the living room. Everyone was watching me, waiting to see my reaction to my gift but I was not too enthusiastic about it. "What's inside?" I asked.

"Just open it", Said my older god brother Josh with a smile. I tore off the shimmering paper and underneath it was my dream come true, a lime green game boy color. As I examined it, I thought. I derived a conclusion and I reached into my pocket and tore the blue wrapping of the smaller gift and inside it was a little box that read "Pokémon Blue Version (only for Game Boy Color)." I was so excited I was speechless. I literally did not know what to do. I just stood there with a huge smile on my face staring at the box. I was stunned. Pokemon is one of my favorite games of all time and with New Year's Eve around the corner; I had plenty of time to try it out.

New Year's was unforgettable. My mom had invited my Godmother over for New Year's Eve. When she arrived, my god brothers and god sister were with her. I was a little upset that they when to sugar land to watch the ball drop without me and my mom was too tired to drive. Therefore, to make some of my own fun I played Just Dance 2 on endless shuffle. Eventually they arrived and we sat down, ate, and watched the music performances on TV. My sister, two god brothers and I played just dance for the rest of the night and I won every match. After a while, we all hopped in the car and drove around looking for fireworks. As we drove, we saw some we even parked in a spot and watched a few. We, "ooooed" and, "ahhhed" as the pretty fireworks shot and leaped across the sky.

I have a lot of fun with my family and friends over the holidays. They get better and better each year.

I love the holidays that I spend with my family and friends. Whenever we come together for a family gathering, everyone is always in good spirits. Whether it's around the Christmas tree, at the dinner table, or by the grill, everyone is laughing, talking, eating, and enjoying each other's company. We all have fun and everyone leaves his or her stress at the office, classroom, or school to relax and have a good time.

SIX STRING JOURNEY
by Frank Eldreth

Unfocused, uncoordinated and an overall lack of patience, this defined my life in the early years of middle school. I became just some random kid, nothing special about me. I didn't fit into any social crowd, probably because of my lack of patience with people. In fact, I felt so impatient I couldn't learn anything correctly I would always want to go faster, or find an easier way to do things. This really affected my grades in school, I knew I needed to get out of the impatient habit I had.

So while visiting my uncle, James, I stumbled upon a guitar. I asked my uncle if he could play it for me. He did. What came out of that guitar sounded literally like music to my ears. Before that I had never seen someone play the guitar in person; only on TV and in movies, so you can only imagine my reaction to watching him play it so smoothly. He saw that I showed a lot of interest in the guitar, so naturally he offered a lesson. He handed me the guitar and said:

"Here why don't you try?"

My 12 year-old voice cracked, "Sure!"

So I grabbed the guitar, sat it on my lap. It felt strange at first, like something broken but now complete. I felt whole, it felt right. Even though it "felt right" my hands apparently didn't get the memo that day, or for the next couple of months. My fingers started off all weak and uncoordinated. I would look at a fret, imagine my finger on the fret and then attempt to do it. I failed every time. My fingers would never go where I would want them to go. They kept trying to do something totally different from what I told them to do. They would not follow my orders.

So of course this process runs through my head as I sit in front of my uncle James. He notices my focus on the guitar.

He simply says, "Why don't you work on this at home?"

A chill ran down my spine, I felt the butterflies topple over in my stomach as I exhaled, "Yes! That would help so much!"

"Keep it clean for me, will ya'?" He said with a smirk.

"I promise, thank you so much!" I said with such I joy I hadn't felt in a while.

So I had my first guitar. At first I practiced every day for about half an hour. After about a month I became completely fed up with my uncoordinated fingers. On top of my misguided fingers, they started off really sensitive so it would hurt when I'd play. So my terrible habit of impatience had caught up to me, I still wanted my own electric guitar though. I lied and blamed the guitar instead of myself. "The guitar is too big for the stuff I want to do with it", "The electric guitar has better sound" blah, blah, and blah these become examples of things I'd say to myself when I would get frustrated with my playing.

Anyways this went on for a couple of months in till my birthday, the day I got my first electric guitar. So naturally I started playing a lot more. I would still get frustrated but it would happen less often. I started getting better at the guitar but my practices stayed the same, random and only for about half an hour. This went on for about 9 months to a year. At that point I can play pretty good but could never focus on any one song. I'd always skip around and learn multiple songs at a time. This becomes very problematic for a guitarist, or any musician, because if you can't finish a song then why should you start it?

Fast forward four years and you'll find me now playing far more advanced techniques and playing full songs. Today I spend at least thirty to forty hours a week playing guitar. My practice isn't as random as it used to be, but I still have a loose schedule. When I get home I play in till it's time for bed, I try to eat before I go and play, if not, I eat just before I go to bed. With all this practice my playing has improved quite fast.

Threw playing the guitar I've gained loads of patience and have found that with everything in life, just as everyone says, "Both practice and patience makes perfect". It's as simple as that. The more practice you put into something the better you will become at it, it's just how the world works.

A CHANGE WILL COME
by Logan Eythell

Slam! My older cousin, Marcus, slammed the front door in my face. Marcus was 5 foot 3 inches and he had a mini afro. He was the type of person who was always smiling. He always wanted to help others but he had his days where he had to be a little prankster. Marcus and I both went to Fondren. He went to Fondren Middle school and I attended Fondren Elementary. He would walk me to school every morning and make sure that nothing ever happened to me. Marcus was rather big, so no one ever picked on me at school. I looked up to Marcus, both in a mental and literal sense, because he was, somehow, always there for me when I needed him the most.

"Let me out!" I yelled,

"I demand to be free." I exclaimed.

We were late for school and Marcus randomly decided to lock me inside the house. At the time I enjoyed seven years of life and he enjoyed thirteen so he always outsmarted me. We were in the front room of our one story house, that's the room nearest the front door. Marcus had scammed me into going outside and then pranked me.

"Marcus!" I cried,

"Why you gotta be so mean!"

He replied with a high pitched cackle.

Marcus liked to pick on me and poke fun at the thing that I used to say and do but I knew that he meant well. He always tried to help me but always ended up hurting me in a funny way. Our relationship, at this time, was strictly based upon fun and games.

"Hey turn left!" He yelled,

"No your other left!" He proceeded to say.

It's now five years later and he's trying to teach me how to drive.

"Why are you yelling at me?" I giggled in a playful voice.

"Don't take your hands off the wheel!" He whined with a stare of stone.

It was the middle of the summer, near my birthday, and he wanted to successfully teach me how to drive. He also wanted to take me paintballing but who knows how that would work out. Marcus just wanted to keep me preoccupied and keep me off the streets, and focused on not only driving but the greater things in life, such as, school and my career choice. Our relationship, at this point, had grown from fun and games to him becoming a role model and I accepting what he tried to teach me. He wanted to teach me about what was wrong and what was right. He also wanted me to learn the difference between acquaintances and true friends. He wanted me to be smart and wise in who I put my trust in and who I chose as my friends. He also taught me that the people that are in my life are in there, my life, for a reason. He said their intention may be good or they may be bad. He wanted me to understand that not everybody has my best interest at their heart.

It's the end of my eighth grade year, and I'm finally graduating. I am finally going to be a freshman in high school, but I'm not the only one who was furthering my education. Marcus, my older cousin, was also going to be a freshman, but he was becoming a freshman in college. He endured nineteen years of age, but I merely scrapped at the tip of my teenage years. I always looked up to Marcus even though he could sometimes be a bad influence, he was still a great role model.

"Marcus what college are you going to?" I asked,

He replied. "I'm going to the University of Texas San Antonio."

"Things are going to be different without you here" I exclaimed sadly.

He then replied with a smirk on his face, "I know, but I'll be back."

He then left in his car soon to be married and have a baby to be named Marcus Jr.

Throughout the years Marcus and I have been through a lot. Marcus and I had and still have a very strong relationship. We are the type of people that learn from others, as well as our own, mistakes. We've had good times and bad times. We've had our shares of up's and down's, but through it all he has taught me to always keep moving forward and never give up. He also taught me the true value of family and that family should always stick together and never fall apart. He taught me the family comes first and nothing should break the relationship that you have with you family. Marcus also, indirectly, taught me how to be a man. He told me that he will always be the same Marcus that he was so many years ago.

RELATIONSHIP BLUES
by Calvin Fitzgerald

I can still hear the music playing and see the look on her face. Oh how beautiful she was. I can still feel the excitement of having fun with all of the coolest people I knew. Most importantly, I can still taste the joy of having a girlfriend. I can sense the fun swarming through the open air of the room.

This moment began in the sixth grade around Valentine's Day. It seemed to be a lot of people at the dance and I made an appearance ready to enjoy the new experiences of my first dance in middle school, whether it meant with or without my "sweetheart." Thinking back to the moments of my early teen-aging life, I wish that I could go back and do everything over again. This day made me realize that my intentions with females would hurt my relationships.

I walked around on the dance floor waiting to hear the hottest singles played on the radio stations. Then a big problem rang in my mind like an un-attended alarm clock. My girlfriend didn't like to dance in public. She always seemed to be quiet, shy and even until this day, she is dangerously beautiful. Although I didn't want to tear apart our relationship, I didn't want to have to regret not being the person I actually was on the inside so I eagerly sought to enjoy my night by using all of my energy on the dance floor . I had asked her if she had wanted to dance, a numerous number of times. She always said no and even told me to go and have fun. I finally took the invitation and danced like I owned every song that played on the sound system.

At that point, I'm sure my girlfriend and her friend began to make perceptions of what type of person I was and how we would last after that day. I'm not one-hundred percent sure of how she felt about me and the first Valentines dance that night. She never explained to me the way she felt after that experience. I danced with girls the way you would see adults dance with each other in a strip club. In my mind, having fun and enjoying my night had become my main focus. Still until this day, I remain unsure of the thoughts that went through her mind. I'm not even sure if I paid attention to her while she waited there. I wasn't around her and I did the most unusual things seeing that she was my sweet-heart. I agree that I wasn't the patient type of person to sit back and mingle with her the whole night. It's not that I didn't want to, but I was just a young kid. I still do the same things in my late teen-age years, and I now consider myself a young man. When will I slow down?.

After the dance when everyone began leaving the area, my girlfriend's friend said, "We saw you dancing with all those girls over there." My girlfriend walked with her in silence. Looking at her sun-filled skin complexion, and staring at her while she ignored me made me realize that I would lose my sweet-heart sooner or later after that night. I had thought about what I did and wondered if I had a good night or a bad night when I went home. I wondered if she would still want to call me her boyfriend or if she would end it.

On top of all of my thoughts, I thought about how much fun I had and still couldn't wait until the next dance. I had danced with the best looking 8th graders and felt like a celebrity in a room full of young people. I thought about the girl I danced with the most and now I think about the way people have changed since then. It was a great night overall now that I think about it.

If I could do something about that night, it wouldn't be to change dancing with my people. It would be to spend more time at the dance with her rather than leave her cold and stuck with her friend on "Valentine's Day."

In that one moment that lasted a couple of hours, I had lost my sweet-heart. All I wanted to do was dance. Now I regret treating my sweetheart the opposite of what a lover does to his love on a special day. That night gave me the blues after all. In my heart lies a poetic inspiration to try and honor that time period in my life that I love most dearly today. Middle School was so wonderful and weird. I wish that I could start all over again and travel back in time to the 6 grade and complete my years all over again. I wouldn't change too many things. Thinking about my years and the experience I had with my ex-girlfriend gives me the blues. The feeling haunts me until this day because I am attached to the beautiful years of my early teen-age life.

The sadness I hoard inside of my mind is for the remembrance of the wonderful times and moments that I shared with the people I loved to be around. Its feels like I danced in that room just a year ago. It feels like I played on that basket-ball only a couple of months ago. Only funny thing about this is that the few months to a year that I suddenly sense in my mind feels so recent but seem so long ago. Time has passed me by and I don't believe I enjoyed the moments and savored the joy of being in middle school enough. That curly head girl had started to really sink into my heart when we broke up. Just as any other day or year, I dream of re-living those moments exactly as they were and changing the necessary things of my life. Why? After viewing my experience with her and realizing how I acted, I feel as if I failed to do my job. I should've kissed her. Now, I've got the old relationship blues.

I SEE THE GOLDEN MOUNTAINTOPS; THEY SEE THE PLATINUM DOLLAR SIGN
by Calvin Fitzgerald

"Encased in a life where I naturally called my home… And out into the world where bright lights were all I had known. God had written destiny and sounded his promising trombones. Fate showed no existence and all predictions read wrong. I was sure to reach success. Into a child I had grown. I breathed a new word. I had waited all along. My head stood high and I sang my first song." – Cali-Cal

In a life where competition meets demand, only the strong survive; only the wealthy write commands.

Hard work and dedication, fighting to be the man; school books and medication, counting money with your own hands.

Statistics reawaken and society labels your name. Fakers want your money and Haters want your fame.

You see the treasures on television and never really understand the game. Introspectively you search for a sign and there's a million others doing the same.

I'm glad I found a door because life gets ignorant and everything positive seems to be ignored.

Shakespeare wrote well when he imagined opportunity, fortune and more.

But, I see the Golden Mountaintops so I'm stepping off-shore.

Success pays me no attention and people show love when they can't find a dime.

Then they recognize your success and pretend they love to occupy your time.

I see the Golden Mountaintops even when my life is on the line.

I look left and veer right because all they see is a platinum dollar sign.

Haters play the game and few people love my name. There were many who looked around me and now the same like to hang. What a shame.

Every single night I pray to God he confirms my intentions to be successful. He sent me a wave of help.

Working hard with little unsupported motivation can always be stressful. If I had never accepted the gifts he gave me, I'd probably be regretful. Some just don't understand, so I speak the truth and they call me disrespectful.

But I know that the destiny which was written for me in the beginning will most definitely appear in satin and Gold.

Terrors of the earth surround me and plan to inhabit my soul.

They said religion is the calling; education is the key. They called me out of name because my destiny didn't seem to cater to their needs.

I look at myself today, in and out a big breath I breathe, "I Am Cali-Cal," and success rests high above the trees.

I see the Golden Mountaintops shining high; un-intentionally waiting on me.

Haters and Failures of life tried to look down on me.

They see me on my grind but don't recognize how close the Golden Mountaintops are lay on the line.

I said, "I Am Cali-Cal," and all they can see when they look at me is a platinum dollar sign.

"They ain't worth my time."

"Bottom Line."

THE KNOWLEDGE GIVER
by Ryan Garner

Death, it always seems to surround us; no matter your age or where you live in the world. No matter how you try to avert it, death always seems to slither into your life. One of the most memorable moments that death seemed to waltz into my life, was on the last day of middle school.

The last day of middle school always seems to be the most emotional no matter whom you ask. Tears seem to dance on the ground as everyone says their goodbyes. On this day though, the loss of friends was not the topic of tears, but the loss of a life. I remember the moment when death made its icy impact upon that faithful school day.

That morning seemed as normal as any other one previous. I remember thinking that this was the last day of my middle school career. When I arrived at school, I thought to myself, "I forgot to bring boxes to move Ms. Taylor out of her classroom." Therefore, I decided to go to her room and tell her of my mistake. When I went to her room, I realized that she was not in her room. "I thought she was going to be out of the hospital by now," I thought to my bewildered self.

Taking a moment to sidetrack, allow me to explain why she was in the hospital. Towards the last month of school, Tamara Taylor began to feel very sick and her body hurt. When she went to the hospital, she was told that she had a blood clot within her upper arm. After a week of taking pills, she started to feel a little better. However, near the last week of school, she began to feel even worse than before. When she went to

102

the emergency room, in the middle of a school day, she was told a piece the blood clot had moved to her heart. She remained in the hospital until the second to last day of school. Tamara only stayed half of the school day before rushing back to the hospital. Now, with that footnote, let us move back to that icy summer day.

I began to ask other students if they knew where she was, and only one had a response for me. When I walked up to my friend Jenny, she seemed in a regular mood; yet her response to my question showed differently.

"Do you know where Ms. Taylor is," I asked.

"I heard that she died last night," Jenny said with a matter-of-fact tone.

"Dude, stop messing with me: is she at school yet," I asked with a sense of non-belief.

"No, she actually died last night. I heard that she died of Ammonia."

At this point, I was in complete disbelief. How could someone so peaceful and so nice die like that? I started to walk back to Ms. Taylor's room and noticed some of my friends underneath the awning. I snaked my way over to one of the benches and slumped down. Everyone was in their normal moods: playing soccer, spreading rumors, or doing homework. Then, Mr. Gil, my math teacher, came over and stopped all the activities instantly.

"What is wrong with all of you? Do none of you realize that someone has slipped from this world," he slightly yelled.

"What do you mean," one of the students asked.

"Ms. Taylor died last night. Yet, instead of mourning, all of you go on, laugh, and play your sports without the courtesy of paying respects."

This is when deaths' icy grip slowly squeezed the joy out of Hamilton Middle School. Everyone reacted in different ways, with the most common being the silent whispers, "She can't be dead, she just can't be." The worst was the first class, which was when I would have had her period. I remember everyone being huddled around Ms. Taylor's computer as her computer was searched through for pictures of Ms. Taylor. At this point, a substitute came in and told us to go outside; that we did not need to be locked in this room of sorrow.

I will always remember the last moments of that class period as I brought out my IPod. My friend Maddy was sitting on a bench along with other friends.

I went up to her, "This was Ms. Taylor's favorite song," I told her.

As Maddy listened to Stairway to Heaven by Led Zeppelin, one group of lyrics forever whispered themselves to me. "... And she's buying a stairway to heaven."

OUR STORY
by Juan Granados

Friday:

Spring is in the air. You can just feel the nice calm breeze as if it was born anew since the last one had died off from the winter that had just passed. Things were different that day I couldn't explain it. However, despite it all; it was a very good difference. The month of March had never made me so happy before and it was because for the first time I had a special someone who had caught my eye. Like a goddess she just came out of nowhere and had a hold of me; hook, line, and sinker. But this Friday was very different. I have been trying to get a kiss from the girl who I want to be mine for the past week, and they all failed because I didn't know how to. It was as if every time I got close something held me back. Was it the fact that I didn't know how because I had never kissed a girl? Well whatever the reason I didn't let it get me down, because I knew that if something was going to happen then the opportunity would present itself. And well what do you know, on that Friday she was walking with me on the side of the school so that I could walk across the street to meet my dad who was in his truck waiting for me. As usual we got to the corner and stopped... I hugged her tight in my arms then I drew back like I always did and faced her with my arms still wrapped around her as usual. I looked at her and somehow my head started turning and so did hers. We drew closer, and closer, until finally... we met together into what had become one of the happiest moments of my life. We departed and my heart was racing, my heart didn't stop pounding that hard until I went to bed that night; that's when she said, "I love you."

Tuesday July 12, 2011:

I had been dating my first kiss, my first love since May 31, 2011 and everything was going great. However, for some reason she had just stopped talking to me. We were both taking the same classes at HCC but it didn't make sense as to why she would just stop talking to me. What happened to the "I love you" and the "Babe I miss you"? My head was trying to just at least begin to try to understand this whole situation and I had confronted her about it the day before. I needed to get my mind off things so I decided to go to a concert with my friends on this day. The day was going really well so far and the time that I needed with my friends was enough to get my mind off of all the bad things that were going on. So we are finally on our way to the Kemah Boardwalk for the concert. My friend and I were having a really good time just cranking the music out and jamming as if there was no tomorrow! "David this song is amazing!" and David said to me "I know bro! Crank it up!" It was then when I came to a conclusion that nothing in the world could ruin a day like that, until I got a text message from her saying, "You know, I was thinking about what you said last night and… I think we should break up." Right then and there my whole world just went crazy! I couldn't think straight and I kept asking myself, "Why now?" "Why here?" and most importantly, "Why me?" why? After I got over the shock a little I asked her why she was doing this, and she couldn't give me an answer. No words could even describe how heartbroken I was. My heart wasn't the same and it was worse because I couldn't brace myself so my heart was vulnerable and unprotected. I still had fun with my friends but after that concert, it was the worst time of my life.

Friday September 30, 2011:

Since school has started we have been talking to each other in "that way" and I really missed her. She had been on my mind all summer and not once did I get tired of thinking of her. I remember that we got out of school on Friday, early as usual, and I didn't see her after school. Disappointed I asked where she was and she said that she was with her cousin and some of his friends. To me, it really sucked because that was the day that I was going to do it. I was going to ask her back out again. I had made a decision to just hang out at the park with some friends with the hope of her coming back to school so that I could talk to her. Well what do you know? She actually came back. We actually did get to talk alone and I did something that I still don't regret till this day. I asked my love out again. Did she say yes? Did she say no? All I can say is that I love her with all my heart.

FIFTH GRADE BULLY
By Mikeila Grant

All through elementary and especially in the 5th grade, I was known as the bully around the school. The school was divided into elementary and middle school. I was of course the bully of elementary, especially since I was in the fifth grade (which was like the senior of elementary). Envy surrounded me as I would walk down the hallway looking tall and lanky while being loud and aggressive to everyone smaller than me. The teachers abhorred the thought of me walking into their classrooms and student became cautious of crossing my path more and more as the years passed by. It seemed like the older I became, the worse my behavior got. There was always this one curious boy who made the wrong decision everyday to test me. But one day, he caught me on the wrong day and at the wrong time. He still regrets it from this day.

We were sitting in Mr. Obinyan's class (he was my favorite teacher ever). It was the last week of school and I was ecstatic at the thought of FINALLY going to middle school with all of my friends (the few that I had) that I've known since kindergarten. Mr. Obinyan was going over the last lesson of the day, fractions (ugh!).I always became frustrated when we did those. After explaining the lesson plan that we were going to do, he told everyone to go to our cubby holes and get out our notebooks and color pencils to help us understand our lesson a little more. This boy named Cameroun Alexander A.K.A. Peanut Head (my little name for him) decided that he wanted to cross that line that no one ever dared to cross because they knew of the consequences. He decided to pull my things out and dump them on the floor like it was just okay. I had to pause for a second I to sit and think as to why he would even fathom of doing that to me, out of all people! My face turned hot pink and my eyes narrowed. I balled up my fist ready to strike him. Seemed like he automatically knew what was going to go down by the way he looked at me but instead of running off like everyone would have, he decided to spread his legs apart like he was ready to take whatever his consequence was. I was kind of proud of him at the moment, but I couldn't let him slide. I was afraid that my tough reputation would dissolve.

As soon as my neck turned to towards him, it seemed like my hand was synchronized with my neck movement because as I moved my neck my hand moved in the same direction fast and hard. Before I could stop myself, my hand was gripped around his head like it was a basketball and I was about to make a slam dunk into the basket for the winning point. And I did, right onto the corner of the cubby hole. The cubby hole corner was hard and sharp. I could tell by the way he squinted his eyes and tears started to pour out like raindrops. Usually I would've stopped but I was so filled with rage and adrenaline to the point where I couldn't stop myself. It finally clicked to me once I saw blood on the ground spreading like a wildfire in a forest with millions of trees that I had gone too far with this one. As I stepped back slowly Ms.Ingles, my principle, charged into the classroom immediately with a wet towel and ice. Everyone was wondering how she responded so quickly to something the teacher haven't reported! She heard the altercation over the intercom. Turns out, she was actually calling me to come in her office so she could congratulate me on not getting in trouble in the past two weeks. I guess I kind of messed that up.

That day happened to be my last day at that school seeing that I was always in the office almost every week and if I'm doing well, every other week. They got tired of it I guess, especially after the last incident. They claimed "that I was a threat to the students in the school" and all that nonsense. So I never got the chance to go to middle school with my friends until now while I'm in high school. Our class had a little get together and I and Cameron became friends again like nothing else happened. Even though it happened about 6 years ago, this was the one memory that me or him would never be able to forget.

THE PROFILE OF NICOLE OWEN
by Andrew Griffin

As I enter the bent solid black gates, I see her walking out of the door, turn to her right and walk off. She walks so proper and upright, usually with a smile or a humorous animated expression on her face. She can easily be recognized by the cat ears, with pink fur on the inside, which she usually wears on the top of her long light-brown hair. You can recognize her by the smooth black jacket, that sometimes has some anime characters pinned on it, or by the cat or wolf tail she occasionally wears. "Hey, Nicole!" I yell trying to grab her attention. She stops to look around, but after a few seconds, shrugs her shoulders and continues to walk.

I run up and grab her shoulder, trying to stop her as she passes by a black table; filled with holes, with a green umbrella overhead. She slowly turns around with a cartoon smile that easily shows her animated personality. As I try to refrain from falling out into laughter, she takes a seat at the table, sitting next to one freshman playing a video game on his Nintendo DS. Being too lazy to try to move, I also sat next to a freshman, wirelessly playing against the first one on his own Nintendo DS. We began to get distracted, by the freshmen and the game they were playing, but snap out of it in no time. I lean over to my back pack and begin to pull out my spiral, with a number of interview questions in it. I set my spiral on the table, open up to the page with questions, and I ask with a sadistic voice "Are you ready to begin?" Nicole just smiles and nods her head. "Let's begin," I proclaim. "What's

111

the first question?" she replies. "Let's start with..." I pause to let the suspension build. I lean in and ask her a simple question: "What is your name?" Without missing a beat, she replies with "Sir Bad*ss Killington." I try as hard as I can to control my laughter so I can ask the next question. Before I ask, she giggles a bit and says "Owen...Nicole Owen." After I finish laughing, I write down her answer and ask the next question. "Where were you born?" Nicole, again without missing a beat replies. "My dear lad, I am from Narnia, the land of magic!" She tried to continue but she started giggling and then said, she was from Frederick, Maryland. I prepare my paper to ask the next question. "What was your favorite game ever?" I asked her, knowing what she would pick. She pauses for a moment to think, and after about a minute she says, "The entire Pokémon series." I knew she would pick a Pokémon game, but choosing the entire series was an unexpectedly answer; even though I would also have had a hard time trying to decide between them all. I decided to build off of her answer from her previous question by asking, "What was your favorite Pokémon out of all the series?"

Again, she pauses for a moment before answering my question, but this time not as long. She raises her head and makes direct eye contact and replies, "Blaziken!" She says it with a confident look on her face. "What's yours?" she asks.

I'm also am a huge fan of Pokémon, and she knows it, so I just came out and told her my favorite Pokémon was the same as hers. We got into a mildly long debate about Pokémon with the freshmen that were playing it next to us. After what seemed like 10 or 15 minutes of talk about Pokémon, we try to rush through the remainder of the interview so she can leave for her trip with the school. "Question five!" I stated with a slightly escalated voice, to make sure I got her attention. "Who was your biggest inspiration?" I ask. "Arceus," she replied back, "the legendary Pokémon, said to have created the Pokémon world himself." Trying not to get carried away in another discussion I say, "next question." "What did you want to be as a child?" "Yes!" she replied. I didn't know how to respond to that, but before I could open my mouth to ask her to clarify her answer, she said she wanted to be "a green fruit roll up Pokémon council leader of the Canto region."

We zoomed through many of the other questions, but when it came down to the last three, we saw the time and realized she only had five minutes left. As she prepared her backpack and lunch to get ready to go, I ask her "Do you consider yourself successful?" Without taking time to even think about the question, she says "Banana I am!" Feeling puzzled decided not to ask again and, I moved to the next question and asked, "What did you do to get where you are now?" She, realizing we still have four more minutes until she needs to walk inside calms down and replies "I took the metro and walked." I began to laugh, as I start to think how that was the best possible way to reply to that common question. She, being in a hurry and trying not to be late, says "I'm sorry but I have to go!" She picks her bags up and walks inside to sign in, and then waits with our friend Brenda as she gets ready to leave.

HE PROMISED
by Erika Gudiño

"Let me carry her", my mother said to my dad as he walked around the room lulling me to sleep with one hand while his other hand was being used to hold up his phone to his ear. "Here, take her I have a meeting at seven o'clock and I'm already late. I'll call you when I get out. See you later", he hastily said as he kissed my mother and me on our foreheads and swiftly left the room. I watched the recording over and over again. I would usually skip all of the discussions between my mother and father. I would go to the ending of the tape where my father would come back to the hospital and sit next to me, "I'll always be there", he promised then once again left the hospital room in a rush.

"She doesn't even see you for days at a time! I bet she doesn't even know you're her father!" My mother yelled to my father. I sat on the stairs watching my parents argue for the billionth time that week and didn't notice that this time it was different since this time my father was carrying a suitcase. When I finally did notice the suitcase in his hand I ran to him. I plead him not to go, not to worry, that everything would be okay by tomorrow. "Sorry Hun, looks like this time it's for sure", He whispered to me in a tired and sad voice. "Don't worry I'll be back for you", he promised.

"Dad!? What do I do next? The pot's boiling over!" I said in an apologetic tone. "Ha-ha! Don worry it's supposed to do that!" he said unsuccessfully trying to muffle a chuckle. We were in our flat in New York where we had lived for 4 years. That night I got a call from my mother whose plead to come back home sounded more desperate than usual. "Do you want to go back?" my father asked as I told him about the conversation with my mother. "Not really, but I guess we can go back for a while. Right? I mean I'll just visit and come back to you", I said as I took a sip of the freshly brewed coffee my father had just made. "Yeah, come back", he mumbled to the table. "Hmm?" I asked in confusion. "Nothing, you'll be back in no time kiddo," he promised, but the look in his eyes looked like he wasn't sure.

"What do you mean I can't go back Mom?" I asked on the verge of hysteria." Dad's waiting for me in new York!" I yelled at her. "No, he's packing everything and moving back to Texas because you will now be living with me", my mother said in a calm collected voice. As soon as she left for work I called my father and to my horror he told me that everything she had said was true, and that he was almost done packing and would be in Texas the next day. "Don't worry kiddo, this is only temporary. Turns out she really missed you and wanted you to stay close to her", my father said in an unsure voice that sounded like it was on the verge of tears. "You won't live with me anymore but, I'll visit you every day and call you at least twice a day. OK?" he promised in an excited voice trying to lighten the mood.

"So then you can't make it today either?...No don't worry it's okay I mean we still have that camping trip next week right? ... Oh I see a business trip? No it's fine. It's fine. OK bye", the dial tone rang in my ear after he had hung up. I slumped to the ground convincing myself that my father always kept his promises and he said he would always be there for me. He promised.

UNTITLED
by Destini Hall-Duncan

I am the only Destini to attend Houston Academy with an "I" ending my name and also up until 2010 I was the only student with the last name Duncan. Yes, I feel very unique for those beings. For reason that the "I" stands for individuality and shows that I will always stand alone. My name plays a lot in my character at school. It's my reason for being so anti-social and why I don't care for friends. I wouldn't call it stuck up or conceited, I just think of it as I'm not afraid of being alone. I always imagined high school as sectioned off by popularity groups and wondered who I would hang out with. Although I wasn't really scared of not bonding with class mates because I've always been easy going with others.

Entering freshman year was great; I made many friends and didn't have any problems with the student body or staff. My younger sister, Paris also went to school here so I let go of the thought of popularity groups and just stayed close to her. I met this one girl name Timisha Jackson, she was a sophomore but we hung out like we were in the same class. She became my best friend; I even begin to hang out with her more than my little sister. Things were going fine but as Timisha and I grew closer I started noticing conflict between other students. After a while I had enemies, well I wouldn't call it war, but there were girls that I didn't connect with. I didn't feed into it much because I knew my mother would be highly upset with my behavior if she knew I had conflict with other students when I should be focused.

The tension went on for over three months till we all could get along. Once it was over I never wanted to be involved in any other high school drama. I decided if there was someone I couldn't get along with I would keep quiet. I am now in my junior year and still haven't been involved in any other conflicts. I believe I've grown to define that "I" even more now because I'm always alone. I can't recall what happened freshman and sophomore years, but I gave up on wanting friends. School was built to help build one's future, not find friends. Having friends at school only makes it more fun, but fun can always wait. I come to school to learn, then I'm off to work, Fiesta, that is.

My name is Destini Hall-Duncan and that's Destini with an "I" because I am an individual.

*If your life turns out half as
great as my moms, then you had
better find some*

A LIFE IN A DAY
by James Harvey

*great people to
share it with.*   *James Harvey*

The clouds were ablaze with that special combination of red, purple, yellow, orange and pink that were almost powerful enough to make a grown man cry. It was as if I were getting a little wink from Mother Nature, telling me that everything was going to be okay. The living room was littered with family photos, "ancient" heirlooms, and things that I used to consider heirlooms. These include a seven year old treadmill, a fifteen year old desk, and a coffee table that had been made 5 years before I was born, but was supposed to look like it was made in the 1950s (kind of like Happy Days, except sixteen years later). There was a light immediately above both my mother and I, which made the room feel like a CNN interview room.

As I sat in the living room playing "Angry Birds", and waiting for mom to get home, I was reviewing the list of questions that I was going to ask in the interview. She told me earlier in the day that she was going to get home at 8:00 so that we could "start the interview and be finished with it at a reasonable hour." Since it was already 7:45, I was having doubts as to whether or not she would come through on her end of the agreement. If I could, I would have put money on her arrival time being around midnight, as usual, but she decided to surprise me with an unusual exhibition of punctuality and sauntered through the door at precisely 7:55.

She had the build of a teddy bear. Now that I think about it, she had many of the characteristics of a mother bear/ teddy bear as well. She is protective of her young, has short hair, is small in stature, and brown. I would probably describe her hair as Ellen DeGeneres' haircut, except shorter and black. The tone in her voice and the look on her face suggested that she was here for business and nothing more, but I knew better. Under that masterfully crafted poker face, that can only be developed over a period of at least twenty years in fierce negotiation with the world, was the excitement of a little girl that was about live her lifelong dream of having her story told for millions to hear. I knew that she would have done this at 4:00 A.M. if she had to; I knew that she would have done it over the phone from China; I knew that she would have done it on a sail boat, in the middle of the Atlantic.

When the time came to ask the first question, I knew that she was ready to answer any question that I would ask, and that kind of trust is what makes a successful interview. Her answer to my first question was very short and did not necessitate an explanation. I simply asked her who some of her influences were growing up and she told me that "they are my mother, grandfather, and my great grandmother". "I was more influenced by the people in her family than by the actors in Hollywood or the politicians on Capitol Hill, or the athletes in the stadiums". Her mother was very supportive and is the main reason that she pushes herself so hard today; she also respected her mother for raising her and three siblings as a single parent. Her grandfather simply served as a father figure to her, but his "simple" role had a very deep impact on her. Her great grandmother taught her to have a good work ethic by having her work on her farm in the summers, which also prepared her for life as a campfire girl.

She later told me that her parents were extremely influential in her development into a mature adult. They also taught her some values to have and some lessons such as "hard work, discipline, worship, how to complete tasks, how to think outside the box, and how to earn anything that I have, also to value the things that I earned".

My mother has many fond memories of childhood that she has been gracious enough to share with me in her interview. The first of which involves her brother/my uncle sneaking out at night to go and ride the motorcycle that he bought using his job money. The story ends with him in the hospital, receiving stitches and my mom getting two severe beatings, one for not watching my uncle, and the other because my grandmother could not beat my uncle. Why don't you fill in the blanks? Another memory includes her learning how to catch crabs. She went crabbing for the first time on a Sunday and she caught three crabs. She also went on her first camping trip as a campfire girl. She learned many things at the camp including horseback riding, archery, rowing, and many other camp related skills. The next and last memory that she shared with me is one of her first experience on an airplane. She won a half scholarship to Washington D.C. with the Close Up organization, where she took a tour of the white house, the capitol building, the National Mall, and some other historical sites in Washington D.C. "It was the greatest and first trip that I had taken out of Texas."

She later told me about her experience with Breast Cancer. "The most difficult part of dealing with it was actually a tie between the physical, emotional, and mental strain of it all." She ended up having to modify some of her major habits to do what the doctors said.

I felt that it would only be fitting to end the interview with what she plans to be remembered for post mortem. She told me that she would like to be remembered for her philanthropy, but she also told me that she really wants to be remembered by her friends and family. I think that we could all do well to take a page from my mother's book. It could be the next bestseller.

LONGING FOR MY FATHER
By Arlette Henderson

On my eleventh birthday while I was in the second grade my wonderful father bought me a shinny, brand new electric scooter. This scooter meant the world to me because it would be the only thing I could remember that my giving father bought for me. I rode my fanatic scooter all around my half way decent, medium sized apartment complex, Foundern Court, and my older, friendly   friends around my inviting apartment complex even rode it too. I was the popular, cool kid in my apartment complex because of the wonderful, brand new scooter that my father bought me. This was one of the blissful times in my life that soon faded away.

Moreover, the years past my loving father started fading out of my life. In those past years I spent numerous amounts of lonely nights weeping in a match- box, purple decorated room in my new apartment complex, Meadow Ridge, because my distant father did not want to partake in my life. I needed my father back. This caused me to wonder why was he treating me this way? For example, my distant father cease to call me in order to receive details about how my day went at school and he also refuse to pay child support. In result to my distant father's non engagement in my life caused my mom to work three jobs instead of one, which caused me to spend less time with her because she was always at work. We barley had a chance to have a normal conversation. My loving, caring mother was always tired but she did the necessary duties   in order to provide for herself and myself.   I hated my distant father with every part of my soul because he could not be a man and communicate or be involved in his second' born life. I eventually went into an depress state of mind. I needed my loving father back so I thought.

Meanwhile, my distant father did not even have respect to show up to my eight grade graduation. This was one of the important events in my life because I was moving forward into my high school years. Why was he treating me this way? He had showed up to every one of my other two sisters' graduations, but when it came down to mine he could not even show his shameful face. At that time when he did not show up I felt notably heart-broken, lonely because all my other friends had their loving fathers for support and encouragement from their loving fathers to keep up the good work, while I only had my humble, great mother and joyful aunties for support to strive for all my goals. He had decided not to take part in this great celebration. I needed my loving father.

After, the eight graduation period of my life I was now in high school freshmen year. My life had taken a serious downfall. I wanted to leave the face of this earth because I felt like my father had left me. For instance, my grades started dropping, I became more depressed, and my relationship with the true living God had decreased exponentially. This action caused my life to be at an abyss point in my life. I needed my loving father, he was the one who had all the answers to my various problems, but now he was the center of rage to all my problems.

I had decided to make a change in my depressing life in my sophomore year of high school. The solution to every one of my problems was that I forgave my distant father for not being in my life. On that day that I forgave my distant father I felt relieved from all the life killing stress that I had because of him. For example, after I forgave my distant father I started smiling more, my grades began to increase, and my relationship with the true living God started to get on track. I also called my distant father and

told him,

"That I forgive you for not engaging in my life all these years."

My father then replied,

"I'm sorry for not being there for you and I love you." I started crying and finally

I said, "I love you to." This was the being of a new, refresh life for the both of us.

Furthermore, I was longing and in desperation of my father, but he eventually came back into my changing life and became my loving father again. When he came back around we talked about the pros and cons of our strange father and daughter distant, but concrete relationship. We promised, from that day to never let our non ending, everlasting bond get weak every again no matter what obstacle came our way.

PAPA VETO
by Airam Hernandez

"We understand death for the first time when he puts his hand upon the one we love."
-Madame de Stael

Death is probably the most complicated stage in life to grasp. Everyone knows that we will die, but no one really knows what it's like to be hurt by it. Death is like a myth, you always hear about it, but you have never been close to someone who has experienced it. Hearing about death does not affect many people because they've never been close to it. When one of your loved ones does pass on, it is like a wakeup call in life. Death makes you understand death, grief, and acceptance.

It was a sunny afternoon, in the summer of 2006, and I was at my best friend's house having a great time. In the middle of all the fun, my mother picked me up without informing me. Usually, I would be upset by her picking me up early, but my mother's eyes were so red I knew I couldn't protest her actions. The whole ride home we shared the silence, mostly because we both knew whatever the bad news was would destroy me. I was really scared to go inside the house; because I didn't want to have the same facial expression my mother had worn throughout the roads. The corners of her mouth looked like they were being pulled downward by an invisible string, and her face had tear trails; starting from her eyes all the way down to her neck. We arrived at the house and my mother sat me down on the couch. My mother looked into my eyes and a pain of sorrow shot my throat and I couldn't speak. A part of me wanted to ask her what was wrong, but the other part of me was glad she wasn't talking. She grabbed my hand and gripped it as if I was going to slip away from the news. My mother could barley form a sentence, but she let me know clearly that my grandfather from Mexico had passed away. She notified me to go pack for the funeral, and when I walked upstairs I couldn't feel any emotion. I remember thinking to myself if it was just a dream or a different reality. I went into the biggest shock in my life. I was just grabbing clothes and putting them in a suitcase as if I were a robot. It felt like a coma for my emotions, because I couldn't shed any tears. I felt my heart breaking, but I couldn't weep. As I was packing I came across a golden purse; it was the last thing my grandfather had given me. I grabbed the purse pulled it to my heart and a tear rolled down my cheek. I never thought much about death because it never affected me, but it was here and it had taken my hero.

Everyone was gathered quietly around the room in their black uniform, waiting for the casket to be brought inside. It all felt like a dream, until four men brought in my grandfather's casket and opened its top. The dream I was feeling stopped, and I knew if I saw my grandfather in that small casket reality would sink into my heart. My grandmother looked so fragile, going up to my grandfather's casket. She placed her hand over her heart as soon as she saw him, and tears flowed down her pale skin. The hand on her chest started shaking and I had to look away. A hand touched my shoulder; and it was my aunt motioning me toward that tiny box that everyone cried at. I didn't want to go, but my feet had a mind of their own. I placed my fingers on the edge of the glass and looked down. My heart never felt so heavy and my eyes never cried so much. It was my grandpa's body, but it wasn't my grandpa. My grandpa always smiled when he saw me, and this body wouldn't even open its eyes. A million emotions rushed through my mind, but they were mostly sad and angry. I was sad because I missed my grandpa, and I was angry at God for taking away something so precious in my life. I was sad because I couldn't say goodbye, and I was angry at everyone for not trying to bring him back to life in some miraculous way.

Every other day, my mornings were spent by a windowsill in my room. I would listen to country music and let my tears flow at the unfair reality of my grandfather not being here. I would just feel the air around my body, and think about how my grandpa should have been feeling the air on this earth also. Even though it was summer, I kept thinking about how the tears against my face were the only warm reality about this earth. I had a very special song that reminded me about my grandpa that would tear the last pieces of my heart. That day I had felt especially sad, and my eyes had been puffy from rubbing them so much. I started half heartedly singing that song, "I wish you were here right now..." as; as those worlds escaped my mouth I felt a warm touch across my shoulders, back, and arms. I felt a sort of happy feeling that brought a light into my life. I think it was my grandfather, trying to tell me to accept that he has moved on. He was in a better place where he felt no heat or cold. He was in a place without torture, sadness, or hunger. I accepted that death was a part of our life and it's not okay to not live your life for the death of a loved one. Your loved one would want to live a happy life and move on from the tears dripping down your soul.

I wouldn't know what real loss was, be aware that death is closer than you ever imagined, or experience acceptance if it wasn't for my grandfather passing away.

NEVER GIVE UP ON WHAT YOU LOVE
by Ashley Hernandez

It's the second half. My heart is racing, my feet are aching, sweat is running down my face; but my head is in the game. I'm having the gut feeling that we will become the new District Champs. This is the biggest game of the season, and my team and I are making the Rivals eat our grass. My "mojo" kicked in and I was on fire. I was making those girls eat my dust as I passed ahead of them. The ball was like a magnet stuck to my feet and it went everywhere I wanted it to. Soon, I realized that I had scored five goals in one-half of the game, and my team was carrying me on their shoulders while I held the District Championship trophy in the air. I have never been more proud of myself; holding that trophy was like holding the biggest glory in life in my hands and no one could take that from me. This was an amazing ending to the soccer season. After that, I was no longer known as Ashley, I was known as the "Prodigy".

Soccer is my life; it is the air that I breathe. I touched my first soccer ball as soon as I was able to walk on my feet. I was raised with soccer, and I will never stop, until I can't move a muscle. I cannot live without soccer; it is like taking my feet away and not being able to walk ever again. I learned from the best, my father. My father is a legend, he's known as the "Master". My father can move a ball with his feet in a way I couldn't even if I had four feet. He is the man I look up to. I want to be as good as him. Bringing home a trophy to my father is like me giving him all of the money in the world, I always brought him a smile. Making my father happy is my biggest achievement. It's like a father teaching his son how to play baseball; the bond, the love, and the friendship of a father and his son that is unexplainable. I have that same bond, but I am his little girl.

It's almost the end of the school year and it's time for the award ceremony. A lot of people stepped up into the stage and got their awards and certificates of achievement. Most of them had certificates for school subjects. Sadly I'm not book smart so I got nothing. That changed as soon as I saw my coach on the stage. She yelled out "Can I have prodigy come on to the stage please". No one ever called me by my name. Every one turns around and stares right at me like if I had a booger on my nose. I was shocked myself, because I never get called up to the center of the stage for anything. I got up and walked up there in a rush as if I needed to pee extremely badly, I didn't want a lot of people to stare at me if I walked slowly to the stage. I despise being the center of attention.

As soon as I got up there I saw my coach shed a tear. "Ashley Hernandez, I would like to present to you and give you this huge honor that no one in the history of our school has ever gotten", she said. She gives me a Soccer player of the year award and my prized possession, a prize that was not mine but I called it mine. She hands me the District Championship trophy. All trophies were school property but the school decided to give me the biggest and best trophy any school could have. Everyone in the auditorium gets up and gives me a round of applause. I turn around and my father is there clapping and crying for me. I run into his arms and I held him tight. His face was very hard to tell whether he was proud or upset, but I hugged him anyway. I have never seen my dad cry before. He told me he loves me in the deepest voice he's ever had with me. Sadly that's all he said the whole time we were there and the ride home.

I decided not to come in the house, I was so confused. I didn't know whether my dad was proud or upset. Seeing a smile on my dad's face is my strength, and knowing that I have no clue if he is upset or happy, makes me weak. This time, I brought him the best trophy I have ever gotten, and I did not see a smile on his face. I didn't know what to say or do. My father brings me in the house and says "We need to talk". I realized this was not a talk I did not want to hear from him. I was barely walking into the house and all I hear is my dad say "you need to give up soccer". I never thought that the person that was the most proud of me would ever tell me this. "Why", I replied. "Didn't you hear me, I said give it up, and this is my final answer!" he yelled. The man that taught me how to play, to be strong, to be brave, to not let people bring me down, tells me to give up. I don't understand. He was the one that got me into falling in love with the sport. He was my coach and I was his follower. I've falling into a black hole of confusion that I feel I won't be able to get out of. Everything seemed so oblivious.

My world was crushed; I ran to my room and shut the door behind me. I isolated myself from everyone. My dad's happiness was the only thing that kept me going and I never gave up on anything, ever. I stopped playing, I stopped caring, I stopped being happy. I didn't want to see another soccer ball; I wanted soccer out of my life. I never thought that the words, "give up" would come out from father. That is what hurts me the most. I was his fighter, I fought for anything my mind was set on to; knowing that now I have no one to support me, drives me crazy. I didn't care about anything anymore.

Soccer season started again, and I didn't even bother showing up to tryouts. This was a new thing for me; I didn't know what else to do. I tried any other after school extracurricular activity, and nothing seemed to represent the person I am. My coach knew the second I was not going to show up to the tryout when she saw me walking around the school without a sports bag. She knew something went wrong. I was devastated by all of this, so I ignored her too. My coach was just as stubborn as I am, so she bothered me until I decided to open up. She talked to me, and she opened my eyes; that I was being stupid. I realized that even if someone is not supporting what you love to do. Do it anyway . Soccer is what makes me happy, but my father suddenly disapproves.

SINGING MAKES A DIFFERENCE TOO!
By Markiesha Hurst

There will be mountains that I will have to climb. And there will be battles that I will have to fight, but victory or defeat; it's up to me decided. Ha ha ha, I look back and laugh at what I did, but at the time when I had to sing it I was thinking that this is a special moment. I was as nervous and scared; as a girl on her first date. I had to sing a song called "Can't give up now" for my fifth grade graduation; while the graduates walked in the church, meaning we were the ones to start off the graduation. My best friend looked at me and nodded to start me off. Overall we sung it beautifully which brought tears to the audience. I felt that we made a difference because people seen a piece of hope in our voice. It's like reading a poem, even though their just words but they have a meaning behind them, a tone, a focus, a path. The time that I took to memorize that song really made me think about how things in my life were going to change. I had a new chapter in life to open; a goal to reach and a task to conquer. I felt so much change in me, in my peers, my wants. It just really made me feel like I had to do better and try my best in school. Singing makes a difference.

Man I wish I would have never got picked to do a solo, especially in front of my whole church. All the kids and grownups are going to see how I sound by myself. At the same time I like singing it's just I get stage fright when I sing by myself. This song I sung was the same song I had to sing at my fifth grade graduation. I chose it because I thought if people liked it then maybe they would have liked it again. It was crazy because my church never knew I could sing and thought that I might be afraid to let them hear me. I wore this pretty purple dress shirt with some nice jeans and dress shoes. I walked up to the mike and the first thing I did was look out to the audience. And my choir director told us to never do that when you're nervous. So I hurried up and looked for her and nodded to Q the music. I started up a little quiet but then people started to say it's alright. So I let my fears go and sung it the best I ever had. When I hit the high notes people to get up and cheer for me. I felt happy because I got out of being scared and sung. After I got through singing people told me that they were proud of me and I did well. One of the kids in our youth choir told me that they wanted to do a solo to get over their fears. I was touched because I made a difference in someone conquering a fear. Singing makes a difference.

My mother is the kind of mom where you have to really do something to wow her. She never likes surprises or anything special but for her last birthday August 4, 2011; I gave her a gift better than money. I gave her my voice, and my love to show her that she was special to me. She was sitting down and I was in another room behind her, and I was singing one of her favorite songs that she always liked. It was "A Ribbon in The Sky" by Stevie Wonder. She liked that song not only because it was beautiful but, because it was her and my dad's wedding song. She really got emotional because she knew that things in her marriage weren't going so great. But when I sung that it made her realize that if my daughter thinks that we should work it out then we should. She said thank you and gave me a big hug and said thank you for letting me realize what I have to do. Singing makes a difference.

My life has a lot of complications to deal with it so, sometimes I try to sing to let out my feelings. When making a difference in life you should do what you feel is right and, because it makes you happy. I hope that everything I do can make a difference and help someone because when I need help I would want some encouragement or guidance. Really singing to me is fun but the thought of me even making a difference with it is a blessing. Singing makes a difference.

FROM SINGAPORE TO THE BEST ROLE MODEL
by Emily Jackson

I jumped off the shuttle bus leaping towards HAIS, an early college high school in midtown Houston, and I'm excited to interview the great Mrs. Ayyadhury. I opened the door to her classroom only to be hit by the usual freezing air conditioning. I walked in the classroom which feels freezing cold, but the room stands balanced out by Mrs. Ayyadhury's constantly open door which welcomes students in. The room is busy with students at Mrs. Ayyadhury's Tuesday afternoon math tutorials. Mrs. Ayyadhury busily shuffles around the room working with students from all grades, helping out with junior committee, and answering my questions. While in the midst of all the dense craziness, the amazing Mrs. Ayyadhury found various five minute intervals to sit down with me to help answer all my questions about her. Regardless of all the flustered insanity of that room there exists a weird rhythm of productivity between all the individuals. Ours was truly an interesting interview, and still probably different than any other interview anyone has had before. Someone might hope their interview has a professional setting with formality while also being absent of distractions. My interview went completely oppositely, and was perfect. I had a sincere smile as I said, "Thank you Mrs. Ayyadhury for letting me interview you today. I had a great interview with you."

Mrs. Ayyadhury is a tall woman but not so tall that she stands above everyone else. Her situation stands on the contrary; she's able to have a

134

strong presence while still being on your level, almost as if you have her full attention. Mrs. Ayyadhury dresses in simple clean attire, usually wearing professional shoes, a nice pair of jeans, all paired with a nice formal or sometimes school shirt. It gives her an air of casualness, but she still carries herself professionally; you won't ever think that she doesn't value her authority as a teacher. Mrs. Ayyadhury's round eyes shape themselves to her emotions emphasizing her smiles, frowns, excitement, disappointment, anger, and hope.

Mrs. Ayyadhury holds herself as someone I as a female look up too. Her relationship with her husband extends its self as one of the most interesting things about her; their story really is beautiful. "How did you meet your husband?" I asked. And without skipping a beat Mrs. Ayyadhury answered, "It's a funny story. I met him while I was on vacation in India." I was amazed that two individuals from different countries met under the rarest of circumstances. Mrs. Ayyadhury often talks about how much her husband means too her. She shares stories of trying times and fun times that she has endured with her husband. Although, Mrs. Ayyadhury's lives in Houston to teach at our school, her husband lives in New York, working on his medical school residency. Even though she often talks about how much she loves her husband she has to live in a separate part of the country from him. I asked Mrs. Ayyadhury, "How has your husband helped you in your life, career, or any other way?". She answers "He never dictated terms to me. He always told me to follow my dreams. He always believed in me." Mrs. Ayyadhury found someone who supports her in life through everything. I see her as a strong woman who works hard for what she wants in life, and won't take anything less than full support from the people in her life. I think that's something every girl should look for in man she wants to marry. One could have guessed you would learn a few things while interviewing such a strong admirable woman.

Mrs. Ayyadhury grew up in Singapore, Singapore with her mom, dad, and siblings. They were an average family who did the normal things families in Singapore did; they went to the movies together, ate together, and split every day for school and work. They had one car and mostly used public transportation for travel unless they were all traveling together, which is something very different from life here in Houston, Texas. Mrs. Ayyadhury misses how in Singapore the food was cheap and still good quality. She misses her family most of all. Mrs. Ayyadhury still does the same practices but here in America she doesn't have the same amount of support. The only family she has in America is too far for them to connect any more than she can connect with her family in Singapore. Something else interesting about Singapore compared to here is their secondary academia. I asked her, "How much education did you receive in your homeland, and how much did you receive here?" and she answered, "I completed my bachelors with honors in engineering in Singapore. When I came here I needed an additional year [according to the American curriculum], so I got another bachelors degree and a masters in mathematics. I'm doing my PhD now here." Mrs. Ayyadhury said she wished she had studied abroad because it would have been a great experience. She thinks everyone should travel. Although when she first came here and was continuing her education she was married with her husband and was not exactly rich as she was a college student. Mrs. Ayyadhury and her husband didn't eat out at any restaurants for six entire years while being frugal through college and trying to make it in a new country. Mrs. Ayyadhury knew how to commit to something and now she's really happy. We should all learn how to commit to our dreams. To commit to our dreams would make all of us more passionate about what we do, then we would all get more things done.

One thing I really admire about Mrs. Ayyadhury is her personality. She has done a lot in her life and it shows through her life experience. Every problem any student comes to her with she has a story and an answer for them, based on her own past. She was once an engineer but left the field. When asking Mrs. Ayyadhury why, she responded by saying "At that point [in time] it was a very sexist environment. Fighting it was uphill. I loved teaching since I was tutoring at the time." Mrs. Ayyadhury liked engineering but chose teaching because she loves it. Mrs. Ayyadhury works with a lot of student before, during, and after school. I think that shows how much Mrs. Ayyadhury loves and cares about what she's doing. At home right now Mrs. Ayyadhury has to take care of her sick mother-in-law, live without her husband, and try to take care of her own happiness. This would probably be easier if she didn't spend most of her day at HAIS taking care of us as students. Mrs. Ayyadhury doesn't complain though. She says herself, "You can be whoever you want, but always be your best. Don't let others tell you otherwise." Mrs. Ayyadhury was raised being told by her father, "Never forget your past, you'll never learn from it [if you do]." That's why today she holds herself as someone so noble, hardworking, and committed.

I think Mrs. Ayyadhury represents a strong woman, and that didn't come naturally. She had to work for her self to be where she stands today. I admire her for her perseverance through hard times in life, school, and work now. That's what makes her such a great teacher. And the life experience she has is what makes her a great role model. She always has the right words to give you the best advice.

FIRST DAY OF KINDERGARTEN
by Destiny James

"You have funny colored eyes", she said. "You're fat and ugly," he said. "You look like a poo-poo head!" Wow, the first day of kindergarten and I am already being insulted by rambunctious five year olds, who can't even spell the words that come out of their mouths! I'm five years old, yet I know how to recite the alphabet, read beginner-level chapter books, count all the way to one-thousand and spell words correctly. Why did my mom bring me here? What kind of a name is Kindergarten anyway? I told mommy this was a horrible idea, she will definitely get an earful of complaints from me when she picks me up. Here I stand in the middle of a room, trapped in this hell-hole of an "educational class", with a bunch of snot nosed kids. The worst part is I'm the only sane one here!

The teacher, Mrs. Graves, yells too much. Her voice sounded like a mixture of a hyper monkey and a female lion protecting her cub. Even when she did not yell, it still drove me crazy to hear her talk normally.

"Boys and girls!" She screeched, "We are going to name the colors of the rainbow. Do any of you know the colors of the rainbow?"

"No!" the class said in unison.

"I do", I said shyly.

Mrs. Graves turned her huge owl eyes towards me.

"Oh, you do?" She asked with a crooked smile.

I nodded.

"Well I hope you don't mind telling the class what the colors of the rainbow are."

All eyes on me, everyone's heads turned towards my direction. The stares felt cold and unforgiving as if I were naked. The red head freckled face boy that called me a "poo-poo head", snickered.

I took a deep breath, "Red, Orange, Yellow, Green, Blue, Indigo, and Violet. My mommy told me to remember the name Roy G. Biv to help me remember the colors of the rainbow."

Mrs. Graves looked at me for what seemed like forever and finally said, "Very Good little girl, now please be seated." Very good? "Very good little girl?" I thought if I did a good job I would get a sticker, at least that's what mommy told me. I'm trying to understand why that poor excuse of a teacher decided to call me "little girl", it's Destiny James, and I plan on being addressed by the name my mother gave me.

Kindergarten work made me feel at ease. Mommy taught me useful information that I needed to know before school started and it actually helped me accomplish assignments Mrs. Graves passed out to us. Russell that freckled face loser that called me a poo-poo head, sits across from me, and I see him having the hardest time figuring out what comes after the letter "C". He notices me staring at him and scrunches his face into a sour expression. After wasting five minutes of his time making faces at me, he notices I ignored him and quits. Being the first one done with the assignment, I counted numbers to myself. As I reached number 120, I couldn't help but notice Lauren stare at me viciously. Lauren sat next to Russell, which means she had a full view of my face across from hers. She reminded me of an "all-American beauty" long blond hair, milky white skin, and bluish-gray eyes. I have golden blonde curly hair and bluish-green eyes but I'm not considered an "all-American beauty", not that I care.

Lunchtime finally arrived, my favorite part of school. The class lined up in a single-file line and Mrs. Graves led us down the hall to the cafeteria. As I began to walk my way towards the nearest seat I could find, I felt someone's hands shove me. I didn't bother to turn around to see who did it because I simply did not care, besides that was a sucky push, I hardly moved. The chicken and tomato sandwich mommy packed for me tasted like heaven on a bun. I could hear Lauren and her little brunette sidekicks talk about me, "Look at what she's eating! It has tomatoes on it! That's Disgusting!" I could care less what they thought about my lunch. From where I sat I could see that they had Chef Boyardee ravioli, a nasty mediocre-Italian cuisine stuffed in a can. Mommy bought that for me once and I hated it, I prefer her home-made cooking rather than processed foods that are sold in cans.

Right after lunch ended, recess began. When I walked outside to the playground I stood frozen. "This. Playground. Is. Amazing." I said to myself. A child's paradise stood right before my eyes. I have never seen a big playground filled with so many activities. There was a Jungle Jim , Monkey bars, Kingdom-castle sized slides, basketball courts, a soccer and a kickball field, a hopscotch court, a sandbox, and a jumping-rope court. I didn't know where to start; I only had forty-five minutes to play before nap time. I, of course, chose the sandbox. When I waddled my way to the sandbox, I saw Lauren and her pals sitting in a circle creating an ugly, lopsided looking sand-castle. They all turned and looked at me.

"You can't play in the sandbox", Lauren said.

"Why not?" I asked.

"You have to have blond hair and blue eyes."

I touched my golden blond curly locks, "I do have blonde hair and blue eyes, your friends sitting with you don't have it."

She looked away trying to find another excuse. "Well you can't play with us because you're black!" She exclaimed.

I have never met a girl so ignorant in my life, the things that came out of her mouth are just plain rude. I looked at Lauren and laughed so hard I almost cried.

"I don't care! I'm still playing in the sandbox you stupid beaver-faced Barbie!"

I found an empty space in the sand-box and hand-crafted the most spectacular sand-castle.

DIFFERENT FACES, DIFFERENT PLACES
By Xzavier Jelks

"No Mother I Don't Want to Leave!" are the words that I shouted when she approached me. This was the place where I grew up and I didn't and wasn't going to leave everyone that I had grown to know and love. Unfortunately, these words were repeated over and over and over again more than times. Every time we moved, I wished it was the last time but it was never the last time. I feel that if I would have stayed in one place, my education level would have been way higher and I wouldn't have a problem with speaking around people that I see every day.

The first move was during my favorite Elementary School, Oak Creek Elementary. Before this school, I had been moved around to 3 different schools. This had been very difficult for me to grasp because there were so many different scenery changes in my life and this was the one place where I finally got a little bit of freedom and I made friends. It was my job to wake myself up in the mornings and to make sure I caught the school bus on time. It was also my responsibility to make sure that I kept up with my house key so that I could get into my home. When we moved, I felt a little bit more mature than I usually was. I had to step and show a little bit more responsibility but at the same time still maintain my usual duties as a child. As I settled in, I made new friends thinking that these would be lifelong friends.. That's when on the last day of school I was hit with the, "We Are Moving Speech!" That was the worst day of my life but on to a new life I go.

When I moved the second time, I moved away but not too far from where I used to live. I tried to take the good with the bad and look at the bright side of the move, but it seemed like I was at the end of a tunnel and the light was too far to reach. One good thing that happened was that I moved a little bit closer to my family. I had access to my aunt and my cousins at any time I wanted. But here I had to change my mind set. It was like I was living in a penitentiary system. If I didn't act a certain way, I was at the risk of getting beaten up or something way worse. All around me was drugs and all the bad things that a child shouldn't be experiencing at a young age. I hated it there; there wasn't anything that wasn't beneficial to my growth as a human being. It was like we were in the Jungle and it was Survival of the Fittest. This time when I was hit with the "We Are Moving Speech," I was very excited. I don't think that my parents really understood how much I really wanted to leave from there and never wanted to come back.

This time when I moved, I moved very far. I went from the North side of Houston to the South Side near Missouri City. I felt better when I moved here because I felt as if I could start all over. I had a new beginning with a new house, a new school, and hopefully new friends. When I was there, I was able to start going out with my friends a little bit more and I had access to more malls and I got to experience more things age appropriate for a teenage boy. The new school that I would attend was James A. Madison High School. The first day of school was much anticipated until it actually came. I was so lost but I wasn't complaining because I loved where I was living and nothing could shoot me down. I felt great until the end of the year when my mother actually didn't give me the "We Are Moving Speech!" she gave me the "You Are Changing School Speech." This was devastating because I was close to all my friends at Madison High School, but another move for me. That is when we found the Houston Academy for International Studies.

In all this I really wish I could go back in time and tell my mother that with the first move, it was traumatize me and would cause me so much pain and anger. But that's not all. I end up moving 3 more times after I moved the last time that was stated earlier. But as long as I stay in the same school, it wouldn't really make a difference to me. The three moments spoken upon were really life changing events for me and wish I could take them all back but its life and you have to what life deals , understand why, and continue on with your walk through life.

MY OWN ROOM
by Tychenellia M. Jernigan

My mom, my sister, and I where all sitting on the couch just wondering how it would feel living in our own house or maybe just our own apartment.

"Mama, are we going to move out of granny's house?" Ikea asked.

"No baby, there is enough room here," she answered, as she thought of my granny's six bed room, two kitchens, two dinner rooms, two living rooms, and two bathroom house.

"But mama, we all share the same small room."

"Well don't you enjoy sharing a room with me and your sisters?" my mother asked.

"Yes ma'am," Ikea said. My granny's house was big enough for my mother and her three kids, but it wasn't big enough for my granny, her four kids, and their children. My mother, my sisters and I lived in the same room. The brick house was so crowded that people would hide food from each other, living there wasn't all fun and games for my sisters and I, because we hated sharing the big house with our whole family. Sharing the brick house with the rest of the family made it seem as if the house was very small. My sisters and I felted that it was time to get out and move. We nagged our tired mother a billion times and more, asking her if we could get our own small or big apartment. She would say, "as soon as I get a better job sweet hearts."

****

"Everyone, pack your bags it's moving day," my mother announced.

"Really mama," I asked.

"Yes, Tych we are moving to Scott Plaza. The money I am earning from my job at AstroWorld is paying enough so that we can get our own apartment," she said.

"Awesome, mama, I can't wait to get my own room." My mother closed her eyes and walked to my granny's room. I couldn't believe that we were going to move out. Throughout six years of my life I lived on Grasmere with my whole family.

When we walked up to the door of our new apartment, my mother took the golden key and unlocked the door. My sisters and I rushed in the house; there were only two bedrooms and one restroom. My mother broke the news to us, saying that we would have to share a bedroom. Even though, Ikea, my older sister, didn't like it my younger sister, Shaelia, and I loved to share a room together.

A few years later AstroWorld closed down and my mother lost the job that was keeping us in our own apartment.

"We have to move out," my mama said.

"Why?" Shaelia asked.

"Because little one, mama lost her job and they say, 'No pay, no stay'", my mother responded.

"Well mama could we get a different apartment?" Ikea asked.

"We will have to search for a new apartment but we have to go now," mama said.

"Are we going to be homeless?" I asked.

"No we are just going to be enjoying the park for a few days and night; until, we find some a new place to live," my mama responded with tears in her eyes. Shaelia walked up to our mother and kissed her on her cheek.

"It is okay mama; we love going to the park," Shaelia said. We were homeless for about two weeks, living at bus stops and parks. My mother searched and searched for somewhere to go but no one would take her in without any money. Finally, my cousin Tonya invited us into her home. We stayed there for two years; while, my mother got on her feet. She went to college during the day, homeschooled us during the evening, and worked at night.

****

"Tych go clean your room!" my mama shouts.

"Mama, I am fifteen years old but I'm going to clean it anyway."

"Girl, talk back to me one more time and I'll smack your lips off."

"Yes ma'am!" I yell. I walk to my room just wondering what makes her think that she is the boss; maybe because she finished school and is a substitute for HISD. Whatever it is, all I know is that I am fifteen and I did not want to clean my room. I just want to enjoy being a teen and go out with the friends I do accept, but she thinks otherwise; as if I really need a clean room to go out to the movies.

Sometimes I wish I was still three; then I'll go back to living on Grasmere, sharing a room with my mother and my sisters. Then I wish I was seven because at the time I didn't have a room at all. I always take back my wishes in the end though, you know, after I finish cleaning my room. Then I thank God that my mama was successful enough to give me my own room.

UNDERNEATH IT ALL
by Alysia Johnson

"Hey Alysia you look so pretty today!" Smiling I reply, "Thank you so much, you know I try." "Alysia I love your hair." Happily I say, "Thank You!" Even though I'm smiling on the outside, I'm really torn to shreds on the inside. It all started with my parents' divorce.

"Alysia wake up!" My mom yelled. Waking up a sleepy five-year-old Alysia was a hassle. "Alysia," My mom shouts again. "Hurry and get dressed it is time for school." Finally, super grouchy I erupt from bed and get dressed. It was just another ordinary day. As I get dropped off at school seeing my classmates gave me an instant burst of excitement. I loved school it was so fun, I had perfect attendance and had never left school early. That is why it was so surprising when I got called down to the office because my mom was there to pick me up. Evident to a five-year-old the look in my mother's eyes instantly gave away the fact that something was wrong. As she strapped me in my car seat we raced home. When we got inside she started zipping through the house. Leaving me dumbfounded standing in the middle of the living room. I watched as she dumped everything in the car except for my Father's things. I wondered why. We never go on vacation without Daddy. Soon after my Dad pulled up, excited to see him because I knew that he would make everything better, I rushed to the door waiting to be picked up, only to be brushed off. He and my Mother rushed to their room to "talk" but all I heard was screaming and yelling followed by a loud, BANG! This was the dresser being flipped over. That did not sound like "talking" to me one bit. This was the biggest fight my parent's ever had and it ended with "I'm leaving you," coming from my Mother's mouth. This was the day she left my father for good and took me with her.

Ever since that day my life has drastically changed. With my mom jumping from job to job and me from school to school, I never knew a stable home. In the process of moving from house to house I do not get to see my father a lot. This hurts because we were close. Now when I see him all I get is negativity. He plays on my insecurities as if it makes him feel better. I often feel he thinks that I am not pretty enough to be his daughter. Since I act a different way than he expects, he's ashamed of me. Not having a male figure around all the time, all I wanted was to feel loved and accepted by one. My mom tries her best to encourage and uplift me but I never feel what she says I never feel is true.

Happy about my new haircut and feeling good about myself I walk up to my Dad's truck to collect my money he was coming to deliver to me. "Hey Dad, I got my haircut, you like it?" I say happy. "Ewwwww, why did you do that and what's wrong with your face?" He says very nasty. Sad I reply, "I like my hair and I thought it was cute and everyone else thinks so too. Dad you know my face has broken out horribly I don't know how to fix it." He replies, "Well you're going to have to do something because that is not cute." He rolls his window up and pulls off without saying anything more. Feeling horrible like I'm not worth anything I run up to my room and cry until I can fall asleep.

I remember days like this so very vividly and it brings back salty memories every time. This is not the first time he has done something like this. I am trying my best to deal with it and get used to it but why should I. This has had a huge impact on me because when I feel like I am not pretty or not worth anything, I always think back on the times where the one male figure that I do have in my life has said hurtful things to me. I think to myself if he doesn't think I'm pretty then who else will. It doesn't help that I have many boy problems and the reason being is because I don't have a male to tell me I am beautiful or to love me like my daddy "used" to. So therefore when I'm in a new relationship I am always vulnerable to lies and often get hurt.

"Alysia, I really do love you." My boyfriend for about six months says. In my head I think if you really loved me why are you with her when I'm not around. Scared to say this out loud because I am afraid he won't like me anymore I simply reply back, "I love you too." Feeling horrible because I am holding back what I would really like to say I do not know what to do. I know my friends judge me and think I am stupid. I just feel like I need a male who is there for me and who I can turn to since I do not have a father. I often jump from relationship to relationship for fear of being alone or to run from the feeling that I might not be "good" enough. "Alysia you are the best thing that has happened to Me." Knowing he's telling her this also I play along with his little game. I just don't know how to end this even though I am not happy. With "him" I feel safe, protected, and loved. When we're not together I know for a fact he is making her feel the same way. Where will I find this again? I often ask myself. That is the real reason I stay.

I have been through a time where in a happy home you feel as though nothing can go wrong and you feel safe with both of your parents there and it automatically gets snatched away from you. How are you supposed to cope? I am in a world or my own place where my father helps me feel insecure whether than trying to help me not feel that way. I am in my own world where I just want to feel wanted by a male who loves me for me. Underneath it all I am not as strong and confident as I portray. The events that have taken place in my life has made me someone whom I despise.

A GRANDMOTHER'S LOVE
by Ashley Johnson

It was Sunday evening when I interviewed her. I remembered because Joel Osteen was on. The room we sat in had an open floor plan with beautiful décor. All the walls were originally white, but over the years turned into an ivory color due to the dust and smoke. The table we sat at was shaped like a rectangle; a bowl of plastic fruit was placed directly in the center of the wooden table. While I was giving the interview, I could hear the television in the background. I also heard the birds twittering in the wind, and the coffee brewing.

As she walked from her lazy boy to the kitchen table, I could see the grayish whitish streaks in her hair. Her hair was placed in a low bun with little hairs sticking out. She had a smile that could light up the room. Her skin completion was a buttery brown, with deep dark brown eyes. She was in her night gown at the time; I watched how it swayed back and forth as she walked. As she sat down the first thing I asked was, "What is your name?" "Dinah Mae Johnson", she answered with a mid-tone voice. I asked her this question as if she was not my grandmother.

"I am an introverted person" is how she choose to describe herself. She loved to see people happy and enjoying life. If there was anything that she could have helped with, she would immediately sign up for the duty. But Dinah Johnson wasn't always this seventy-seven year old woman.

On a small farm in Hallettsville, TX, Dinah lived with her other eleven siblings. While on the farm she lived as a normal child. She went to grade school at Steven Mayo Colored High School. But, because my grandmother was an African-American back while segregation was going on, she was forced to attend an all black school. Not only did she live on a farm, but she spent a lot of the year harvesting and working on the plantation. She hated the summer time the most because there was an increase in the work load.

Some of her daily chores were to chop wood, stock up on house supplies, get food and other supplies to last through the winter, learn how to cook, pick cotton, help furnish for the family, and because she was one of the oldest children, she had to help with the other children.

My grandmother was a part of the day and age, when being black was not acceptable; but she fought through it. This is one of the reasons why I admire her so much. She did not allow her skin color to determine her future. She was not allowed to drink from certain water fountains and go to different places, due to her race. She would tell me the story of when she went to the movie theatre; she was forced to sit at the top (balcony). They let the white's sit at the bottom because there were emergency exits. Therefore if a fire was to breakout they could escape more rapidly. All of these things were normal for her to live with, so she didn't see that much wrong with it at the time.

After she graduated from high school, she decided to move to Houston, TX to get a job and get greater opportunities. When she first moved there she lived with her grandmother for a while. Later she went on to move with her Aunt Sweet, up until the time of her getting married. She meets her husband, Joe Bill Johnson on the city bus while traveling to work. After two years of dating, they got married in 1957.

Dinah lived the average married women life. She went to work, as a maid for Miss Helen Stevenson. At this time she was getting paid $25.00 a week. After years of working for Miss Stevenson she resigned. She soon went to work for another family as a maid where she earned $35.00

a week. I asked her "How did you feel at this time of your life?" "I was content." She felt as though this was the way her life was meant to be.

In 1965 she had a son, by the name of Michael Johnson. She listed becoming a mother as being the most fascinating time period in her life. She loves her son deeply, and is very proud of him. "I don't think I could have done better", she went on to say.

On top of her being a married mother, Dinah loved to travel, and she took a fine liking to sports. She went on a beautiful cruise to San Juan, Saint Coy and other beautiful Islands. Her favorite singer of all time was the famous Neil Diamond. My dad says she used to listen to all of his records 24/7. Dinah was and still is a beautiful person inside and out, and I am thankful for having her in my life.

She resigned from being a maid for the Herring's, and went on to work for the city for better wages. She took courses at a trading school, to secure a good job and with higher wages. She worked for the city for 15 years, and then resigned. She soon started to do temporary jobs for about four years; soon after, her husband got ill, and passed on in 1995. He passed, a few months after I was born. But though this tragedy happened, Dinah still keep going. She worked at the blood center, and helped my father take care of my brother and I for many years.

She got tired of the city life, and decided to move back to her hometown in the early 2000's. Dinah is now living in Hallettsville, TX where she is living her life peacefully. "How do you feel about the turn out of your life?" I asked her at the end of the interview. "Well I'm at peace with what I have done", is what she replied to me. I love Dinah Johnson because she is a great woman, and I know I can always count on her when I need her. She has never let me down, and has always been there for me, even when I couldn't be there for myself.. It's not one person in this world that inspires me more than she does. I love her with an everlasting love.

Life Ways
By Israel Rodriguez

MY DAD
by Altaniece Jones

Many come across that one person who inspires them to become whoever they want to be in life and supports their dreams one hundred percent. These people often time have the ability to make you want to reach for the stars. For me, that person happens to be a middle age male, who is 5'8, and loves the Football Team the Dallas Cowboys. He has always made it a priority to make sure that I stayed on top of my school work and continued to follow my dreams. Everyone knows him as the loving and kind person who is always there to help others and give them advice. Lending a helping hand is something that comes natural for him. This person happens to be my Father. He has always taught me about self worth which has stuck me from my child hood years.

Alton Jonathan Jones was born on September 20, 1963 to Alton and Leta Jones. As a young child he enjoyed school describing it as " One of the best times of the day for me." When asked by family members what he wanted to be when he grew up, he always replied a football player. Being apart of The Dallas Cowboys football team was one of his many dreams. During his spare time he enjoyed watching football, reading and writing, and listening to rock and roll music. Alton, stressed that listening to rock and roll music was something that calmed him down on a daily basis. Throughout his childhood, Alton was always helping others around the neighborhood and being a model brother for his younger sister Jennifer and younger brother DeUndre. "I was always helping my Mothers friends unload their groceries and help them take out their trash. It was something that my Mother enjoyed seeing me do."

Along with his mother, Alton looked up to his older cousin Gerald and of course his father. When asked about his run-ins with trouble, family members explained he was never in trouble, always doing something good. By the time, Alton was 17 he had found a good church home and was looking forward to graduating. Things seemed to be going very well until tragedy struck. Right at the peek of adult hood, Alton was diagnosed with Ulcerative Colitis. A disease that causes inflammation and sores called Ulcers in the lining of the rectum and colon. His dreams of being a football player was now crushed. This disease made him lose weight and made it extremely hard to walk or do anything for himself. During the difficult time, Alton was surrounded by family who prayed and took care of him. He was hospitalized 6 times, all times being in ICU(Intensive Care Unit). He explained how he felt during this time by stating "Sometimes I felt like I wasn't going to make it, I felt like at any moment I could just pass away." Alton knew he had to get well for his family and continue his life. With two life threatening surgeries at a young age, Alton was determined to make his self well again. "This was when my faith in God got a lot stronger" he said.

After months in the hospital, Alton was able to return home and continue his life. He knew that wouldn't be the last time he would be hospitalized but he continued to pray for his health. Although, Alton wasn't well, he still felt the need to help others in any way that he could. Just a two months after surgery, he begin volunteering and looking for a job. It didn't take long before he found one.

Dealing with work and the healing process didn't come easy but with the help of a special person. He made a full recovery. Alton met Talitha by accidentally calling the wrong number. Through their brief conversation he found something special in her. After calling numerous amounts of times, he took her on a date. From that day on they were inseparable. She helped him become a better person and helped him with anything he needed. Shortly after meeting, Alton was hospitalized once again but this time even longer. His one true love was there throughout everything. When asked what made him want to embrace life he replied "When I met your mother it made me want to embrace life. I actually found out the true meaning of love when I met her." During his stay at the hospital, Alton knew he wanted to get well in order to do something he had been wanting to do for a while. He had wanted to propose to Talitha. Shortly after being released Alton and his sister Jennifer made their way to jeweler so that he could pick out a wedding ring. On September 8, Alton and Talitha were pronounced Mr. and Mrs. Jones. This was the beginning of a very happy life.

Completing my father's life story wouldn't be right because it hasn't ended yet. Sharing all of the information above truly explains why my dad inspires me. For him to go through such a hard period during his life really gives me motivation that I could overcome anything. Although my dad wasn't able to follow it dreams, it doesn't stop him from helping others follow theirs. His kind spirit is something that over power everything. His last remarks of the interview was "Altaniece, never give up on your dreams. No matter what anyone else tells you. And remember I will support you one hundred percent!"

MI ABUELITA
by Nazreen Kashani

When you see her she is usually running around like an antsy old woman, trying to do everything she can because she is the only one who can do it "right." Standing at an average height with aging skin and a boy haircut with her white and gray hairs, I see her as the most beautiful grandmother with her natural beauty. She can be described as the kind of woman who thinks us younger ones, like my mother and myself, do not know how to clean or do anything right. Nothing personal; just an old woman stuck in her ways. I live with her now, as I have for almost my entire life, and I love her like my own mother.

Her life started on a bumpy road and turned into a spiraling course through adulthood, overcoming one obstacle after another. Since the time she was a baby, her family was extremely poor, living in a small home with only 4 rooms. Her mother lived in sickness and they would never get a chance to go anywhere. She and her siblings each had two changes of clothes and one pair of shoes. She almost never saw her dad, since he was away at sea, working on different boat ports.

"I missed him, constantly cried about not seeing him, but I knew he was working to keep us alive."

Hearing about her childhood, made me feel as if I did not know the true life she lived and the struggles that carved the rest of her life.

"There were some good and funny times though, like when my baby brother was being born. Back then, births were done at home, and my mother told my siblings and I that a plane was going to come with my baby brother. We would always be running around in the yard looking for the plane, and one day when they sent us away to our aunt's house we came back and saw our new brother."

I thought to myself how much of a sheltered life she had as a child, not even told the truth about where babies came from. It explained to me why she sometimes wonders why I do the things I do in this day and time. I felt as if I somehow now understood her better than I ever had. It was simple. She grew up in a different world than mine.

She went to school until fourth grade, walking to and from alone, and not being able to have fun as a kid. After fourth grade, her mom left her to work at her cousin's house.

"It was as if she sent me away, but I loved it there because my aunt would make delicious food. My mom always made the same stupid rice and beans and I hated it. The bad thing was I did not attend school when I lived with them, and unfortunately I never went back, ending my education at fourth grade."

When she returned home, after living and working with her cousin for a year, she felt like she fell into the same old thing she had escaped, having to eat the same thing, and do nothing. So she decided to try something new.

"I worked selling bread but people would steal from me, so I never made much profit. I didn't care though because I would get myself a taco and that would be my delicious meal." Her schemes over the simplicity of obtaining a meal really opened my eyes to the amount of things I have in my life and how I should never take anything for granted.

"I got pregnant the age of thirteen."

She had a baby and he died after a few months because of a bad shot given to him from a doctor. The sad time came and passed quickly, ending with her second pregnancy. My Aunt Clara came about soon after the incident, my grandmother having just two years of being married. Clara's dad was sick the day she arrived, came to see her the day after, gave her money and left to find work. She never saw him again. The way things worked out after that eventually led her to end up in the United States working for a family cleaning and babysitting a sick child. Cleaning and housework was all she had ever learned to do. She eventually left working there, met my grandfather and got married.

Life with my grandfather felt unbearable to my grandmother. She repeatedly left because of his alcohol problems, but always came back because he was ultimately the father of their children and the only life she knew.

"I'm not sure if I loved him."

I had no prior knowledge of my grandmother's true feelings towards her deceased husband; it was heartbreaking listening to her, because I never expected those words to come out of her. Sitting there, in the very room I had the most amazing times growing up with my grandpa; I was discovering something that had been kept a secret from me.

"Life now is way better than back then, but I'm always working, if it's not taking care of your uncles' kids that are living with us, it's cleaning up after them."

She spoke as if her wings of freedom had been cut off immediately after they had been given to her. She now has the responsibility of three of her grandchildren, just like she had the responsibility of me when I was left there. Probably one of the things that hit me the hardest was when she said:

"I'm no good at anything. I'm useless because all I know how to do is clean."

I felt like my heart shattered into a million pieces. Breaking into tears I stood up and went to give my grandma a hug. She seemed cold and emotionless. I had never seen this sad side of her. I love her and see her as my inspiration in all that I do. She keeps me going, on the road to becoming something, because she never could. She raised me almost my entire life and taught me most of what I know and I thank her.

THE SYSTEM
by Clare Legg

The pencil sharpener is full. I just sharpened my pencil, and, now, the pencil sharpener is full. This can only mean one thing; it's my turn to dump out the pencil shavings. This seems silly, but, as of three weeks ago, dumping out the pencil shavings once the pencil sharpener is full is the coolest thing to do in Mrs. Behrend's second grade class.

I've just moved to Houston from San Diego, which means I'm the new girl. The new girl who currently only has one friend, and she's absent today. You would think that the bright-and-shiny new girl from the glittering oasis that is California would be immensely popular, that kids would be lining up around the block to be her friend, but no. The boys and girls in Mrs. Behrend's second grade class could not be less impressed with my tan skin and blonde hair. All they care about is Avril Lavigne and dumping out pencil shavings.

So, I wrap my small hand around the smooth plastic vault containing these strange six year olds' most precious possession. You see, in Mrs. Behrend's second grade class, pencil shavings are like social currency. The more pencil shavings in the pencil sharpener at the time of the dumping and the more times you dump, the cooler you are. I am the only student who has yet to dump the pencil shavings.

This is my shot, I think. Once I have emptied the pencil sharpener, I'll finally be cool. Everyone will immediately accept me. Instead of having one friend, all twenty-one students in Mrs. Behrend's second grade class will be begging to be my friends. All I have to do is dump the pencil shavings. I pull the little plastic box out from the pencil sharpener. I begin to tilt the box and let the shavings inch their way to the edge. And, finally —

"Kuh-lare, what do you think you are doing," squawks a high-pitched voice from behind me.

"I'm, um, dumping out the pencil shavings."

"Oh my gosh, Kuh-lare, you can't dump out the pencil shavings until the pencil sharpener is full. Everybody knows that!"

It's Brelan Owen. Not new, vicious, popular Brelan Owen. I should say something. Explain to her that the pencil sharpener, in fact is full. So, if she could kindly move aside, I'd just go about my business dumping pencil shavings. I can't, though. New girls aren't allowed to disagree with popular girls. Apparently, it's written in a handbook somewhere.

She grabs the box of shavings, her bubble gum pink nails scratching my hand in the process. She then proceeds to dump the pencil shavings! She didn't even sharpen her pencil, which means she stole my chance to dump the pencil shavings and consequently stole my imminent popularity. Brelan Owen is a popularity stealer.

I can feel face get hot as Brelan walks back to her assigned seat with the kind of satisfaction that can only be caused by ruining other young children's lives. I wipe my sweaty hands on my overalls, and it takes everything I have not to cry. I'm already the new girl; I can't be a cry baby too. I risk a glance to my right and see that Chris Farrish, super cute and nice Chris Farrish, is looking at me with sad eyes, like he pities me. I hate Brelan even more now. Not only did she steal my popularity, but she embarrassed me in front of Chris.

I want more than anything to run over there and rip that disgusting smirk off her face. Better yet, I want to collect all of my stolen pencil shavings from the trash can and make her eat them, every single shaving. I can't though, because in that same omniscient handbook, directly below New Girls Are Not Allowed to Disagree with Popular Girls, it clearly states that new girls are also not allowed to defend themselves from popular girls. I don't have to defend myself, though, because apparently, Hailey Sellers is going to do it for me.

"Brelan! You didn't make Clare stop dumping the pencil shavings because the sharpener wasn't full, you did it because you wanted to dump the shavings yourself. You are a mean girl, Brelan Owen, and the next time the pencil sharpener fills up, Clare gets to dump the shavings," she orders.

The small smile on my face that formed during Hailey's speech turns into a full blown grin when Brelan actually apologizes. Hailey turns around and smiles at me, and during recess, she asks me if I want go on the tire swing with her.

I, Clare Legg, bright-and-shiny new girl from San Diego, California, beat the system. I have gone from one friend to two friends in Mrs. Behrend's second grade class without dumping a single pencil shaving. Eat your heart out, Brelan Owen.

UNTITLED
by Ashondra Lewis

I remember it like it happened yesterday, the day I almost lost my brother. I was seven years old and he was nine. I lived with my grandmother at the time. One Saturday morning during the summer of 2002 my aunt called and asked if we wanted to go to the beach and of course we did. I was so excited. It was my first time ever going to the beach. I imagined looking like the beaches that I had seen on television and movies. I even expected us to have fun like they do on television and movies, but boy was I wrong.

When we first arrived to the beach I saw the beautiful white sand, I couldn't wait to take off my sandals and walk through it. While walking in the sand the first creature I saw was a crab. It was the first time I've seen something so red and tiny. I wanted to touch it, I would have too if my mother told me not to. In a split second I turned my attention away from the creature to the water. The water wasn't clear with beauty. But it was clear and as fresh as salt water could be. The wind was blowing so smoothly I could feel the breeze flow through my body. I couldn't wait to feel the warm water pressing against my feet, the waves pressing against my body, the sun hitting my face, shining light into my eyes.

A beach greeter came by and explained the rules to my family. I didn't listen, I just wanted to run and feel the waves brush against my little seven year old legs. I did hear one rule and to me it was the most important one. The greeter said "Don't go too far into the water, because the waves will pull you back". It seemed as if he was talking forever. Blah, blah, blah, blah when will he be done talking? About five minutes later he finished talking. My cousins and I ran into the water. I felt like Ariel from "The Little Mermaid." The waves were warm and soft, it felt like the feeling you get under the covers during the winter time. I felt the seaweed touching my toes. It felt really slimy but I didn't care I enjoyed the water. I enjoyed life on the beach.

It's been almost two hours since we've been at the beach. Everything's going so smoothly. We built sandcastles, played with a beach ball, and enjoyed the water. The adults were sitting at the table drinking and talking while my cousins and I were playing in the water. Suddenly we hear a kid saying "There's a kid out there drowning". I laughed a little because he sounded very country, and he was short and stubby Of course like the noisy little kids we are, we looked to see who's drowning.

None of us expected to see what we saw next. It was my brother. Everything after that happened so fast. It was as if time was speeding up. My mother ran into the water but I could tell the water was heavy because she was slowing down. I couldn't imagine losing my brother this way. We were so close and I don't know what I would do without him.

All these thoughts were running through my mind. I wanted to be like Superman and save him myself. In reality I knew I couldn't save him because I couldn't swim myself. I kept saying to myself, " what can I do?" A minute later, I see my uncle rushing into the water like he was a speed racer. Seconds later he came back with my brother in his arms. I cried, but they weren't tears of sadness, they were tears of joy. My brother was safe and sound on land and out of the water

After that we left the beach so fast and never went back again. That had to be one of the worse days of my life. From that point on I realized the dangers of having fun and that life is too short. That experience changed me. It still affects me until this day. That day is one of the reasons why I'm so cautions when I go to the pool or when I'm near any type of water. People can say I'm scared, but I want to live to see more days and have more adventures in life. It seemed as if all the little things my brother and I fought about didn't even matter anymore. The only thing that really mattered was no one was lost that day. Aside from that experience I was just happy to have my brother in my life and I will never take him for granted again.

UNTITLED
by Juan Lopez

The chilling wind attacks my skin as my mother walks in through the front door, immediately closing it. She genuinely smiles; taking this interview as a silly game. That is one aspect of my mother I always admired; her smile always has a way of calming not just me, but any creature that lays its eyes on it, down. We take a seat in our relaxing blue colored living room; she hands me a nice, warm cup of atole (a very solidly but liquidly Mexican drink) she had prepared earlier. Pictures of all the precious family moments line the walls and the tables next to the couch. She lets out a sigh as her stare lingers on my older brother's Marine boot camp graduation portrait.

She is dressed casually, wearing a simple white t-shirt and sweatpants. "Sorry if I don't look properly dressed. I just finished washing the car; I don't think I have to impress my own son", she jokes around.

I laugh with her, "It's fine mom; no point in making this awkwardly professional, and we see each other every day after all. But since the people reading this don't know squat about you; just tell me a bit about yourself."

"I was born on December 17, 1976 in a small town in Mexico. I had an amazing childhood. My father; oh where to begin? He had so much money; one of the richest men in Mexico." "How rich exactly?" I ask "Millions upon millions! I got anything I wanted with a snap of my finger. All of our maids hated me for being so spoiled. My father made sure I had the finest clothes, toys, anything. He was such a strong, powerful, yet gentle man. He would always pick me up from school and carry me on his shoulders all the way home. I miss him terribly," she shifts her body, this subject is obviously bothering her.

"Are you okay to talk about this?" I personally know her history and how horrible it turns out. "Yes. A week after I turned fourteen, he committed suicide. I can't celebrate Christmas without thinking of him,. Terrible, terrible things were happening to our family. It was all the witch's doing," she spits as she says the word "Witch."

"Can you elaborate on the witch?" I ask her. My mother's heartwarming smile disappears, a hateful scowl taking its place, "She was my father's business' partner. She would always do some sort of witchcraft that would guarantee my father's success. She was an awful, ugly woman and always slapped me when my father left me in her care. There is no way to prove it, but I know she cursed my father."

"Do you really believe in magic and all that nonsense?" I question her. "I saw her do things, evil, but magical things. Nothing no machine or normal person could do. I know it seems farfetched but I wouldn't lie about such a thing."

The atmosphere feels colder now; I try to move the interview in a different direction, "So tell me how you met your husband, Preciliano Lopez" "Well after my father's death; my mother, baby brother and I moved to Houston to get away from that cursed town. We moved to Houston and I started attending Milby High School and was placed in the ESL program. Funny thing was; I didn't learn anything in that class, and all the teacher ever did was show us movies from the 1950's.No, I learned how to speak English in three months by watching the show *COPS*. At first it was just curse words, but I caught on. Anyways, I met your father at a club where we danced all night," she's smiling now, remembering fond memories. "I didn't know dad could dance," I interrupt.

"Oh he can't! He was stepping on my feet all night. No, the reason I decided to give him a chance was because unlike the other boys that were all after me; he was a man. After a while we started going out and it was just such a sweet thing. I can't remember being happier. He would pick me up from school and one time this idiot guy who convinced himself he had a chance with me was so jealous, he threw a rock at your father's new car. You're father jumped out of his car, chased and tackled him down. After that day that idiot never looked at my way again. If it weren't for your father, I would have been such a broken girl."

The ominous tone dies down as my mother remembers fond memories, "I visit our tree every now and then. We had our first kiss under that tree and he carved our names into it. It's right outside Milby. Everyone gave me heat for dating him, Oh he goes to Austin High school, if you didn't know Austin and Milby were huge rivals at the time. Oh there was so much fighting between the two schools because of us."

"Fighting?" This is the first I hear of it.

She laughs, "The guys from Milby were mad that some random guy from Austin got the girl that they were all going after." -Side Note- According to my mother she was one of the most beautiful girls there, I've seen her high school photos, and I'm not going to disagree. –End of side note- "So they started fighting your dad's friends and eventually guys from each school would have big fight club type brawls. Never too violent, no deaths, it was kind of playful."

"So what happened?" I can guess the ending.

She shifts her legs a bit, "Well your father and I ignored all the stupidity and just did our own thing. I got pregnant, but it was out of choice. I wanted a baby because I felt a bit empty after my father's death and my frame of thought was that a baby would make me feel whole again."

"You don't regret getting pregnant at such a young age?"

"Oh no. I was ready and I would do it all again if I could. People expect you to fail in these cases, but I proved everybody wrong. I am still happily married to your dad. I raised four healthy, intelligent kids. I am happy." Her trademark smile is back.

I couldn't help but admire her and all the struggles. After everything she has been through, she still holds her head up high. "So that is about it; most of my life story in a short interview. You better make me sound good or I'll ground you!" she jokes around.

OLD FRIEND
by Juan Lopez

Dedicated to my first love and first heartbreak. You made me into what I am today.

You make the hole in my heart
not feel so dark
the pain in my chest
you put it to rest
I can't thank you enough
my life was so rough
until you came
and made it all okay.

I remember the nights
we had our play fights
oh how'd we lay in my bed
your head on my chest
and you'd count every beat
one two and three
and I would just smile
knowing everything
would be good for a while.

I just think about how
I found someone so wow
with a beautiful face

with such natural grace
when our hands intertwine
I know that you're mine
and that's fine
because you're worth all my time.

Now you're out living life
and I'm left behind
I'm glad we had our own day
But there's nothing to say
Oh I'll surely miss you
and even though I'll never kiss you
again,
such a wonderful thing
had to come to an end.

FIRST GLANCE
by Juan Lopez

The warm home glow of Christmas Eve

To the beautiful blooming fields in spring

She creates a delight so unknown to a heart in such need

In temperance though I make a haste to bring

The random complications

Of a fool's emotional intentions

As the thought of red embarrassment lingers

The mere idea vicious like an angry wasp's stinger

But my young heart must have its way

While my idle brain has no say

There I go; each step towards an angelic creature

A simple yet stunning beauty in each feature

What leaves my mouth next might betray

The shattered nerves led astray

Courage be with me now

Let her have a smile not a frown

A loving god must have answered

A selfish prayer for his servants; a true master

For the lovely scarlet wore a smile

It was that smile that took us for miles

Dedicated to S.

HE IS MY BROTHER
by Marylu Lopez

"Big brother what are you doing?" I shouted, "You forgot this piece!"

"Be quiet and let me do my work!" he shouted with a harsh voice, which quickly turned into laughter.

My brother kept cutting pieces of my curly hair, piece by piece. Watching the curly fry pieces of hair fall, was just as amusing as watching a rainbow for the first time. Suddenly the door opened revealing my mother with a bright smile which quickly turned to a shocked frown. My brother and I knew we would be in serious trouble. Are we going to get a big whooping today? I hoped not.

She dashed towards us and took the red scissors from my brother's shaky hand, "What are you doing with this?! I told you not to touch them! AND YOU," she turned and looked at my frightened almost crying face, "look what you did to your beautiful hair! Everything is uneven!" My brother and I looked at each other. We didn't think it was that bad. "Little girl we're going to make you bald! You heard me bald!"

I began to cry. What would the other kids in kindergarten class think of me? They're going to make so much fun of me. "I don't want to be bald, mommy," I wanted to say, but all that came out was high-pitched wails. That was when I first saw my brother step in.

"Mommy, it was me!" he stated, "I forced her to let me cut her hair. She didn't want me to, but I made her," he said with a straight posture revealing a King Author like confidence.

I stared at him as if he was a crazy hero. Why would he do that? Does he not know she is going to get the chankla and spank him with it?! But at the same time, that was when I realized, he always has my back. He is the best person ever. He is my brother.

I dreaded walking home from school. The blue castle isn't the same castle as it was before. The walls seemed to scream louder. The plywood squeaked with every movement. Worst of all, my brother always locked himself in his room. He turned sixteen last month, but he has a face of a bankrupt thirty year-old. Wrinkles covered his face, there is always an unmovable frown, and his eyebrows grow angrier after words are exchanged.

My little brother and sister, at the age of eight and nine, do not understand why their brother was always being so grouchy. They don't understand why their big brother was always nagging at them to do their homework, brush their teeth, and take a shower. They don't understand why he never seems to smile. They don't understand why he's acting like a father when they already have one.

However, that was not the situation. The father we all once loved was in prison from drunk driving and our mother was suffering from loneliness. I was originally not supposed to know this information, but if you care so deeply about family, you want to know the problem and ways to solve it. Therefore, if there isn't a father or mother to take care of kids then you must act like one yourself.

My brother, no matter how stressed he was with his own homework; he would always help his three younger siblings, even me. No matter how obviously tired he was, he would always somehow regain energy to try and play soccer with us. No matter how horrible of a cook he was, he would always make food whenever we were hungry. This thirty year-old teen is the best. He is my brother.

"Press the 'x' button dummy!" I shouted, "Ah! No! Look what you did! You made us lose!"

"Maybe if you told me three minutes ago we wouldn't have lost, donkey," my older brother stated with a sly smile.

"Nah excuses! Give the remote to someone else, you suck!" I laughed.

The single roomed box apartment was filled with a gleaming ball of happiness. Who knew after all of the two years of nonsense he dealt with my mother and father would lead to this?! He now has a loving girlfriend and a two year-old son. The living room is filled with playstation 3 video games and cheerful memories of his own family. The aura is as pink as there can be.

His posture shows security. His smile shows his energy. His broad shoulder shows how serious he can be. He is just like a normal eighteen year-old! It's as if he drank a whole fountain of youth! Now, he lives his own life with his own family. This doesn't mean he completely forgot about his younger beloved siblings and his parents' divorce, oh no. That is simply impossible. He does intervene into our parent's business when he feels comfortable in order to keep his stress level to a minimum. His strength to deal with any situation is admiring. He truly is the best. I am glad to have him as my brother.

A FLIP OF A COIN
by David Lujan

Someone can have many friends, but not that many true friends. These true friends are your best friends, does whom you can trust and not only see them as friends, but part of your family. One does not choose their friends, but one does choose their best friends. If you truly look at your best friends and your old best friends, you will acknowledge that they share the same characteristics. This means when you leave your old best friends and make new best friends you're not really leaving them in a very weird way they are living though your new best friends, because they share the same characteristics as your old best friends.

Life always gives you options, this day I had two options or as I like to call them two different paths. These two paths had different destinations; one path had a destination with my friends while that other path had an unknown destination. As I recall it was a Friday afternoon, I was at my best friend's house, Francisco, and the other guys were over there too: Carlos, Luis, Eduardo, Benjamin, Desmond, and Victor. We were at Francisco's house playing soccer, we had just finish playing, and we were cooling down from Houston's desert heat. Francisco said, "Does anyone want water?"

Everyone responded, "YES, please." He went to get us water and I went with him. I was walking right behind him, but I saw my pack back on his couch I decided to move it to his room. I didn't see that my backpack was open and the letter fell out, when I came back from his room, Francisco had the letter in his hand.. He said, "I think this is for you bro, from Houston Academy…High school?" he handed to me. I took it, and I told him, "It's from some high school that I apply to, no big deal" but what I didn't tell him was that I was applying to different schools, because Furr High School I had no future and I was not planning to go there. He took the letter from my, open it and read it. He looks at me and shows me the letter. I read "David Lujan has been accepted to Houston Academy…" I was surprise that the school accepted me, even though I was not trying to be accepted. My best friend asks me, "What are you planning to do David? Dude, are you willing to leave everything behind, I know you were lying about this not being a big deal. I know you better David you can't fool me! So are you leaving everything behind, friends and people who love you, why are you starting over from the bottom if you already have something?"

I reply, "I don't know dude, maybe I just need a fresh start for me, I just don't know!" I walk out of his house into his front yard. As I was outside, I look at the sky and ask myself, "Why am I leaving my friends behind? I don't need a fresh start." I was so confuse I couldn't think straight that I decided destiny to choose my path. I reach to my pockets and pull out a quarter. If it lands in heads it means that I stay with my friends because I will keep my head up with no shame and not be a traitor to me friends. If it lands in tails, I will choose the unknown path and walk in shame. So I tossed the coin, fate had played her rolled in life; the coin had landed in tails. Destiny had chosen my path; I had to leave my friends behind.

She had brought me to a lake to spend my last few hours with my friends. The great lake's breeze had hit my face and I had reminded my about the countdown to zero. I had less than two hours to say good-bye without saying good-bye to me friends. All my friends and me had played every type of game and I try to make this day count as the last day on earth. Talking to the girls, I most care about, telling them to never let themselves down because of a guy, and that they are more guys in the world. With my best friends, we did what we always do be boys, horseplay and play fight. As my last day with my friends ended and the countdown reached to zero, it was time to walk a lonely path to the unknown.

Walking this unknown path, I met my new best friend. The first day of school, I had met martin he was family friend. In 5th period, Martin and I were talking and he introduces me to his new friend Jose. We started doing work and talking about games. Suddenly this Asian person comes to us, Jonathan, and asks, "Ya'll play call of Duty?" Everyone nods; he starts talking to us and joins the group. Everyone was arguing that they were the best player in playing Call of Duty. While we were discussing in my corner of my eye a see the door opening and Joseph walking in, but in reality I didn't knew him or his name. The teacher assigns him to sit in our group. Joseph was a very sociable person that he rapidly fit in and join our conversation. Now our conversation was not about who was the best player in call of duty instead we were discussing what was the better video game console; Xbox or PS3. As the conversation when on Joseph said, "Let me get someone to back me up." He called his friend, Gabriel, while he was approaching us I thought of him as a mean looking black person. He came to our table talking about how Xbox had a better online play the PS3 in the process he made some jokes. In minutes he had join our little group. Throughout the entire period, we were laughing so hard that my stomach was hurting, by the end of the period we were best friends. I had just not only made friends but I had just met my best friends in high school.

When I had met my new friends, I saw my old friends. It's weird, but I saw my old friends in my new friends because they share the same characteristics. In Gabriel, I saw my friend Victor both share the love of games. In Jose, I saw Francisco both men are genesis and like to socialize. In Martin, I saw Carlos both like to play spots. In Joseph, I saw Desmond both men have character. In Jonathan, I saw Eduardo both are Geeky. So in the end I didn't leave my old friends, they were reincarnated in the personalities of my new friends.

O BONG CUA SU CONG HIEN
(The burns of dedication)

by Joseph Mabasa

I remember one fine crisp afternoon when I was drawing in the living room. I drew a lot as a child; it was my favorite thing to do. My parents always had me turn on the little desk lamp when I drew because good lighting was key to not developing bad eyesight later in life. As the six-year-old version of me transferred the various wacky ideas and inspirations jumbling around in my miniature cranium onto the paper, I noticed the heat coming from the lamp to my hand. What in the name of Charlie Brown is this? I put down my reliable drawing utensil, the pencil. The lamp gave off heat but was more moderately warm than hot. "Hmm, I wonder how hot that lamp is if at all." The six-year-old I thought inside my head. Without further thinking, I quickly touched the lamp…why? Because I can that's why, "For science!"

"Ow!" I let out as a cloud of breath escaped. The lamp was scorching hot and singed the side of my hand. I had just touched the hand of Hades and he wasn't feeling too nice that day. I learned how things tend to be even hotter at the source of heat as I ran to the sink of the kitchen. I hastily turned the cold-water handle until it could turn no further. The cool and calm water spilled upon my hand and relief came over soon enough. Man, that blanking hurt. I let that water run over my hand for at least several more minutes. Afterwards, my hand still felt pain, but to a lesser extent. I put a damp napkin over it and continued my doodling time. People draw, thugs doodle. To this day, I carry a mark on the side of my right hand from my act of ignorance as a child during that event. So my dreams of becoming a hand model burned up as well that day. Well at least I'm a live and now I know.

A few years pass and I am now nine. "I have a paper clip, an adapter for a power socket, a power socket, and a mind full of boredom." Little I thought to myself. This already was a set up for not the brightest of all actions. So here I am, inside the house once again with the limits of doing well thought out things in the day are expired once again. "Well I know metal lets electricity travel through it and the socket needs a wire to one side to the other to work. Hypothetically this should work." Little I said, probably in a simpler way, inside the mind of awesomeness while not consulting the brain of critical thoughts at all. I bent the paper clip into a U shaped wire and carefully stuck it into the adapter. So now it links correctly from one side to the other... now just to plug it into the socket to confirm whether or not if I was right. I plug the adapter in by holding the makeshift wire to secure as my hands yell out, "For science!"

"Ow! That worked but I kind of wish that it didn't!" Everything went black for a solid three seconds. A jolt of very unkind watts ran through my body like a boss. The Wrath of Zeus hath been unleashed unto thy self. I grab a napkin and vigorously take the adapter out the socket. Then it's time to sprint to the sink and crank up the cold water handle. I now rinse my now realized burning thumbs. I let the water run over my thumbs for a prolonged time. They still burn but it's now somewhat bearable so I tie a damp napkin and watch TV to get my mind off of it. My thumbs were left with marks from where my blood was burned and it hurt to do things with them for a week which was pretty bad because I like my thumbs. Well at least I'm alive and now I know.

A while passes over time and I am now 15. I'm with two of my closest friends Jose and David at Jose's house for the science fair project. We have recently discovered how to make water undergo the process of electrolysis to separate it into the extremely flammable element hydrogen. We craved this element for scientific means so much. The idea was to fill the bottle with hydrogen then launch it like a rocket. The empty soda bottle (rocket) that collects the hydrogen over time while in our bucket of strainers and wires connected to a car battery charger was filled to our satisfaction. Not the ideal setup for our purpose but fairly resourceful. Jose takes the bottle and is very careful not to let any hydrogen escape it. He puts the bottle on the angled launching pad which was a stick dug into the ground, once again, not the best setup, but certainly resourceful. Guess whose job it is to ignite the rocket? Yes, it's mine. The ingenuous method of launching the rocket was merely to stick a lighter under the rocket. I walk over to the rocket with lighter in hand and kneel down on the rough grass to ignite it. My hand reaches over to the rocket filled with an extremely flammable element. I say inside of my head, "For science…"

"Boom!" The rocket pops loudly at the end and takes off in flight across the yard. Oh cool, I hurt in no way what so ever. Just as planned. I watch the rocket with my friends unscathed as we exclaim sounds of excitement and jubilance for the finally working rocket. We all run to see how far it goes afterwards. I'm still alive and have successfully constructed a device with launching capabilities and useful purposes together with my two friends.

I now realize that I used to be curious with my, "What would happen?" and, "What if?" ways of thinking and was somewhat impulsive and a bit reckless at times. I've grown with more years of experience and knowledge now. I'm still the same way which I like, but the difference now is that I have more access to more useful, promising, and occasionally dangerous methods. I don't care because I like knowing how things work and I'm a person for science.

UNTITLED
by Lauren Macedo

Many might use the words charismatic and charming to describe her, but I use mom. Her description might also include loving, generous, and proactive, with much more. To me she is the closest thing to a SUPER HERO. Her always present bright smile, her vibrant big eyes, and ease with words have marvelous powers. Sometimes I wonder how is she capable of placing words in the most perfect place. And how can a pair of eyes and a simple smile pierce your soul. But her most major super power; probably her secret weapon, is her intuition. She has the capability of giving the most perfect advice without knowing anything about the issue. She knows how to use all her powers very well. In occasions, without knowing her advice drives people into action for change.

Like a super hero, my mom is always on the run. Thankfully she always has time for me, her child. "I didn't even know I was expecting at first. It took me about seven months to figure it out. Maybe that is why you turned out to be such a weird little child." The smile in her face proofs the existence of my mom's goofy side.

THE SILENT BOND
by Jazmen Massie

Every day I am forced to listen to my mother's voice. If she wasn't yelling she was back to her usual mono toned self. Unlike my mothers, my father's voice was of the ones I rarely heard but I always knew exactly what he was going to say. My dad's approach was always more subtle than my mom's when it came to talking to me. "I'm always here for you princes", is what he said every time we spoke. I could never see it then but it was something about me and my father's relationship that didn't relate to me and my mom's.

My mother being a single parent and raising me on her own without my dad was a struggle, but she never complained. Although I appreciated her efforts I always longed for the stable existence of my father's presence that my mother's long term boyfriend couldn't give me. I did everything to make my mother proud of me. When I was appreciated I felt as if I was on top of the world, but it was also her who made me scared of rejection. She was never shy of telling me no and keeping me away from what I wanted to do as her way of protecting me. I longed for my father to save me. I remember the time I got my first C on a progress report in the 8th grade and my mother was furious. She said "I'm so disappointed in you." I never shied away from trouble as a child but it was never anything major. I was never a disappointment. From then on I got in trouble constantly for pretty much everything. Just because my mother never wanted to me to be like my father she came off stern and strict towards me being her only child. She felt as if she had to protect her baby from the dangers of the world, and because I was the one child she had I was her main focus besides work. It was kind of like she didn't want me to rebel and become a bad egg like my father.

I could never run to my father for help because he was never there. Until this day he has been in and out of jail since the day I was born. It's weird how although my father has two other children and I am the middle child, but to my father I am favored most. It's almost a contradiction how my father was practically never there physically but always said to me "I'm always here for you princess." And I always believed he was. I could tell him anything in complete confidence and he listened and never judged. It took me forever to be that open with my mother. I'm sure if she knew how close I feel toward my father she'd be distraught. It took a lot of bad situations and emotional break downs for me and my mother to have the bond we have know. Although it could have started off earlier than it did I'm glad we have the understanding we do now.

I had been going to visit my daddy in jail with my grandma and other siblings since I was 7, so seeing him in that kind of light grew on me after a while. The first time I went the feeling was too much seeing him like that. I remember fighting back the urge of my tears as they pierced my eyes with heavy water flow. I hated being emotional around him and showing him that I couldn't bear seeing him like that. "Don't cry baby girl I won't be here long." He said and I could only think of all the other hundred times I had heard that but I nodded my head with approval. When we left I hugged him really tight and wished he could walk out with us. As I turned to look at him before he could say the words he always did I said "I'm always here for you daddy." And left before my emotion of tears ran down my face.

Regardless of my father's past I still loved him for being my dad. As much as I wanted to resent him I couldn't because I knew it would only hurt me more. I knew he had to live with his own past and never meant to hurt me or my brother and sister. Although he was always far away from me, my father and I had a close bond that was invisible to everyone but us. He holds a special place in my heart and no matter how far he is I will always know he'll be here for me no matter what the circumstances may be. That's why I love him so dearly. I will always hold a special place for him in my heart.

PEACE BE STILL
by DeNae Maxie

Slam! The door shuts. My eyes pop open. Boom left! Boom right! Boom left! Boom right! She's making her way up the stairs. She makes it to my room. She slings the door open. After analyzing my room she finds it spotless, nothing to complain about. She flicks the light off and slams my bedroom door close. Boom left! Boom right! Boom left! Boom right! She stomps back down the stairs. Three minutes later I hear her yelling at the top of her lungs.

"DeNae! DeNae! Get up and come help me with these groceries!" Three minutes pass and I still haven't got out the bed. "I'm waiting! Don't make me have to come back up there!" She shrieked.

I force myself out of bed. I dully walk downstairs to help with the groceries, just so I don't have to hear her voice anymore. The whole while I'm putting up groceries, she's nagging, yelling, and complaining.

"Who dirtied up all these dishes? Whose week is it to wash dishes? Whose clothes are these hanging up? Put the groceries up right! Make sure you fold the bags and put them in the pantry!"

I hate it when she does that. She comes in making all kinds of noise, killing the quiet in the house. She knows I'm tired and exhausted from the school day. All I want to do is go to sleep. It's not like I'm slumbering for the rest of the day. I simply want a rejuvenating nap. Then I'll do the dishes. Then I'll sweep the floor. Then I'll clean the bathroom. Then I'll scrub your back. Then I'll wash your feet. Then I'll get on all fours and scrub the kitchen floor with a toothbrush. That what she makes me feel like: a slave. I don't feel like her daughter who has feelings too. I don't feel like her daughter who gets tired too. I don't feel like her daughter who gets to spend time with her. There's rarely peace in my house. Something's always going on.

"Happy Birthday to you! Happy birthday to you! You look like a monkey. Annnnnnnnnnnnd you smell like one too." My family sang to my brother. "Make a wish, Taedy! Hurry before the candles go out." My mom excitedly expressed. Whewwwww. He blew. I helped him. I also made a wish too. I don't exactly remember what I wished for. Maybe it was for a doll or a pink Barbie car.

It was his 12th birthday and I can still see the cake as if it were sitting in front of me. It was chocolate with chocolate topping and blue icing with the words "HAPPY BIRTHDAY TAEDY" written across the center. It was my dad, my mom, my brother and I sitting in our 3-bedroom apartment. We were gathered at the kitchen table singing and laughing. My mom put a birthday spread across the kitchen table just to give the house a more birthday feel. We never did anything extravagant for birthdays. We just simply gathered as a family to celebrate. But it didn't matter.

It was still fun. It was still peaceful. There was so much love bouncing off the walls you had to get a piece of it. My dad lived with us then. I was such a daddy's girl. I still am. I can see the days where I would go to sleep on his stomach. That was the best sleep ever. I'd cry when he went off to work. I missed him that much. I wouldn't let anybody call him while he's sleeping. They'd surely get the dial tone. My daddy needed all the sleep he could get. My mom would simultaneously laugh and apologize for my rudeness when the caller would call back.

"You move like a turtle. Just like your father. You inherited all his bad traits." My mom rambles on as I sat the salt in the cabinet.

I'm thinking to myself: Maybe I wouldn't be moving so slowly if I just hadn't been rudely woken up. Let me try waking her up out her sleep. She would moan, groan, and yell some more. Then try to put me on some ridiculous 6-month punishment that she'd forget about in two weeks. I hate when she tries to bash my father like that. She tries to talk about him like he's a bad dad. He's not. He's been there for me at the least. Some people's dads don't even want to be associated or seen with them. Not my Daddy.

"When you're done, take the dishes out the dishwasher and put them up. When you're done let me know, Imma give you something else to do," she says as she kicks her feet up on the comfy couch.

I guess Daddy sheltered me from the things I should not have seen. The things I should not have been around; the other side of her. The side that is not so happy so she yells. Or maybe the fact that daddy was still around is what kept Mama sane. Maybe she misses him too. I'm pretty sure she does. She still tells me "I loved your dad and I still do." Maybe if things were back the way they were I'd get some rest. Maybe if things were back the way they were I'd get some peace and that feeling of love like I used to when Daddy was around.

MY ROCK
by Nia McCardell

As I sit across the table from him, I take notice of everything. My father's deep, dark, masculine complexion, his thick eyebrows, the deep wrinkle that runs through his forehead and the protruding veins that showed on his hands. The way my dad sat in his chair with a confident glare in his eye, even the way I began to fidget with my pencil, caught my attention. We were on his territory now (which he had considered all of his children's' house, but still…). I was fearless, he unnerved, and at the same time I was nervous, he cautious. Throughout all the 16 years we've known each other, this was the first time we both had to prepare for a confrontation, and this was only an interview! As the smoky room from the three or four cigarettes surrounds us, I peered through the fog and dove in with my first question.

Travoyie McCardell, known as Troy to most and "daddy" to six, is a hardworking man who, lives and works in Houston as a truck driver, during which, he has "driven as far as Michigan, Florida, Washington, and many other places." He smiled and said "I have been driving trucks since I could drive cars, and it is a very peaceful job that allows me to get away." He was born in a big 1 story house along with one sister, one brother, and a host of cousins and relatives. Over the years he has become a deep thinker and one that likes to observe, and then take action. He has numerous personality traits, and when asked how did he get his personality, he responded, "My mother and father were the driving forces of my personality. They always reminded me about morals, values, and respect". I knew his answer was credible because those are the types of things he has instilled in me throughout the years of my life.

One of my dad's hobbies is to watch sports on TV. He loves football, and when asked what his favorite team was, he said, "I love football, Dallas Cowboys, Baby!" I asked what other sports was he interested in and he said basketball, stating "I like to watch basketball, just because it is a sport that requires extensive amounts of teamwork, and I love seeing people work as a team." He reps the LA Lakers, something that I wasn't too proud to hear considering the fact that I'm a Boston Celtics fan myself. After we chatted about favorite teams, I decided to go deeper into his own little team: his kids. I wanted to know more about how I became to be. I asked about the whole process of me getting here (by the way, I'm not speaking on the birds and the bees). He said everyone was running around, nervous and on alert about everything, while he was just calm and patiently awaiting my arrival. I asked him what his first words were when he held me, and he said, "I was like 'Oh Snap!' I was a father for the first time." He said that he wasn't scared; he was just "chillin'" Finally, I asked him how he came up with my name, and he said that at the time, he wasn't really concerned with my name; all of his focus was on me.

At the end of the interview, I asked my father if he had anything to add, and he simply said no. He then backtracked and said, "Have fun in high school, and don't be messin' with them boys!" I ran the whole interview through my head a couple times and figured out a couple thngs about my father that hadn't clicked in for me fully in the past. The moral of my father's story is that 1) You can make life whatever you want it to be, 2) You can change bad situations and make them positive, and 3) Treasure what you have because it won't be there always. I sat and listened as he talked about his children, describing them as "something so innocent, something that the world hasn't had a chance to alter." He says "I love how each one of my kids has their own unique personality, they are all different and I treasure them and their attributes." I didn't learn anything more that what I already knew, but I did realize his one true love is his children and that's really all I would need to know; that he loves me and he would do anything for me.

If you look through the contacts in my phone, you will not find a contact labeled "daddy", "dad", or "father". You will find a contact named "MyRock" because that's what he has always been for me; a grounding force through all of my troubling times. His place with me is sealed with a kiss in my heart, where it will remain forever.

UNA MENTE DE LA CULPA Y ROSIE: THE LEGEND OF DIEGO SANTANA
by Nia McCardell

Prologue

Bump, bump, bump…CRASH! "Ouch!" thinks baby Diego as his world, which was once known as his protection, is now abusing him. Screams can be heard, although he doesn't know or fully understand where they are coming from, and the significance of them. All he knows is something is tightening around his neck and squeezing the life out of him. Suddenly, he feels a tug, a pull, and a smack and then he is creating the sound he once heard before.

Soon enough, Diego is outside playing with friends he has known his whole life. Growing up in the streets of Panama City is no joke, and these are the boys who have helped him through the lies, fights, and thefts that took place around the neighborhood, even though he is only 13 years old at this point. Uh oh! There's another window. He is now running from the house with the angry old man that has the special shot gun for the neighborhood kids. As he is running, he looks out the corner of his eye and sees his crush of two years, Rosetta.

"Que paso Rosetta?" Diego yelled as the old man shot at his knees.

"Hola Diego!" She replies as her cheeks turn a beautiful red. He smiles, winks, and watches as she whispers something in her friend's ear. She likes him back and he knows and thinks about this as he continues running from the old man.

Next thing Diego knows, he is 18, in a familiar place, one that he was in once before, the room where he had last seen his mother. Ahh, the emergency room. Yeah, it all came back to him. This is the room where he lost his mother to 18 years ago. This was the room that his dad had left him in and now it will be the room where he will bring his own little piece of life into the world. He hears Rosetta screaming in pain, and all of the actions of the past six years are coming back to him. Everything is happening so fast. Wait! What is that? Diego hears crying, then a tug, then a pull, and a smack, and now sweet little Diego is thrown into the real world.

Chapter 1

"Come on mija," Diego said as he guided little Rosie down the street. They were out for ice cream, just as they would do every Sunday afternoon. This father-daughter time would usually consist of walks to the ice cream parlor, Rosie hopping over curbs, and spilled ice cream all over Diego's shirt. It was worth it though. She was his angel.

As they were walking, Diego noticed the sun was setting and more and more all black cars with tinted windows were passing by. He knew what this meant. As he guided Rosie back to their apartment, he thought about what the night would bring once more. Night was the time when all his regrets were and where his double-life began. He got home, with Rosie in his arms, put her in bed, tucked her in, and silently kissed her on the forehead. Then, he proceeded into his room to change into his business suit, with his attached rifles, and walked across the street to be what he has been for the last three years since Rosie was born: a Drug Lord.

Chapter 2

"Aye Diego, what you want me to do with this tonto?" asked Diego's right hand man?

"Eh, deshacerse de esta basura…" Diego replied as he turned his back on the man that owed him over 1,000 dollars in illicit drugs. "Take him out," he ordered.

"No please," yelled the man, "have mercy!"

"Why should I give you mercy?" yelled Diego.

"I have a little girl at home. Please don't take me away from her!"

As Diego thought and contemplated about the man's plea, Rosie crossed his mind. Then he thought about his life a drug dealer and how he affected other people's life, and then proceeded to tell his goons to let the man go, with a threat saying if the man didn't have his money by next month, he would be severely injured. Diego's main man didn't like the fact that he was being so nice to the man, and this upset him. At that the man left with plenty of thank yous. After that he kicked everyone out of his office, and thought about his life, his lost love Rosetta, and how he would possibly give Rosie the best life her little heart desired.

Diego knew that even though she was above him in heaven, Rosetta was not happy with what he was doing. His long time love was killed by a rival gang during a drug shoot-out. Rosie was only 6 months when it happened. Diego knew what he had to do to provide for Rosie and also make up for the loss of her mother, and the only possible way to do that was to become what had destroyed his perfect life.

Diego also knew that the gang that killed Rosetta, knew where he lived. With this information, it was enough to keep Diego on edge about everything.

Chapter 3

One night after Diego tucked Rosie in, he went across the street to do some filing for his drug paperwork. As he got up to get something to drink, he got an emergency call from his main man saying that the mob that killed his wife was calling him out in the middle of town. At that,

Diego rounded up his boys and strapped up his guns.

On his way to town, Diego noticed that it was silent and no one was in sight. He came across the area where his main man told him the ruckus was going on and found a note attached to a post. it read:

Dear Diego,

We have your sweet little angel Rosie. To get her back, bring 2 million dollars in cash and all of the drugs you own. If you do not comply with these rules then your daughter will die the same way your wife did. Meet us at the old warehouse on the corner of 49th and Ridgewood.12:00 sharp.

103 Mafia and Your Main Man

Chapter 4

At the sight of this Diego screamed into the night sky, took the nearest car to his reach and sped of to the location on the note. Tears and rage filled his eyes and the thought of his little girl made him press the gas even more. As he turned the corner of 49th street, he saw Rosie and three men holding her back, one of them being his so called "main man".

"Give me my daughter back you....you asesinos!" screamed Diego.

"Come get her," Said the leader of the mob, "if you have what I asked for".

Diego then remembered that he didn't have what they asked for because he sped off as soon as he read the letter.

"Give her back to me I said!" Diego's voice was now cracking.

"I'm not gonna say it again mijo! Give me the money and drugs and you will get her back!"

They were yelling back and forth and Rosie was crying harder and harder.

"Papi! Help me!"

Out the corner of Diego's eye, he saw his main man pull out a rifle and point it a Rosie. With a quick grin on his face, he cocked it back, and put it up against her head.

"Diegoyyy....say good bye!"

"No! Don't do this. We've been down for each other since we were 13 man. Don't do it!"

"You're weak, so I'm gonna kill her, then you!"

With that the gun went off, and all was silent.

Chapter 5

Rosie's limp body fell to the ground with a soft thud and all eyes were on the corpse.

"What did you do that for?" said the mafia leader "She was just for the threat!"

Diego watched as his "main man" and the mafia leader argued. He watched and thought about how his only joy was dead, how the mother of that joy was gone, and how he was about to leave his final mark in the world. He pulled out his rifles and shot everything in sight. They tried to shoot back, but by the time they pulled out their guns, they were annihilated. The last man left was his main man.

"Diego, man you know I love you. Don't do this" he begged

"You are weak. You killed my daughter, and now you must die."

With that, he shot him dead. Diego took a look around, and saw what a life of crime and drugs left him, turned the gun on himself, and pulled the trigger. His body fell right next to Rosie's, with closed eyes and a tear-streaked face. All that was left was the yelling of the old man with the shot gun at some kid who had broken his widow again. This is the legend of Diego Santana.

THE LAST ANGEL
by Kaelin McCoppy

The room is kind of dark and there is not much lighting there is only one window and it is really big but the blinds are never really open. When you enter the room, it feels really cold and sometimes it feels as if you're not the only one in the room. The bed is facing you as soon as you walk in and the sheets and headboard is a dark color. In the opposite direction of the bed are some of his old clothes, shoes, and his motorcycle helmet; blue which was his favorite color.

His name was Terrence Smith, he was six foot one and was brown skinned, and he had black wavy hair and big brown eyes that seemed to glimmer every time you would see him. He was born December 13, 1979 his mother Sharon Smith and father Darcy Smith, they couldn't be more proud to give birth to a healthy and beautiful baby boy.

"I will never forget the day that I gave birth to my first born child and when I laid eyes on him" his mother Sharon said with a cold stare. "He was so little when I held him and he was also fragile and I cried when I first held him". "I cried because I loved him so much and I couldn't wait for our journey together to begin", his mother said with a smile and a chuckle.

Little did she know that he wasn't going to be the last child she would have. She gave birth to two more boys Brandon and Darcy Jr. and one girl Ulrica who was the baby and the only girl. "As he started to get older, he always loved to help me take care of his little brothers and his baby sister. "He would always be my little helper" his mother said with a smile.

"When he was a little kid he was always making me laugh and he would always do silly things, I knew he had a good heart."I guess it was a way for him to cope with a broken home and not having a father". "He probably felt like he was going to make our family better even though his father left us", she said with a questionable look in her eyes.

When he started high school at M.B. Smiley his life was starting to look up, his mother and gotten remarried to a man named Anthony. He gave all of her children the sense of a father figure in their life since they didn't have one. Terrence played football, basketball and he ran track for M.B. Smiley high school, the same year he met his best friends Donnie Sanders and Glen Ashley. He couldn't have been happier in his life he finally had the family that he always wanted.

"As he started getting older I could see my little baby boy becoming a man, he was so happy to be in high school", she said with a chuckle. "Secretly, I wanted him to be the first to graduate high school and also to set an example for his younger siblings. I wanted him to give them hope that they can do it and that they can graduate high school. ". "I never wanted my children to give up, I wanted them to try their hardest no matter what".

When he was in his sophomore year, his younger brothers started to head in the wrong direction and he knew that he was the only one who could stop him. He tried his hardest to keep him on the right path in life and told him that his education is very important. He kept up with his siblings grades and helped them with homework daily. Terrence graduated high school with his best friends and family at his graduation, he proved to his younger brothers and sister that they too can graduate high school. All they would have to do is to try hard enough. "I was so proud of him, that he graduated high school", his mother smiled "That was the happiest day of my life to see him graduated, and succeed in life" his mother said.

After he graduated he felt that he should pursue his long life dream of being a truck driver and travel the country, since he was so use to being in Houston all of his life. He was on the search for a truck driving company and he started filing out applications.

Finally, he got a break in his career a local truck driving company called National Freight Line called him and asked for an interview. "I took him to National Freight which was down the street from me house" she stated. "We were both excited and nervous, but I knew he was going to get the job" she grinned. "About a week later they called and they said he got the job" his mother said.

Everything was starting to go fine he finally got the career he wanted and he had two kids a girl and a boy. He was finally having the perfect family he always wanted and nothing could stop him. He was always happy and smiling. "Every Mother's Day he would buy me an angel and I would put them in the living room, I stocked them on a shelve and showcased them" she said with a blank look. "The angels he bought me were so beautiful and I adored each one of them so much" she said.

"The last Mother's Day angel he bought me was the most special to me" she said. "It was huge and it had pink wings with glitter and it lights up and the wings move too" she said with enthusiasm. "That was my favorite angel by far and it sits on the top shelve and I hold it with high honor's" she said. "It was around after his birthday when I had a terrible dream about him" she said with a chilled voice. "I remember in the dream he was in apartments and the apartments were by train tracks, and he was shot and killed" she said with tears in her eyes.

"When I woke up from the dream I was in shock and I was crying, no one would want to have a dream like that about their child that was so real". She said with confusion. "I told him about the dream I had and he was in shock to". " I told him to be careful when he leaves the house". "About a week before Christmas he started to ask more about death and what do they do when they cremate your body" she said. "For Christmas all the family got together and had a Christmas party, he was so happy and telling jokes we were all having a blast" she said. "I will never forget that day" she said while she shook her head.

"December 31, he came home from being on the road and it was night time we were watching T.V. together" she said. "We were also making fun of each other like we always do" she said. "We stayed up for quite a while until I told him I was going to go take a shower "she said. "When I got out of the shower I noticed that he wasn't in the living room and I thought maybe he was in his room, because his shoes were still in the living room". "I went back in my room and went to bed". "I woke up later with the phone ringing and I answered, it was Terrence he was murmuring and it sounded like he was in pain" she said. "Mama I been shot" he said. "Stop playing" I told him. "In that instance I knew that he wasn't and that my dream had come true" she said.

"My husband and I rushed to the hospital, his brothers and sister later arrived" she said. "We had to wait in the waiting room, I was hoping and praying that he was going to be okay" she said. "When the doctor came to us and I looked into his face I knew my baby wasn't alright" she said with tears. "They told me the bullet was in his lung and they couldn't save him because it would be too risky" she said. "Everybody broke down and especially me can you imagine losing something that you gave birth to, a life you brought into this world" she said and paused.

"I went into the room to see him and he was already gone and I noticed his eyes were still opened and I cried and kissed him on his forehead, when I looked at him again I noticed that his eyes closed" she said with anger. "The worst thing was losing him he was my first born and I loved him so much, I just hate he had to leave me so soon" she said with a glimmer of hope. "When I saw him being buried into the ground it was like I lost a piece of me and he took it with him "she said. "He was my angel that I lost."

A MOMENT FOR LIFE
by Remington McKnight

During my family vacation to Orlando Florida my cousins, sister and I got the opportunity to spent the day at Disney World. My favorite part was going on the Buzz Light-year space ship roller-coaster. My whole life I wanted to go to Disney World just to ride this roller-coaster that I had saw on TV, so at that that exact moment I was extremely filled with enthusiasm.

After already spending a day in Florida not doing anything my cousins and I were very excited that we were going to Disney World. As soon as we heard pots and pans rattling in the kitchen we all woke up and jumped out of bed. After we gobbled our breakfast down like it was our first meal in a years we stormed into the room and quickly got dressed. Then we were off to have a day filled with fun. As soon as we got into the parking lot and saw all the rides and rollercoaster we were amused with excitement. After we stood in line to get inside, we all ran for the first ride we saw which was the Shrek rollercoaster. The Shrek ride was amazing it was made like we were in a swamp. When my cousins and I got off of the Shrek roller-coaster ride, the Buzz Light-year roller-coaster quickly caught my eyes. I pointed the ride out to my family and we took off towards it. I was so excited to be able to get the ride, I did not even mind waiting in the long line that stood before me. While standing in the extremely long line to get on the roller-coaster my family and I talked and joked to consume time. We even decided that we wanted to get on the Sponge Bob roller-coaster right after, since it was right next to where we were. As I got closer and closer to the front of the line I felt as if I was about to jump out of my skin. I was even more motivated to ride the exciting roller-coaster once I saw how extremely fast it went and how it sped off into the spooky dark tunnel. By that time I was excitingly jumping up and down like a three year old watching cartoon network. Once my family saw how dark the tunnel was and how tremendously fast the ride went, they were kind of spooked out. I teased them because it was way too late to turn around at this point. We finally made it to the front of the line and I was so happy I did not know what to do with myself. I thought to myself "this is the ride I have waited so long to get on, and now it is really happening." As I watched the people before us get off the roller-coaster my heart started to beat twenty times faster than it was before. Instead on walking to get into the ride, I got in so fast it almost looked as if I jumped inside. It seen like forever before the ride started because the workers had to make sure that everybody was secured in their seatbelts. When the roller-coaster started to move I burst out into a loud exciting laughter. Inside the tunnel, it was so dark I could not even see the person sitting beside me. Everyone screamed very loud as the ride took us father away from the light. The ride jerked us spun us around in circles and even made us go down really fast backwards. The part of the ride I will never forget is when the roller-coaster dropped down so fast that I really thought that I was going to fall off. My sister immediately grabbed my hand so tight I began to feel my heart betting inside of it. The ride felt as if we had been falling down for about ten minutes, and as soon as we stop falling the ride jerked us back extremely hard and came to a complete stop. As I got off I felt like my heart had now fallen into my stomach. My aunts and uncles we so mad that they got on that ride t (they said they were too old for all of that), but despite the adults everyone else had an awesome time.

To this very day I still think that the Buzz Light-year roller-coaster is the best ride ever and I will always remember how much fun I had riding that ride. If I could I would go to Disney World every day until my hair gets grey just to get on that ride. If I ever get the chance to go back, I am sure that the Buzz Light-Year roller coast would be the first ride I get on.

LOCKED UP
by David Mondragon

I was locked inside an outhouse, terrified and shocked, just a few feet from the house and yet no one came to help. I remember thinking, "why, why is this happening to me?" No matter how much I cried for help, there was none. No matter how much I begged for mercy, I received none. In those moments, I began to subconsciously image how this whole mess began.

This all took place in Mexico, and I was at my grandma's house. They were having a party, so tons of people where there. Everything seemed normal. Anyways, I needed to go bad. Yes, I needed to pee. I went to the hallway and turned to my left to try to open the door. When I shook the handle I heard a voice, "El bano esta acupado" said the lady in Spanish. The rest room is occupied. Dancing around from the unbearable liquids inside of me, I ran straight the hall way made a left into a room then out the back door. There I met my cousins... one which I didn't like.

We were both 10, and also around the same height. To be honest, it's not that I didn't like him; it's more like we were rivals. I mean since we were little, we use to fight and challenge each other to silly things. Sometimes it got out of hand and we ended up in some serious trouble. Anyways he was there along with some strangers, who I presumed where family. We talked a bit but not much, I was in a hurry. The backyard or the back of the house was like a patio, and in the corner was the outhouse. I ran towards it but stopped at the door. It's like I knew something was going to happen. In that instance, I stared at the door and the whole world faded away. I looked at the handle and saw a locking device. This meant that the door could be locked both on the inside and out. "A lock on the outside-" I wondered, "what purpose does that serve?" However, nature was calling and I did not have time to ponder on such thoughts.

Once I was done, I unlocked the door from the inside, put my hand on the handle, and pushed out. I tried and tried; yet the door would not budge! At first, I did not want to believe that I was stuck in a dirty, stinky, space tight outhouse so I kept trying to open the door. After a while, I began to feel trapped like a caged animal. I screamed, " Ayuda, Estoy adentro del bano! Alguin abren la puerta!" "SOMEONE PLEASE OPEN THE DOOR" where the only words that could escape my mouth.

I put my ear close to the door and heard nothing. The sudden loud burst and random laughs disappeared leaving nothing but silence, I was alone or so I thought. I began to look around and saw the thing that terrified me most. There were two huge spiders in the top corners of the outhouse. As soon as our eyes made contact, I lost it. I was scared, frightened, and hyperventilating. I pushed the door again trying to open it while still keeping an eye on the two beasts above me. They were big for spiders, I've never seen one like that, and its legs were huge too. The spider's movement, however small, never escaped my eyes. The thought of it coming down and even touching me threw me into frenzy. I started banging the doors, yelling at the top of my lungs, red faced, tears running down my face, and slime out of my nose. I stopped, tried to regain my composure but every time I stared into the top left corner, I went savage. At the point where I felt all hope was lost, a light shined in the door, and a figure stood before me. It was my aunt.

I felt relieved and most importantly saved from those two monsters. She welcomed me into her arms as a mother does to a child and I hugged her as my savior. She helped me inside the house and told me to calm down. I sat in the bed, in the room right next to the back door, with a perfect view of the outhouse. When my heart stopped beating fast, tears stop falling, I began to think who could have done such a thing? Although the torment was over, my mind kept thinking "who? Who would do something like this?" Even though somewhere in my mind I knew who did it; it was Luis.

INTERVIEWING ENRIQUETA NAJERA
by Lorenza Najera

The gravel driveway, tall old trees, vivid green grass, and black gate surround the small brown house. On the porch there are dark green, iron chairs with a black cushion stationed on their laps. Pots with pink flowers are stationed on the small steps of the front porch. The white iron gate overlaps the brown wooden door that opens into the living room. In the room there are two brown leather sofas, a flat screen TV, a glass lamp, and two tall shelves that are adorned with picture frames and small glass figures. The aroma of my mother's cooking comes flowing into the room, and I inhale the delicious smell that's so familiar.

My mother's short, shoulder length, brown wavy hair compliments her large, round, light brown hazel eyes. The lines drawn deep into her forehead shows that she worries and cares. Her light complected face turns bright red with her laughter. Her name: Enriqueta Najera. She might seem very shy when you first meet her, but eventually you will see her other side. Her other side is very loud. If she knows you very well, she will let you know what's really on her mind. If she doesn't know you very well, she might just stay quiet and be nice. My mother can be described as a very calm person who likes to play around with people.

She was born on February 1, 1955 to Fidencio Gallegos Alcalar and Lorenza Gonzales Hernandez in the Santa Maria ranch located in Coahuila, Mexico. She has a large family of eleven: eight sisters and three brothers. When asked about her relationship with her parents she answered: "Mmm. Well...good. I get along well with them, I talk with them. When I need something or when they need something they call me to tell me if I can help them with whatever thing they need." Her childhood was fun and even though she didn't have everything she wanted what mattered was that she had her parents. She was happy with that, even if they lived in a small room and didn't have much. Another topic that she talked about was her education and her large family. Since there were eleven children her parents couldn't afford to buy them many small things such as toys. When I asked when was the first time she fell in love, she giggled and laugh, her face turning bright red under the lamp's orange gleam. After she stated, still giggling, that it was at the age of thirteen when she had fell in love, I asked her who. She said in a soft, low voice: "Do I have to say the name?" We both laughed and I nodded my head to answer yes. She lowered her voice and answered, "Well Carlos Manuel Samaniego. He was the first boy I met, the one I fell in love with the first time." Unfortunately she had to end the relationship, which had lasted for a couple of years, because of her move to the United States. Once she got to the U.S. she started working to maintain herself. At the age of nineteen she was a servant who babysat and cooked for an Italian family in Texas. After that job, she then spent ten years working for a company that made diapers and twenty-three years at an auto auction company as a detailer.

One thing that I believe is important to bring to attention is the fact that she did not have the opportunity to finish her education. She was able to stay in school until the eighth grade, and then her parents could no longer afford to pay for her to go to school. As a large, low income family, all the members had chores. Since there were lots of children, each and every one of them had a duty. One would wash the clothes, another would clean the dishes, and another one would cook the food, and so on. In Mexico, most parents if not all, would discipline their children by giving them a whooping or grounding them. Discipline was practiced in my mother's family. If one of her siblings didn't do what they were told to or did something bad they would get punished. I believe that the discipline her parents had on them made them all hard workers like she is.

Unfortunately, one of her sisters, my aunt Lorenza Gallegos Najera, passed away in 1994. In that same year, after her younger sister Lorenza passed away, she found out she was expecting a baby. The baby would be her fifth child seeing she already had three boys and one girl. The pregnancy came as a surprise to her. At first she thought there was something wrong with her and maybe she had some kind of disease or sickness, but when she went to the doctor to get checked she found that that was not the case. She was a 40-year-old with four children, and three months pregnant. When she got the news, she made a promise. She promised that if the baby was a girl she would name her after her deceased sister, Lorenza. A couple of months later the baby was born. It was a baby girl, and her name would be Lorenza, just like her mother had promised. When I asked what she felt when she first saw me she replied: "Well...When I first saw you I was filled with joy because you were going to be my second daughter because I only had one and three boys. But..." At that moment, my mother's gaze drops to the floor and her eyes begin to form tears. I as well felt her strong emotions and my eyes began to water too. A moment of silence passes by and I'm watching her. I'm watching the emotions on her face as she slowly starts to weep. She slowly tries to steady her emotions so she can answer my question. I can see that this has to be something very strong because she wouldn't be crying for any reason. With a small lump in my throat, I patiently waited for my mother to find her voice again. She then answers, "Although you didn't come into this world with the hope that we would be together, your father and I, but anyways it gave me joy that you had come into our home."

My mother, Enriqueta Najera is a caring and understanding person. She is a very hard worker and can truly be a sweet and wonderful woman. She has the patience to deal with all of her grown children and all other problems and situations in her life. Her caring and generous heart makes her one of the most important people in others' lives, especially her children's and her family's. She is sensitive and kind and has gone through a lot. She is truly a person that I see as a role model and whom I look up to. I'm glad to have her in my life. I don't know what I would be without her.

CÓ ANH – THE PERSONALITY OF A MAJESTIC ANTELOPE
by Jonathan Nguyen

The hordes of ragged clothes and half eaten noodle cups filled to a height just as a towering skyscraper. The atmosphere of the living room seemed to create a disgusting cloud of vial smells that seemed to cringe the nostrils. And there lie the wastelands of clothes that seemed to entrench the living room floors. The couches seemed to tower the never ending clothing. However, none of this stopped the all mighty aunt Anh from taking the time from her busy schedule to provide me with an interview.

She is young in age, about 27 years old to be exact; she is a very radiant woman at first glance. Her cheeks glimmered through the room with skin as smooth as new born baby's butt cheeks. Her dark brown hair glistened through the dimly lit room, it was voluminous just as it was entangling. And through her eyes, I saw the confidence of a lion, the image of a lion protecting her cubs from hundreds of ferocious predators. This only made it even more anticipating to finally interview her. It was nerve wrecking at first, but as I asked more and more questions, the awkward bridge seemed to break down. It felt as if the room was heavy as a polar bear... enough to break the ice.

English was the primary language of her household. She was born into an American society that seemed to shape her entire life, however, her parents saw this consistently tried to entrench her into their roots. It was a hard goal, and frustrating in fact, her parents struggled so hard for their daughter not to become Americanized. However, it was a goal that was non-existent. Her parents, being native born Vietnamese civilians, always told her lessons taught in Vietnam. Lessons of struggle, anguish, and overall good; they were stories like "The Rebellious Boy" and "The Wicked Robbers". Anh said that they tried to shape her into the way of a "traditional Vietnamese girl". But living in America, she did just the opposite. She became strong and independent.

When my aunt started the first years of school, she realized she had no friends and couldn't really socialize with anyone up until high school. She was a social outcast with no social antiquities. Her elementary through middle school years seemed to be like a hellish abyss of endless torture. Each day would be another long wait to the next; with no friends she sat alone at lunch every day. It was a depressing time for her in fact, but as she progressed through school, high school that is, she began to socialize more often and even get boyfriends. She was popular in her opinion. I asked her what popular meant to her and she said, being able to be happy and enjoy every day of your life because of the friends you have, not the ones everyone wants. One of which, turning out to become the first love of her life.

My Aunt was a realist; she believed that all decisions were made because chosen to be that certain way. In which I agree is very true actually, seeing as how when people have their regrets, it was their fault at the time for creating those regrets. She quotes, and a good quote I might add, "It's because at one point you wanted that moment to be the way it was, because you were the one who chose that decision." She believed that one shouldn't take things for granted. All throughout her life, she has lived with 3 siblings that she loved and cared for no matter what the scenario. But no one person would get one something, it'd have to be shared with everyone. Clothes, food, toys, all of them had to be shared. She believed that all the things you may have now, may not be the case in the future, so take everything that is given to you and cherish it. "Cherish it like the fat boy cherishes cake" she would say.

Up until this point, my aunt has lived her life to the fullest despite the bumps she had to drive through along the way. Cracking jokes whenever the time is right, she makes the ideal candidate for the journey of life. She is married to a man named Jason Lai, and she enjoys his "company as well as his money". She really takes the meaning of life to the heart, and pierces through it like a arrow through the skin of life. She works as a successful physician's assistant, with the long-term goal to become a surgeon. She understands the twists and turns of life and doesn't back. She is a true inspiration. She is, my aunt or in Vietnamese, Có Anh, and she, has faced the testaments of life.

I REMEMBER
by Cydney O'Neal

I remember that day like it was last week. It started off normal, besides the fact that my mom was out of town, but other than that, I woke up to a normal day, or so I thought. My dad woke up my brothers and I urging us to get dressed and ready, my grandfather was supposed to come home from the hospital, so we were headed to be with him and my grandmother at their home. We pulled up to the familiar brown house and saw quite a few cars parked out front. "He's gone, remember when Mr. Morris died, it was like this," my older brother Dalen said as we got out and started our way up the drive.

I walked ahead into the house, pretending I hadn't heard his statement, and found myself face to face with a crowd of aunts, uncles and other relatives. My grandmother approached me as I walked down the hall to the room trying to find my grandfather, but I didn't see him. Something was wrong.

"Where is he, Where is papa?" I asked, my smile slowly fading away when I saw my grandmother's puffy red eyes. She slowly shook her head as more silent tears began to stroke her cheeks, not even able to say the words. I couldn't understand; so many thoughts, questions, and comments invaded my mind with confusion. I started to feel light headed so I backed to the long white wall for support and I slowly slid to the ground when the tears started to flow. Everyone leapt at me thinking I was going to fall faint into the world of unconsciousness, but it was much worse, it was a world of grief, confusion, mourning, loss, and disappointment.

I remember I cried by myself upstairs in the middle of the floor. I remember my brother Blake locked himself in my grandfather's closet and sobbed on the floor under his clothes. I remember my brother Dalen, sat at the dining room table dazed with red puffy eyes while my grandmother sat rubbing his back to comfort him, and silent tears flowed down his face. I remember my brother Austin sat with my dad, not crying, but he questioned everything that came to be of that day my grandfather left us. I remember my four year-old brother wondrously walked the house, as he watched his older siblings with question and confusion as he tried to figure out what was going on, and when my grandfather was coming home. June 7, 2008, I remember that day, that was the day I lost someone close to me for the very first time.

Now-a-days it's easier to talk about him without tearing up. "You know papa would flip if he saw this kitchen," I tell my grandmother looking through her half empty pantry. My grandfather never let that pantry or fridge go anywhere near empty, especially if he knew his grandkids were coming. "I know Cydney, We'll go grocery shopping, and get some more stuff," my grandmother replies. But there is only one thing missing from her statement, my papa, and without him in the kitchen unpacking or bringing in the groceries, things will never be the way they used to.

I can't fill the emptiness of his positivity not being there. There could be a hundred plus people in the house, but I can still feel the empty space that my grandfather use to fill. I will always feel that feeling of something missing, something empty, and something lost. I can feel the hurt, the grief, the mourning, the loss of emotion everyone had from that day three years ago.

"What you doing watchin' my TV lil Negro girl?" my grandfather asked humorously sparking up playful trouble. "Hahahahaha, why do you call me that, I have a name," I reply. "That's what you are, a little Negro girl," he says laughing so hard his belly starts to bounce.

"I'm telling," I say teasingly. "Grandmother, papa's picking on me," I yell down the hall for my grandmother to hear, and with that comes my three year old brother trotting down the hallway to my grandfather, walking away with him to the kitchen. The same kitchen I saw my grandfather cry in for the first time explaining to me that he will always be able to watch over me, and protect me, even though he was barely able to manage himself with the cancer that had taken over his weakened body.

My grandfather had his favorite chair in the corner of the living room, directly in front of the TV. A green comfy recliner that I always found him sitting in; whenever he was needed. It's weird to go over and plop down in that chair these days, even though it's in a different location, and he isn't here anymore. I feel like I'm taking his spot, like I'm just forgetting it was ever his chair, even though that isn't the case, that I'm actually sitting in that exact chair for the memories and comfort it brought me when he was here. It's like he's holding me as a little girl all over again.

I remember waking up to my grandfather's prayer's echoing off the bathroom halls through the closed door to the bedroom. I remember squeezing in between him and my grandmother in their big comfy bed listening to his loud yet comforting snoring that use to be my nighttime lullaby. I remember going in the kitchen and being hit by the strong smell of my grandfather standing over the sink peeling and cleaning chit lens. I remember going into his closet and standing on my tip toes to reach the top shelf holding the sacred juicy fruit gum and lifesaver candy.

I remember going with him to the car wash, and talking about everything my little head consisted of. I remember that exciting gut feeling as a little girl when he gave me a couple bucks to spend at the store. I remember his prickly cheeks, pale skin, limp body, and skinny yet fragile state as I kissed and hugged him goodbye for the last time. I remember losing it all in one day.

THANK YOU, DAD
by Vanessa Ordonez

I remember that day like it was last week. It started off normal, besides the fact that my mom was out of town, but other than that, I woke up to a normal day, or so I thought. My dad woke up my brothers and I urging us to get dressed and ready, my grandfather was supposed to come home from the hospital, so we were headed to be with him and my grandmother at their home. We pulled up to the familiar brown house and saw quite a few cars parked out front. "He's gone, remember when Mr. Morris died, it was like this," my older brother Dalen said as we got out and started our way up the drive. I just got out of the shower; Mom is getting me ready for bed. Dad still isn't home. "It's getting late, Baby," mom said, "let's go to bed." She turns off the lights and lays next to me and holds me as we both drift off to sleep.

Bang! Bang! Bang! Dad is knocking on the door. I can't tell time yet, but the red numbers on the clock say "2:47" and its dark outside. Dad is yelling "Open the door! Who are you trying to hide? Let me see him!" I'm confused; it was only me and Mom in the house. Dad is going crazy. Mom opens the door not knowing what to expect.

Then suddenly my Dad charges at her as if he was a bull, knocks her down, and starts beating her like a punching bag. Mom is crying and screaming. Tears are falling from her now lifeless eyes. Blood is secreting from the lips that would comfort me those nights when Dad wouldn't come home.

Mom breaks free from the bull, grabs me and runs to the car. Dad is chasing us. Fortunately he didn't make it on time, so he decided to throw a lime green plastic chair at the car instead of trying to continue in his rampage of abusing my Mom.

Now we're driving with nowhere to go. Home isn't safe, we don't have any money, and it's late. We parked at the local park near my Grandma's house. Mom rolled down the windows and came to the back seat with me. I could feel the cold air brush against my face. My Dad is the wind. He too is cold, cruel, and unmerciful.

I don't understand why he hit my Mom. Who was he looking for? Why did he get home so late? Why were his eyes so red? So many things I don't understand. So many things I wish I didn't see. I can't decide whether it was my fault or my Mom's fault that my Dad was acting this way. But for right now me and Mom are drifting back to sleep in the back seat of this small car while this cold air continues to mock us.

I'm four years old. I fell asleep last night in my warm bed, in my house, in my Mom's warm comforting arms. Now I lay in the back seat of my Mom's cold car. My innocence is gone. I no longer have a Dad; my Mom is no longer the loving, compassionate person she once was. Her eyes are scars, marking the beginning of troublesome life not only for my Mom, but for me as well.

Reflecting back on this as a 16 year old, I learned to let go of the anger I once had for you, Dad. I realized that because of you I wanted to do better in school and actually make something of myself. The idea of turning into you scared me and made me want more for myself, so I thank you for that. You taught me to never depend on a man for anything. Most importantly, you taught me to forgive, which is something most people cannot do.

Dear, Dad. I forgive you. I forgive you for never being there. I forgive you for: never wanting to be with your family, for choosing drugs over your daughter, for all the stealing and all the lies you told, for all the crimes you've committed, and for all the pain you caused. I finally understand that it wasn't my fault that you weren't a father to me. It wasn't my fault that you threw your life away, but thank you for influencing my decisions for the better.

A DAY AT THE CON
by Nicole Owen

I remember walking through the J.W. Marriott hotel, with its pastel yellow walls and fancy-looking mahogany railing. The halls were filled with con-goers, and I had to push past more than my share of Narutos, the occasional Bleach character, an Ash Ketchum (who threw a Pokéball and tried to "catch" me; I was not amused), and a man in bright yellow spandex with tiger stripes (terrifying experience) on my way to our Artist Alley table. Soon enough, I had reached my destination: a folding table with a navy blue tablecloth draped over it (presumably to hide any deficiencies it may have had). On it was a towering heap of Yaffa blocks, which are little cubes made of metal that looked more like tiny birdcages than anything else, stacked one on top of the other. Each was sporting a dozen or so prints I had drawn. It was certainly odd to have my art, which had until this point usually only decorated the inside of my sketchbooks, smiling back at me from the boxes in their fully-colored glory. It felt unreal, like it wasn't mine at all, but that I was in fact staring at someone else's prints.

As soon as I came into view, a blonde head popped out from behind the various pictures and art supplies scattered across the booth. She pushed her glasses up and carefully adjusted the pink wig and tie of her Amu cosplay (anime character costume) as she stood to greet me. It hit me just how short she was, standing at just about five feet, a bit short for a ninth grader.

"Nicky! Biscuit!" she squealed, using my mom's (much-despised) nickname for me, despite her being a full month younger than me. "Come on! I need help organizing these prints!"

She gestured to a massive pile of papers, all of which were copies of the prints we had on display. I agreed to help, though my organizational skills were arguably just as bad as hers, if not worse. After we had completed this task, we sat down and started fiddling with the numerous PrismaColor markers Haley had brought with her. We (and by this, I mean "I") began making the commissions sign. I had just finished the "Add another person for an additional 50% of the commission price!" when I realized that it was oddly quiet.

The others in the Artist Alley explained to us that, as it was a Friday afternoon, business was going to be pretty slow. Saturday was the big day for everyone down here. The people here today had come for the events, mostly, like the Kazda concert (turns out the drummer and guitarist were pretty cute~) and the cosplay contest. Anyone who was in a buying mood had made a beeline for the dealer's room. The hall we were in was pretty much empty. In this time of extreme boredom and awkward silence, I thought back to how it all started.

From what I remember, it began on a sunny day at Pin Oak Middle School. I was a little sixth grader at lunch with my new best friends, Haley and Amber. I sat in silence, trying to eat a sandwich (which I preferred to call a "sammich", being eleven) and doodle on a scrap piece of paper at the same time.

"What do you mean you don't know what anime is?" Haley asked, a look of intense disbelief plastered across her (then eleven-year-old) face. "You're drawing it right now!"

She jabbed her finger at the piece of paper I had been sketching on. I glanced down at it.

"Oh. So that's what this is..." I mumbled back, pretty embarrassed. I didn't want to admit that I had learned to draw from some old book and had never actually watched an episode of anime before. Amber, who was sitting across from me, let out an exasperated sigh.

Her eyes narrowed to slits as she examined my expression, which was blank as usual. Finding no hint of humor or sign I was about to laugh to indicate to her that I was joking, she sighed, rolled her eyes somewhat dramatically, and wrote something down on a piece of paper before she passed it to me.

I flipped it over and read it. On it, in Haley's messy handwriting, were the words, "Naruto www.anilinkz.com".

"What's this?" I asked, honestly curious.

"It's an anime called Naruto," she replied patiently, sounding like an adult trying to explain something to a child. "It's about ninjas. You should watch it."

"But I-"

"DO IT."

I looked over my shoulder awkwardly, just in time to see Principal McDonough's shiny bald head used as a mirror by some twelve-year-old girls searching for something to fix their hair in. Amber and Haley were still staring at me (and possibly judging me). It seemed like I was the only one in our group who didn't know what anime was, actually.

That day, I was anxious to get home and see what this "Naruto" was. I dropped my backpack on the carpet with a loud thud, where it rested against the pale orange wall just underneath the painting of New York my mom had gotten a few years back, then made my way to our desktop computer, which was perched on one of the counters we never used in the kitchen. I pressed the power button, and the machine booted up with a whir, followed by a low hum as Windows loaded. Eventually, I was able to get online and begin watching the first episode.

It took a while to buffer, but as soon as it did and I was able to start watching, it was pure magic. I swear, that's what it was to my little eleven-year-old mind. Magic, like how Pringles taste. Magic, like unicorns, rainbows, and unicorns throwing up rainbows. I am not exaggerating. In that moment, I decided that this was what I wanted to do with my life. No, not be a ninja, though that was (and quite possibly still is) a close second. I wanted to draw manga and anime. I was a sixth grader with a plan, and god help whatever tried stopping me.

I snapped back to the present, startled, as Haley jabbed my arm with her finger. Dazed, I looked around again at the pastel walls and numerous tables in the hallway. Oh. I was back in the present, with the anime convention, not at home waiting for the next episode of Naruto to be released.

"Hey, I'm going to go stretch my legs. I'll be back soon, okay?"

I nodded, still kind of out of it. She yawned and stood up, stretching her arms and back, then wandered off down the hall.

I put my head down with a sigh, still pretty bored. I couldn't wait for Saturday, because then I'd at least have something to do. I was about to start napping when I heard a soft fluttering sound. I looked up in time to see one of the cheap dollar-store magnets (it's sad how cheap we are) fall off, followed by a particularly colorful picture. I decided I'd better pick it up before it got lost somewhere.

I got up and went to the front of the table, then crouched down and rooted around under the tablecloth to retrieve the picture. I snatched it up, then grabbed the magnet and put them both back up on the blocks. I took a moment to gaze back at the wall of prints and remember all the work we'd put into them. Naturally, the first memory that popped into my head was from last week, when Haley and I had been working on the prints that now adorned the front of our booth.

The memory in question began took place on a Saturday night. It was the weekend before the convention, and Haley was flipping out. Thus far, the only thing we'd really done was come up with ideas for pictures, and she was getting stressed out. I had the opposite reaction; I was (apparently) way too okay with our progress. At Haley's request, I agreed to begin working on several Shugo Chara prints (Amulet Heart, to be precise) while she started sketching out the rough drafts (she insisted on having me do all the final drafts, as she has convinced herself that her art isn't as good as mine, which I have to disagree with, to be honest) for me to complete later. Soon enough, I had created what Haley considered to be an acceptable Amulet Heart picture, which she took and began coloring. I stopped working for a moment to look around her room for inspiration, as her walls are quite literally covered in anime posters and wall scrolls, with the occasional cosplay wig thrown in for good measure. To the far right, I saw a wall scroll of Mia and Kite from .Hack// (a sci-fi anime about a computer game gone wrong), then a glossy poster of Lelouch and Suzaku from Code Geass (ah, memories! I remember the rebellion of the Elevens!), and even a promotional poster for Kingdom Hearts 358/2, which partially covered a scroll from Kuroshitsuji (featuring Ciel and Sebastian, both of which are made of some odd mix of awesome and insane... well, Sebby is, anyway, as Ciel seems to be mostly just insane). Looking at all these posters by successful anime artists, I felt a surge of energy and encouragement. Heck yeah, I got this. I could totally do this. This was the first step on my way to achieving our dreams, mine and Haley's, and failure was not an option. I got back to working on my Pandora Hearts picture.

The next day, we woke up at the crack of dawn (well, I did. Haley got up even earlier). I'd completed several more pictures before passing out the night before, so I started coloring the backgrounds. Haley had no suggestions as to what they should be, so I just decided to pick the most amazing thing I could come up with... Straight up RAINBOWS. Aww yeah.

Haley thought it was glorious, so we did that for the entire Shugo Chara set. We continued this drawing and coloring cycle for a good four hours before my mom came to pick me up, by which time I had started on my sketches for all of the prints. It was a very productive weekend.

I'm pretty sure that by the time I finally stopped reminiscing, I had been standing in place for about ten minutes and had sufficiently freaked out the other artists in the hall with us.

"Hey. Nicky. Nickyyyyyy." I heard Haley's squeaky, girly voice.

"Yeah?" I replied, trying to play it off as a careful examination of picture placement.

"What are you doing? You're just standing there, staring. It's kind of creepy." Yup, creepy. That's me!

I think I turned a bit pink. "Oh. Umm... sorry. Just fixing a picture that fell."

She nodded skeptically, then went back to her chair. I did the same. I was about to lay down and sleep again when Haley elbowed me (abuse!). "Nicky!"

"What?" I grumbled, glaring up at her from the table (I was much too lazy to sit up and glare properly).

"People!" she replied excitedly. Yeah, that's the kind of day it had been.

One of them, a Zabuza cosplayer, wandered up to our booth and began looking over our display, which made me more than a little nervous. Haley greeted him in a sing-songy voice, "He-llo~," and then I started tuning them out, pretending to straighten some papers and organize some supplies (I was really just moving stuff around for lack of something better to do). I heard Haley unzipping a bag and getting some money out. She tapped my shoulder.

"Hey, Nicky, go get the Pandora Hearts print. You know, the one with Break on it."

I looked confused and glanced up. The Zabuza waved at me in what I assume he thought was a cool way (he pulled it off better than most "cool waves" I've seen in my day, and I've seen a few), then looked down and started examining the sword he had with him, looking for dents or signs of damage.

I quickly retrieved the requested picture (which happened to be my favorite, the one I was most proud of at the time), which I handed to the Zabuza. He asked us to sign and date it for him, so we did (Haley later told me that in that moment she'd felt like a celebrity, which I found funny because I'd felt the same way for a second). He stood there awkwardly for a second as Haley got him his change, then he smiled at us again and walked off to participate in cosplay chess (that's what he told us when he was waiting for the print, anyway). I was frozen for a second after that, until Haley broke the silence.

"Hey, Biscuit, we did it~!" she said, grinning at me.

"That we did," I replied, feeling sort of proud.

Then we reached into the cooler so we could celebrate the sale of our first print with a bottle of strawberry Ramune. Cheers.

PERCEPTION: IN A NEW LIGHT
by Gabriel Pena

On a humid summer afternoon, I gazed into the eyes of serenity. The cool bendy grass under my blue striped towel made a soft crumbly sound as I brushed away the damp sweat off my forehead. The wispy yet gentle breeze swept across my baggy cotton t-shirt on my back. Birds flew across the cloudless deep blue sky. Sounds of the many violins, percussions, and wind instruments fluttered into the ears and mind of the listener, me. My breathing pattern even synchronized with the serene music. One glassy surfaced, red balloon slowly drifted into the seemingly infinite sky. Sounds of the passing cars were faint, yet the glowing laughs of distant children were eminent. The smell of the fresh green grass tickled the hair follicles in my nose. Every breath rushed gallons of humid air into my lungs. A hot breeze grazed against my skin. Bizarrely, it felt chilling. All the senses in my body seemed to have been united as one, creating an entrenching visualization of my environment. I actually felt as if I tuned into my surroundings. What opened my mind the most was the large green hill, which seemed to graze the very edges of reality and fiction. This moment is where my mind roams, my soul is free, and anything can be plausible.

Time seemed to be motionless. Like a prehistoric bug in sap, or an icicle hanging off the roof of a house. Yet I seemed as free as a seed falling from a tree or a skydiver hovering over the ground below. When these contradictory terms are working as one, you can experience every moment at its fullest potential. Taking in every sound, sight, taste, smell, and touch to another level. The environment around me suddenly seemed extraordinary. The wind lazily stroked each blade of grass, birds chirped in a sonorous tone, cars drove leisurely, and clouds drifted slowly.

In a desperate attempt for achieving something spontaneous, in order to take advantage of my new found ability, I stood up tall in the blink of an eye. I stood as tall as a sky scraper and felt as solid as a mountain. My crimson red skateboard kneeled at my feet. With its gummy Hasoi rocket wheels, silent Swiss bearings, and maneuverable industrial trucks in all its glory. As I concentrated, I picked up my board, and took a quick step forward. Little did I know that this very step would begin my voyage towards the concrete path that laid ahead of me at such speed? Contrasting colors were embedded into my vision. Waves of light and sound clashed and swirled, slowly settling down like the ocean after a storm.

My surroundings blazed past me and blurred by. I pushed and pushed as I seem to defy the very laws of gravity. I felt weightless. The textured concrete squares went by like slides of a flip book. My hands were perched behind my back like a statue. The path suddenly changed from smooth concrete to paved brick. My destination was prematurely met as I slowed down to a complete halt. My surroundings slowly went back in focus. The wind that once pressed cool air in my sun burnt face, and blew my baggy T-shirt like a flag in the midst of a hurricane, suddenly stopped. I kicked the tail of my board and it glided into the grip of my left hand.

At that moment I took a breather to think. "Did the past events leading up to this very moment open up a door for me?", "Was the key to enjoying life, time, and experience right in front of me the whole time?", "Is the key to enjoying life just paying attention to the detail around me, as well as focus on the emotions in me?", and most importantly, "Is this combination of emotion and reality beneficial?" These are all questions I thought to myself very diligently. I focused all my concentration and thought on the subject matter and discovered something remarkable. What I have discovered in myself was, enlightenment.

Finding out new things about yourself is a very prestigious event. Especially when you learn more about how your mind works and perceives life around you. In my experience, I opened the gate of my emotion, and perception of my environment. This experience would be impossible to learn forcefully, it happened spontaneously. But, this skill allowed me to see the world in a new light. Even if I am in a dreary setting, I can walk with a skip in my step and a smile on my face. I think positively, and that is how I see the world around me. With this mind set, I can achieve whatever I put my mind to, enjoy life, and positively affect others around me.

TALENT SHOW: RAP
by Gabriel Pena

Well I'm just going to tell you what I got to say,

I'm a make my rhymes clear as the light of day.

Started freshmen year with a smile on my face.

Things are going fast; I'm a pick up the pace.

No more staring at a wall or empty space.

Some days are a bore, but not a chore.

Your potential is imminent, I'm new to poetry but I'm going to finish it.

Seniors and fish got along all right.

Matter fact you could say we were tight.

This is the only school without even one fight.

Until now, there's only been one kid that wasn't so bright.

But, I'm not known to call people out.

My main goal is to tell y'all what I'm about.

Smooth talking will get you a long way,

But, debate skills made me what I am today.

This school has a strange crowd.

Honor Rollie's chillen at the park in the shade of a cloud.

Morning Announcements is the usual ritual,

But sometimes the announcer's voice sounds seemingly fictional.

Kids on the court playing their favorite sport.

On a rim with no net, no sound even when they hit wet.

Ball bounces over the fence into the freeway.

Kids running in the street, cars don't give them any leeway.

Yet, we do what we gotta do to stay true to our value.

The step team, wants to gleam, like a laser beam.

Making a beat with their feet and hands.

Hours of work go into meeting our demands.

They like to dance and we like to watch.

I'm a take a chance and step it up a notch.

This school is so small, you could hear a pin drop.

I'm not saying it's not loud, but words travel in a crowd.

I do what I want to and get good at it.

I like to leave the audience ecstatic.

So I'm a change my stance and even break dance.

Hopefully, I'll leave y'all in a trance, I'm a leave it up to chance.

Thanks in advance.

I'm a try a trick.

Don't worry it be quick, maybe even sick.

Good enough to take a pic.

UNTITLED
by Hailey Phillips

One afternoon I wasn't feeling too well, my mother would always take me out for ice cream on Saturdays. This one day I just told her, "No mommy, it's okay. Maybe another day?" I never said no to my ice cream so she automatically knew I wasn't feeling well. She checked my temperature and sure enough I had a fever. The second my mother saw that I had a fever from the thermometer, I was wrapped in two thick Disney blankets and she was by my side feeding me hot chicken soup. I remember all I could see was my leopard print picture frame of my closest friends because I was stuck and wrapped up so tight from the blankets tucked in around me. I was listening to my favorite band "The Cheetah Girls", they were the best. I loved cheetah print and they were girls singing and dancing about wild cats. And if you knew every lyric you were considered one of the popular girls' in 5th grade.

"How's my princess feeling?" My mom would constantly ask me. The way my mom was always by my side, so caring and comforting. There was never a time I wasn't being nourished and loved by my mom. Her warm and loving care never let me down and she was always there for me, one thing I'd never forget.

After Ballet practice my mom and I would from time to time go to the park, just to relax and reflect on our day. I had practice just about every day, but only on Thursdays would my mom and I be able to have our alone time just to catch up and bond throughout the week. My mom is a Constable Police Officer and is a workaholic. We hardly had free time with our schedules. It was killing me because of the fact that my mom and I were inseparable. There was this tree that we always sat under and listen to Pandora on my mom's phone singing along like sisters, "I got a pocket, got pocket full of sunshine. I got a pocket full of love and I know that's its all mine. Ohhhh. Ouwh, oh." As my mom and I played around, she helped me with some of my 8th grade mathematics homework.

"Hailey, you need to practice so you can get better and learn on your own. So, give it a try." She said with a smile after she had explained to me how to work out the problem. I hated math, but my mom always knew how to explain it to me in a way no one else could. I could always depend on my mom to be there for me. I got a little hungry while we were bonding we went to the bistro across the street and met "her friend", that later turned out to be her new boyfriend that I was meeting and she wanted my approval of. It seemed to be a lot of small talk.

"So I hear you love Ballet." He said.

"Yeah. I do, it's like my life. I've been doing Ballet for years now." I explained proudly.

"That's great, then I need to see how the pros do!" He announced.

"Well, I do perform in the Houston Nutcraker every year, since the 4th grade!" I exclaimed theatrically motioning my performing hands to the side. "So where do you work?" I questioned.

"Im the manager of the Lowes in the local area and I engineer my very own workshop back at home." He boastfully mentioned.

"Back home? What do you mean back home?" I wondered.

"I was born in Honduras and I came to the U.S for college." He explained. "I love it in the states, everyone is kind of in their own world, doing their own thing. If you want something you can work hard for it and earn your way to the top." He remarked smiling at my mom.

My mother's face just got red and she changed the subject. I couldn't quite remember about what. I could only think about how much he wanted ti be apart of my mother's life. From then on, I was completely quite. I just continued to analyze every little thing he did. I kept thinking, "I don't know this man. Why is he even here?" Rolling my eyes, "Look at him, he just walks like he owns the place. A little to arrogant for my taste." I went on and on. I knew for my sake he had to go. He wanted not only my approval but my mother's complete heart.

Even though I knew how to fake a smile or two and just be as cordial as I could be, I felt betrayed that my mother would even think it was okay to invite someone else to our fuse time. This was the day he invaded our alone time and came along with us everywhere, the day my heart tightened, I'd never forget.

"And again! 1 2 3 4 AND 5 6 7 8!" Ms. Beth demanded pointing and showing us our places as we practiced our routine for the performance. "Good Job. Now were gonna take a 15 minute break until the guys get here for the stunts. Continue to stretch girls." She said walking off to the dressing room. We started joking around. Joanna pliéed into Samantha's arms and caught her.

"Britt, you and Hailey give it a try!" Samantha yelled across the stage. Brittany and I looked at each other, match up, and I darted at her jumped pliéed and posed. Everyone thought it was perfect. "We always made a great team!" I said while Brittany put me down.

Everyone started partnering up, even the girls that were doing the stunts with the guys. Our stage was huge but with all of our girls at once wasn't too good of an idea. Someone counted off and we all ran to our partner and pliéed. My friends Joanna and Samantha crossed in front of Brittany and I which wasn't such a good idea.

The second we intercepted, I jumped, we all collided and fell on the hardwood floor. Yet I fell right on my tailbone and Joanna fell down on her left arm. This stunt takes a lot of power to perform. The ones who were performing the stunt actually build up the strength and speed for the stunt which resulted in us getting hurt so quickly. The pain was beyond excruciating, and nothing like I've ever felt. All I wanted was my mom by my side. Samantha yelled to Ms. Mary Beth. She already saw the emergency issue and immediately called parents and the ambulance. I was trying to control as much pain as I could. A few moments later I looked up and there was my mom by my side holding my hand. Finally I had my mom and to me that's all I needed. "Just breath princess, everything's going to be fine." My mommy said. Even through all the pain I had, I knew I could manage just knowing my mom was right there beside me. The one thing I'd never forget.

POEM
by Filipa Ribeirinho

Life is a road. That's what it is.
You never know
    The best way to go;
    when it rains, should you stop and find shelter, or should you open
your own umbrella and fight the weather yourself?

Life is a road. That's what it is.
You never know
    What's next.
    Can shortcuts be trusted or are they just wrong choices you have to
distinguish?

    So many detours.
Life is a road. That's what it is.

THE PERFECTLY IMPERFECT SIDE OF ME
by Alba Rios

Everyone pictures the perfect family, the mom in the kitchen, the dad mowing the lawn, and the kids playing in the backyard. All my life I pictured my family like that, but that was something I would never reach no matter how hard I tried.

"Abort the kid, it will only bring us more problems," said my 'so called' father.

"I would never do that!" exclaimed my mother.

"Then choose between me and the kid," demanded my father.

"I choose my kid you can leave if you want, the door is right there, get out," my mother said with nothing but rage in her voice.

I was in the womb but I could feel that my father didn't love me. He didn't want me alive. He didn't want me at all. Her never caressed by mom's belly or talk to it. My mother on the other hand would comfort me and speak to me. He left slamming the door behind him. I could feel my mom crying and I felt the tears running down her face. "I will make sure you never have to say that you wish you had him in your life, I'm going to make it out and give you the best life possible," my mom talked to me, while unknowingly I moved through her womb. When I was born, I felt the love my mom had for me was immense even though my father left her because of me. He didn't even show up to see my mom give birth to me. He walked away from my life forever and now that I was out, I could feel it as much as I could feel the warm, soft hands holding me.

The next five years were hard especially since my mom started dating my stepdad. She made me meet him and she knew that I felt so opposed to anyone who tried to take the role of a father with me. Since the first day, I saw him I told him, "Why should anyone love me if my own father doesn't?" He knew what I spoke of but he didn't reply his expression was the one of a man who is confused.

In December, we moved in with him. As my mom packed I unpacked, I refused to go with anyone who wasn't my father. I cried the whole way to my new home. I didn't want to go with them I wanted to stay where I was. As the tears rolled down my pale cheeks, I remembered about my mom crying when she was pregnant, the hate I had for my father was the same but he was still my father, I couldn't let anyone just walk in and take the role my mom had played so well for five years. I always had the same line going through my mind, "Why should anyone love me if my own father doesn't?" As I got older, I asked my mom, "Where is my dad?" "What? He's in the living room," she responded. "That's not my dad and don't ever say he is!" I ran off crying. The story about my dad changed every time I asked, one day he was dead, the other he was in either Mexico or McAllen, and so on. The lies never stopped and I honestly grew tired. I became the hardheaded child that no one really wanted to speak to, but I managed to keep going. Every time I got an answer I would end up mad and saying, "And then you wonder why I'm like this." The rage I carried myself with was unbearable sometimes and I would cry it out.

No one was responsible for the way my father took things but I still took out my anger on everyone. All that rage made me blind and made me very aggressive, to the point where all I wanted to do was fight everyone. My mom brought me up with lies and I felt as if my life had been a lie since the beginning. I couldn't bear with the thought of never finding the love I was looking for from a father. Even though my stepdad tried to I always shut him away, and he began to grow a grudge against me.

His last strand was the day I was going on vacations to México. As I was getting in the SUV he told me that he was going to miss me and to be careful. I turned around and told him that I wasn't going to miss him that he could go on and get to stepping because I didn't care about him. I went as far as telling him that I regretted that mom met him. I could tell I hurt his feelings but I didn't care I just sat back and talked about what awaited us in México. "I'm done trying to satisfy someone that will never be satisfied," said my stepdad to my mom. "I'm sorry she's just so ignorant," replied my mom. "I am not ignorant I just say things the way I see them I don't hold anything back, I'm just too realistic for you," I said without the slightest hesitation. I honestly did not see how anything made me ignorant but I just moved on. I grew older and started the toughest years of my life, the teen years. Many people say these are the toughest and honestly, I believe they are as well.

It's hard to keep your head up when you see all these kids walking around with their dads and talking about how their dads just gave them this or that. It hurt a lot to be the odd one to say, "My dad never bought me anything." When I turned fifteen, I talked to my aunt about how I wanted to find out where my dad lived so I could see him at least once.

She started telling me that she knew where he was. I was very excited about the news and we began to talk about how we would go and see him without my mom knowing. "We will go when you get out of school for the summer, we will pretend we are going on a vacation to Mexico," she said. "Okay, I will be ready," I responded. The plans were set and I made sure that I wasn't going to have summer school classes so the plans wouldn't be ruined. Maybe this was never meant to be because my aunt died May 14, 2010. A month before I got out for summer vacations. A month before I finally got to see who my real father was. All my hopes of finding him went to the gutter. I was so sad and mad that this had happened. At her funeral I went up to the casket and began saying, "Aunty, please tell me this is all a dream. Say that you're just sleeping and in a month we are going to go find my dad just like you promised," I was sobbing and I felt my world crumble and break into a million pieces.

The last hope I had in finding him banished from the planet. I felt like my aunt died with all the hope I had so I became angry and all that went through my head was, "And they wonder why I'm like this. Why should I love someone when my own father didn't love me?" I am now sixteen and I'm still looking for my father. I'm not interested in finding him because I would want to get to know him, but because I want to meet my stepsisters. My family tells me that they look like me. Sometimes I wonder if he ever thinks about me. He has my reflection in his daughters. I don't think he ever wonders how I'm doing since he never wanted me in the first place. Ever since my aunt died, I have felt a gap in my heart get bigger and bigger, but they say, "What doesn't kill you, makes you stronger," but if that saying was true, I would be as strong as Hercules. I will one day get through it and understand what love is even though he was never in my life, and I hope that day is soon.

INTERVIEW WITH BATMAN
by Israel Rodriguez

He was always crazy. That's why I had to interview him; he's the only one with a good story to talk about. The only problem is that he doesn't hold anything back and didn't censor anything at all. It was hard to interview him at first since he's always worked late nights, but when I got the chance, he thought it was a joke. Like always, he just goes with it but just with his own attitude. Before we even started the interview he told me, "Israel, this better be your home work or I'll beat you down." (He said something else, but I censored it) I just laughed and said, "I know." When I started interviewing him, I noticed that he dressed up like he was ready to go cruising around the neighborhood or go hang out somewhere. He dressed in a skull t-shirt, gray skull jacket with a black hood, good but saggy jeans with his expensive sapphire black Jordan. He also looked like he just came back from work just with his hair all spiked up from gel, piercing on his eye lashes, lips, and tongue. As always, he had his expensive Converse glasses and with a face that would one make him look stupid or two mad at everything. So, right before I started interviewing him, he took my rolling chair and makes me sit on the floor in my room like a dog. I already knew this was going to be funny and a really stupid interview.

So, I asked him some questions that were supposed to be easy to answer but, instead he made them seem like mathematical questions, which really sucked. The first question, he answered with ease. "What is the happiest moment and saddest moment in your life?" He says, "The happiest moment in my life is when I became a dad", then he answers the last part like this, "The saddest moment in my life is when I lost my first candy." He was giving me a sad face that looks like a little kid will his spines on my chair (and he was actually serious about the answer he gave me too). I'm just laughing at him and I just continue on with the questions. The next question he answers with ease until I got to the next question. I ask him, "Who has been the kindest to you in your life?" Then for about 5 minutes he just sits there in the chair saying, "Uuuuuuuuuuuuuuhhhhhhhhhhhh...I don't know?" Then finally answer the question with another question and it was, "I don't know, you tell me?" I'm just giving him a face that says, "Are you really serious", and then he gives a face that looks like a stupid kid's face that says, "Yep." All of a sudden his fiancé comes into the room (whose name is Cecelia) saying, "Are you serious!? What about me?" He answers her with a stupid response, "Oh ya, I forgot about you... I'll say a maybe." That's when she started to attack him and he starts screaming like a girl.

The interview continues with him either answering the question with a simple answer, some serious long answer, or with a really stupid response. I ask him, "How do you know that the person you're going to marry is the One?" He just answers it with the most simples response, "I just do." And nothing else. He answering a serious response to the question when I ask him, "How would you like to be remembered?" He answers it with a pretty long and serious reason saying, "I want to be remembered as a person who never gave up in life no matter what came into my life as I was growing up and that I was proud of myself. Just lived life to the fullest you know." I then ask him another question, "Do you have any regrets in life?" He answered it with a stupid face of a kid saying, "I didn't take over the world. I tried to you know." (At the same time I'm laughing at his responses) Then I ask him, "Is there anything you've never told me but want to tell me now?" And he tried to be funny by acting stupid and not knowing what to say. Then he answers the question, "Ya, if you die before I do, tell me how it feels." I'm just looking at him with a mean face and he says, "Hey, you're the one asking the question, I'm just answering them like I want to, Ha-Ha!!" Then I ask about his time with his girlfriend (who is his fiancé), "What were the best times and the most difficult times?" He answers the question saying first, "When we had a good time..." Then he answers the last part by saying these, "...the worst of times is when she became pregnant, man the beast came out!" Now I thought his response was really funny but it was pretty messed up. Then It got funnier because she came into the room saying, "WHAT!? And she started to attack him again. I almost lost it through all the laughter. It's also funny because my door has no lock or even a door handle on it so anybody can come in or just listen to what's going on in my room.

The rest of the interview went pretty good with him giving me some good response. I ask him, "Do you think about dying? Are you scared?" He answered the question with a really smart response, "We will always die someday, that's why you got to live life to the fullest so that you won't have regrets in the end." Then I ask him another question, "What does your future hold?" He first answers the question by saying, "Only time will tell." Then he adds on by saying, "You can never know what will your future hold. Only god knows and if someone tells you other ways then don't lessen to them because they're going to trying to control your future. The decision you make in life will affect your future. That's why you have to live a good life and just life in your own boundaries. Israel, if you really want to have a good future then go to school and get good grades, respect mom and dad's decision, do what you know is right in life, alright. Don't mess up on me Israel because I trust you, believe in you that you will make it in life, and make a difference in these world. And if you feel alone or want to give up, then don't forget god here to help you and your family is here too. If not, then I'll kick some senses into your butt so that leaves a mark on you. But ya, only time will tell you know." I took all that he said series and wished I was as wise as he was, even do he had a bad background. He was the only one that believed in me, the only brother I felt I had. It was a good thing my room was dark, because I stared to have tears in my eyes. But I think he notice it because he shouted, "Hey! You better not be crying fool or kick your butt." I start smiling and say, "Ok"

The rest of the interview goes great and pretty funny. When we finish I notice something, he wasn't affected by the interview at all. He looks like when we first started, all calm with a bored look. As always, he just does something stupid and leaves my room a mess. I finish it all off by saying to him, "Thanks Jose." He just say, "Anytime fat white boy." Like that, the interview was over but not the craziness of it all. I always try to act stupid around him but he always wants me to be as marcher as I'm supposes to be. That why I chose him, because even do he's crazy, he's the wisest person I know. That's why I'm honored to call him my older brother. But I still think he's stupid.

NOT AN OPTION
by Kesley Rodriguez

"I give up! I can't take this anymore!" I constantly told myself ever since I got on this rollercoaster called High School. From watching movies and TV shows, high school seemed to be all about doing whatever you felt like doing. From staying up all night on the phone gossiping about senseless stuff that happened on that very same day, to beating up someone for looking at you the "wrong" way. It seemed as though education was the last thing on almost everyone's mind, except for the "Geeks" and "Nerds". However, for me, yet I was different.

Ninth grade was my first year every being in a public school. The system was totally different from the Montessori way that I was accustomed to. Instead of me having the freedom to learn at my own pace and not have to worry about getting a bad letter grade on a so-called report card, I had plenty to worry about. "Am I going to fail this class? What if Mom doesn't like my grades? What will she do to me?" Were the prevalent questions I frequently asked myself. My family expected so much from me. My older brother did really well in high school and my parents expected me to fill in his shoes or possibly do better. I tried my hardest. I considered myself different from my other classmates which may have explained why I only had a few friends. I sacrificed my social life for a good letter grade on every report card.

I remember one beautiful, warm, and breezing day in ninth grade I got my very first report card. When I looked at it, my whole day turned and flipped upside-down into a stormy abyss of mixed up emotions. I had all A's and a B in IPC. Some may consider that good, but to me, however I felt absolutely ashamed. I didn't get a perfect report card and I had to show my Mom my grades. When my Mom arrived to pick me up from school, I was in complete dismay of just the thought of even showing her my grades. In result, the car was filled with utter silence as my head was buried in between my arms for the entire ride home. When we finally reached home, I looked up at our pink and off-white checkered front door and knew there was no turning back now. I was scared to show my Mom my report card. Fear ran all throughout my body. As soon as I got in the house I rushed into my bright fuchsia pink room to try and recollect my thoughts on how to show her my report card.

"Mom?!" I yelled across the house in a worried tone. "I have something to show you!"

She answered back, "I'm coming dear, what is it?" She arrived in my room, staring at me. My nerves began to build up. I slowly reached out my hand and said, "Sit down Mom," I told her as calmly as I could, and so she did. "You love me, right Mom?" I asked just to make the room less tense. "No matter what I do wrong, right Mom?"

"Come on girl. You need to hurry it up. I have dinner cooking on the stove, and if it burns you're going to be the one who has to eat it." She said with her neck rolling in somewhat of a "Z" shape motion. I took out my report card and tossed it at her and yelled, "I GIVE UP!" She picked it up and said, "Oh my Kesley-"

"I know! I know Mom! It's completely atrocious!" I blurted out, "I give up on life! I give you permission to disown me." I was close to tears.

"Honey, this is a really good report card babe," She tried to ensure me that everything was fine.

"Mom, do you not see that big fat B?! It's totally killing me!" I couldn't understand why she wasn't mad at me. I pointed at the B on the paper, "Do you see this?" and all she said was, "Honey, don't give up. Just continue to do your best. Don't let one B put you down. Don't give up!" From that day on I tried to remember those words, "Don't give up".

I remembered those words for rest of ninth grade and continued to get better and better, until the middle of tenth grade. I was tired of working hard. I was tired of just doing home work and missing out on my social life. It was around thanksgiving break when I had a gut feeling that my grades had dropped. On Thanksgiving Day I woke up with an empty pit feeling in my stomach. My intestines felt like they were twisted and mangled around a splintered filled tree trunk, yet as if I was chained to it; chained to school work, and the work wouldn't let go of me. That ugly gut feeling made me wonder if I had bad grades. I checked my grades right before leaving for thanksgiving dinner at my Aunt's house and sadly sure enough I had a C. "I can't believe I have a C!" I repeated and kept getting upset with myself. "That's way worse than that B that I freaked out over," Is what continued to run through my mind on the way to dinner. When we finally arrived at my Aunt's house a sweet smell of pumpkin pie and pecan pie filled the air as they welcomed us into their home with plenty of hugs. The atmosphere was greatly filled with love. But sadly for me there was only one thing running through my mind, "A bad grade that was worse than a B. How can this possibly happen?" I asked myself all throughout dinner. My Aunt could tell that something bothered me throughout the mean, and so after dinner she sat me down to talk.

"What's wrong Kes?" She asked

I replied, "Nothing is wrong Aunty."

"I can tell that something was eating you up at dinner," She insisted. "Just let me know so I can try and help you."

"Aunty, I GIVE UP!" I exclaimed, "I've been trying so hard and I checked my grades before I let the house and I have a C Aunty!"

She put her hands on my shoulders and said, "Look at me. You can't be perfect, I'm not perfect, and sure as hell no one else can be perfect. You just can't give up. Don't give up! Keep trying your hardest and it will all pay off eventually." I then thought back to when my Mom said the exact same thing, "Don't give up." Everything then seemed so clear, "Don't give up!"

Everything was going well, I finished tenth grade with really good report cards and, "I give up" was nowhere in my vocabulary. The ending of my tenth grade school year was absolutely great, so great that my social life turned for the best and I made more friends. After the 2011 summer break, I was eager to go back to school and meet up with them. I was then a junior in high school, still surviving one day at a time with a new view on things.

My family and I were going to surprise my Grandmother on the day before school began. It was a nice bright and sunny day, the perfect day to hang out with her and relax before the long school year. As we walked in the nursing home the smell of old people and baby powder was prevalent but for some strange reason it was homey. We saw her in her wheelchair talking to the receptionist as we all called out, "Hey Granny!" as she opened her arms looked for a hug.. Later that day, my Grandmother and I talked alone.

"So you ready?" She asked.

"Ready for what Grandma?" I asked.

"The school year is about to begin young one. New challenges, obstacles, and more report cards, so I ask you again. Are you ready?" She asked with a stern tone.. My Grandmother had always been a strong and well educated woman. Whenever her voice got stern it's a sign to listen, and so I did.

I confidently replied with a smile, "Yes, I'm ready and I WON'T give up!"

OIL
by Maya Rueda De Leon

"One-two cups of rice. Two-four cups of chicken soup or water, what else do I need?" I ask my sister anticipating her negative answer.

"I don't know, you are the one cooking" her reply was exactly as I thought, arrogant.

"I wasn't talking to you! I was just asking myself, you know... to kind of force myself to remember." I reply murmuring already getting angry at her.

"Whatever." she said giving me a cold back. Every time it comes to cooking, even though she is younger by tree years, her cooking always turns better than mine. She is always showing off how good she is at cooking while I cook because she knows I know. It's not that am not good at it, I just don't like cooking. Cooking is dangerous.

After cleaning and washing the rice the next step it's to let it dry for a while and then gild it. The gild part it's easy if I make normal rice but am not cooking "normal rice." Today I'm cooking white rice at my style meaning that am only using whatever I can found in the kitchen. "The rice is going to toast if you don't add the chicken soup" my sister said, again with her arrogant tone.

"I know it's just that... it's just that..." I couldn't answer. I tried to ignore her but ignoring her it's like trying to ignore that you live in a world with other human begins, which is impossible.

"It's just that you still afraid of oil. I'm right?" She grins at me like she had won something for being right, because she was right.

When I was nine or ten my mother started to teach me how to cook. At that time my little sister wanted to learn with me but the stove was bigger than her and my mom didn't let her. My mom taught me the basic of cooking during a week and the week after I was going to start cooking. The dish that I was going to cook was empanadas, they look like fried tacos. That night my sister was also "making" the empanadas but my mom didn't want her to help, she was afraid of my sister getting burn with the hot oil because she was very short at that time and didn't understand much about cause and effect, instead my mom let my sister help because she really wanted to put the empanadas in the hot pan with oil.

"No it's not that! It's just that I don't want to end up with a mark in my face" Se didn't reply back. I knew I had hit her with my words. I turn to see her expressing and she was already getting mad. She wasn't mad because I insult her face having a tiny mark, the mark wasn't even big. She was mad because behind my words I was calling her a fool.

She wanted to put an empanada in the pan with oil but because she was really short and the stove big she needed help. The last things that I remember it's going to the restroom for a short break while hearing my mom telling my sister to watch out with the pan because it could burn her face. I was washing my hands when I hear a horrible crying. I run to the kitchen and my mom was hugging her while she was crying. Since I was also little I got really scared because when I saw my sister, she was crying like someone was killing her. After that day my mom couldn't make me cook because I refused in every way I could. I was traumatized because of that incident to the point of not standing next to the stove. When I turned 15 my mom was determinate to make me cook and force me, literally, to cook.

"I am just teasing you. Sorry I am really nervous right know, don't interrupt me" I say trying to calm the situation. Carefully put the chicken soup in the gild rice.

"You made it Maya! This time you weren't afraid of the hot oil; one step towards you goal of becoming chef." My sister said proudly. She was really happy of my "step"

"Wait! 'becoming a chef' when did I said such a thing?" I asked confused. She was just laughing because this time I wasn't complete scared of the oil. This time I was only sweating.

TEMPORARY SITUATION
by Genevieve Sandoval

As I walked through my torn down house, I was fully aware that there were nails along with broken glass everywhere. In the year of 2001 a tropical storm named Allison traveled her way through the city of Houston but I felt as if she had only targeted towards my home. I was only 5 years old, but I remember everything. I remember having a Rottweiler, Chihuahua and a cat that we had to get rid of because we could no longer care for them. That's every child's worse nightmare. I remember going to the dollar store to buy new clothes because our belongings had been demolished. I remember these pink sandals with green flowers on the top that my mom had bought me; she looked at me in the eyes and said, "I know these aren't the ones you like or want but they have to do for now." I nodded yes in confusion. I remember I walked down the dark hallway with a flashlight in one hand and my mom's hand in the other; we were in search for my dad. He had packed what he could save and asked my mom, "Are you ready?" Neither I nor my brothers knew where we were going; we pulled up to my grandma's house. This was quite strange because her and my mom weren't at peace. Little did we know we were going to be living in the tiny trailer behind the house for quite some time. There was only one tiny bedroom and there were five people desperate for a home. As we walked in to the run down trailer I could hear my mom as she repeated,," This is only for a little while we'll be home soon."

The knowledge of every mother is unrecognizable for most children, however I could see my mom did what was best for her family. She swallowed her pride to make sure me and my brothers were stable and happy. Months went by and the house was still a wreck due to construction, but there was one bedroom completed. We packed our belongings and moved back into our home. We all slept on two twin size beds that had been placed on the floor. My two brothers on one, me and my mom on the other and my dad on a pile of blankets next us it remained this way for about 3 months. Our home had finally been complete and we were all excited to get our own bed rooms. We were back in school and things started going back to "normal", then my family was torn apart in a matter of a day.

I came home to back and forth yelling between my parents I knew they had been arguing lately but it had never reached this level of anger. I was convinced, if I went to my brother's room and put my head under the pillow that it would all stop because I could no longer hear them being unhappy. I was stupid for believing myself because by the time I knew it the cops were at my house telling my dad, "Sir, I'm only going to tell you this once, you need to leave this premise immediately!" I chose the wrong time to open the bedroom door because when I did my dad was walking out the front door. Many thoughts ran through my little naive mind." How could he leave me? I'm daddy's little girl! He's not supposed to leave me! He didn't even tell me bye." I remember that night my mom decided to sleep with me, usually my dad did because I was still terrified of the dark but he was nowhere to be found. I couldn't help but be furious at my dad for leaving my mom with 3 kids. Before I closed my eyes my mom told me "Everything will be fine, I promise. Everything will go back to being normal soon I promise. This will always be your home; don't let anyone tell you different." I nodded in confusion because I didn't know what was going to happen. My mom's voice brought comfort to me when I needed it the most. A matter of six months went by, switching from apartment to house everyday was not fun, so my dad moved back in but things were not normal. I started getting use to the fact that things would never be perfect but I knew my mom tried her hardest to make them be. As I grew up I resented my father for leaving and my mom became my best friend.

Years had passed and everyday had become a routine, I would wake up go to school, then go to dance practice and go home for bed. My everyday plan was thrown off one night because I didn't come home. My dad was at work and my mom was at the hospital with my cousin. He didn't have anyone to care for him so my mom decided to step up. My Wednesday had started off completely normal as I was at school my mom called me asking "do you think you can stay at lulu's tonight?" I said "yeah that's fine" But in my mind I wondered "what's my life turning into am I really being placed in a situation that I had to be independent and strong on my own?" I went home to grab some clothes, feed and kissed my dog for a temporary goodbye, then I left. The next day I was waiting for a call or text from my mom or dad but nothing was received. I went to school disappointed, when all of a sudden my phone lit up. I had gotten a text message from my mom saying," Do you think you can stay at Lulu's till Saturday?" I replied with a "yeah . . . that's fine" but in my mind I thought," Do I have any other choice?" One day passed at a time and I learned there was no easy way out of this situation., I knew my mom was doing the right thing, therefore I couldn't be mad at her. Friday morning I got another text message from my mom saying" Thank you for being so strong through this all you truly are an amazing daughter. I know you're not happy with this TEMPORARY situation but it will all be over soon I promise than you can come back home with me,"

It seems as if my whole life I was placed in temporary situations. My mom always knew the words to tell me to keep moving forward. I was fully aware that I had a place to call home. Throughout my life I constantly heard "Everything will go back to being normal soon I promise." I remember every detail of every predicament I had been placed in and it had been in the same home. I still walk the same hallways that had been torn down by the storm, the hallways that my dad walked through before my opinion towards him changed, and the hallways that had been abandoned for a couple of days. Memories are memories weather they're good or bad I was just lucky they're all in one place. That is the place I call home.

DEDICATION AT ITS PRIME
by Angelica Scales

As my mom and I pulled up to her house, I grabbed my; tape recorder, note pad, and pencils as I prepared to exit the car. When the car finally stopped I said my goodbye's and closed the door as Destini's mother walked outside to leave for work. She spoke to me and told me to go right on in, and that Destini was up stairs in her room. As I entered their home I proceeded down a hallway that led to the stairs. I could smell her aunts cooking and hear the grill sizzling underneath the chicken breast while in route to her room. As I walked up stairs I heard Beyonce's new song "Party" playing loudly and I knew that the room with the pink door and the mirror on it was where I should be headed. I walked through the door to see Destini with her books and work spread out on her bed.

Little did I know, I had just walked into a fashion hall. There were designer retail bags and photos from fashion magazines all over the walls. This girl was obsessed! On a day where she was just relaxing, she wore an ancient printed shirt from forever21 with her designer sweats and her ancient printed house shoes. She had a long, dark, weave in her hair that she pulled into a high ponytail with a bang that covered nearly half of her face. Once she saw me she stood up and gave me a hug as if she hadn't seen me in days. She is tall, light skinned, and ambitious which was proven by her "Wall of Goals". She proceeded back to her bed but she didn't walk in steps. She strode. She looked at me with those chinky eyes as she turned down her radio and said,"You getting thick, you must be eating!" I don't ever take anything she says too personally because I know her personality. One thing about her is that she doesn't hold back much, if anything. She is loud, not ashamed of anything she says or does, and bold. She asked, "Are you ready to do this interview?" I replied, "Don't I look ready, but it's just your profile love."

Destini Fasha Duncan-Hall was born in the 90's like me, but times were completely different for her than they were for myself. Growing up she was a lonely child. Her only friends were her cousins and her brother. She was raised in Trinity Gardens where there is so much negativity and a lack of faith, but to come out of that a beautiful, independent, young woman is a blessing. She says that this is where she got her "Zero Tolerance for BS", that it's also why she is so tough and so hard on others. She is a strong believer in tough love. Her motto to life is "No Pain, No Gain. But don't let too much pain come your way or you might get hurt!" She has a big heart but she doesn't let anyone take advantage of her. She says that, "Kindness is the key to so much in life, but it could also be the cause of your down fall." Words like these are why I consider her to be wise for her age.

Lots of people see seventeen year olds as children, but with as much wisdom as she has you have no choice but to see her as a young adult. I would never doubt her ability to do anything or think that she will not do something that she said she would. Since I have known her she has never gone back on her word. There are many words that could describe her and put her in a category with millions of other girls, but she deserves to be in one of her own. Destini is a one of a kind type of girl with a one of a kind type of personality. Not too many people are brave enough to always speak their mind or open up to almost anyone about anything. She sets a great example for young girls our age not because of her grades, but because of her diligence and her desire to not half do anything. If Destini is going to do something she is going to put her all into it. You may find lots of girls similar to her, maybe even some who are better at academics or juggling their schedule. That's you, but I only know one her and that's enough for me.

I wouldn't say that she is my role model. She isn't even a person that I would say I look up to, but she is my inspiration to be a better me. She showed me that hard work does pay off and that I don't necessarily have to be the best person in the world to do what she does. Destini Fasha Duncan-Hall is a diamond in the rough and she is not afraid to admit it.

MY LIFESAVER
by Jonathon Schnur

Memorial Herman will forever be my life saver and scary exciting place to be. Because When I was younger, sometime back in fifth grade, I would get sick a lot with my horrible migraines. So I would miss a lot of school, well I would use this to my advantage and would lie sometimes saying I was sick to get out of school because I hated school with a passion. Well, the one time I decide not to fake my mother doesn't believe me sadly and I ended up in the disinfecting smelling hospital known as Memorial Herman. As you might know Memorial Herman is a very large and has a haunted feeling to it in the night time. I woke up in the morning on a school day with a nasty stabbing pain. And so I begged my mother to take me to the hospital she only took me after threatening me, "If there was nothing wrong with me that I was going to get a spanking."

When we first entered the hospital I felt a great rush of the freezing air conditioned breeze hit us, And when we walked through it the feel couldn't be any scarier so many sick people sitting around, people getting rushed in by ambulances, my surroundings were terrifying. Up until we reached the happy colored kids area but even there, there were kids screaming bloody murder. So we signed in with the super nice clerk at the front desk and she took us back. I was sobbing in pain so finally they gave me pain meds as I lay on their nice comfy metal framed beds. I passed out I guess because I don't remember a thing.

As I awoke to them pushing my comfy bed through the hall it went from dead and bleak which was the adult area to a very fruitful and happy area, which was the children's area. They had a fake forest park and as I passed through it, it looked like a different dimension because the floors and trees were so colorful. But then I made it to my room where it became dead and bleak again. They gave me a clicker so I could inject myself with morphine every 6 hours when I would click it you could smell the strong smell of alcohol then I would become relaxed. Also in case you didn't know if you never been in the children's area they have the prettiest doctors so I guess you can say I was in heaven due to how I was being treated. And when it was finally time for me to leave the heavenly nice nurses checked me out and gave me an awesome green stuffed giraffe which was there mascot memorial Herman was and will forever be a life saver.

ADIEU
by Emma Shahriari

Light slanted through the blinds, illuminating her cold, hard eyes. She concentrated on something I could not see, a place I could never reach. The room was enveloped in silence, like a heavy cloud, frowning upon even the fan for its gentle whir. There was a piercing stillness, yet inside I was screaming. Words and repressed emotions fought and tore behind my teeth, shredding my throat and snapping my bones in their desperate, heedless rage. My lungs felt ready to rupture, tear free from inside my chest and rip me open, spewing all my poison into the already charged air. I couldn't possibly hold this back, not any longer. I had to open my mouth and let loose this insanity. Nevertheless, my jaw was locked, my body frozen. She did not speak. I barely dared breathe.

Her dainty legs were folded beneath her far too slim frame, her skin almost glowing in the lengthening shadows. Was she really only a girl; sitting dejectedly on my floor, refusing to acknowledge my existence, like a put-out child? It seemed as if she focused hard enough on that far away place, she and I would cease to be anything more than a bad dream. Such a child, such an old, damaged child was sprawled before the fading light of my window, pointedly avoiding me.

She looked just like a doll, dressed up with thick, chalky make-up and ruined, over-dyed hair. It was just a costume, a disguise for that frozen creature inside. Of all of the incredible people I had seen, I had never known anyone more beautiful in all my life; I knew I never would. She looked so frail, so fragile, as if with just an embrace I could crush her bones to dust and destroy her. It wasn't until I looked into her eyes that I felt the strength emanating from her. Her gaze dared you to try and touch her, to see if you could break her. It had taken one look for me to know that she would never be broken. Never.

But that voice, those words that just disintegrated to nothing in her mouth? "I'm going to miss you." Barely a whisper, so quiet I couldn't be sure if she really said it. Where did that voice come from? That was not the voice of the fearless, tenacious, stone-like women I was used to. A tinge of desperation colored those syllables. That could have been the voice of a child, a teenager. I could have even imagined it to be the voice of an 18 year old girl, someone who was vulnerable and scared.

And then I heard it, that resounding crack of miles of ice shifting apart to let out a small bit of human. A tear slid down her cheek, even though she tried to hide it. I shifted forward, I was going to put my arms around her and tell her it would be all right; and it would be all right, because I could, and would, make it so.

My lips moved, words formed. I could say this, no matter what was on the line; the ice had cracked, if only for a moment. This was my chance. But my tongue refused to move, my lips were glued to one another. I could feel my rage beating relentlessly on the walls my jaw and lips had become. I hadn't known it was possible to feel so close to exploding, bursting into a thousand shreds of myself from the sheer pressure of those intangible things called emotions, and still remain in one, unmovable piece. The seconds were ticking by like sand in an hourglass; an entire future slipping through my fingers like smoke as I hesitated.

Silence, stillness. I wanted to tell her that I'd change my mind, I would fix everything, and she would have nothing to fear. I could take it back, couldn't I? Pretend it was all just a joke? There would be no reason to wait if I never left, right? Did I really need to go on exchange in a foreign country for an entire year? How could it be worth losing what it had taken me so long to build? Was I really that selfish, that I could choose to exile myself far away from her, when she really needed me? The rustle of paper and the cold caress of the fan suddenly became unbearably loud and glacial. Her perfume was choking me, that warm mix of vanilla and flowers which so deceptively gave the illusion of warmth. I was so close to her, frozen just behind her. If only I could break through the invisible wall between us, renew whatever it was we had lost in those horrendous moments since I told her why I wouldn't be here come September.

I reached out, the tips of my fingers only inches from her hand. I just barely heard the ever so small rasp as her breath caught in her throat, and her entire body tensed. It was the smallest of movements, an almost imperceptible shifting of her shoulders, the nearly flinch-like movement of her hands as they reached to pick at her bracelets; but it told me everything I needed to know. She was building her wall again, freezing the warmth that had for only a second tasted fresh air and possibility. I found my arms could move, and they immediately wrapped themselves around her, ten seconds too late. Her perfume enveloped me, that beautiful warm scent that fooled me into believing the impossible; but her skin was as cold as ice. Her hands gently disentangled my arms and she stood up, turning to face me. I looked into her eyes and saw only ice. She was gone. I was too late.

UNTITLED
by Emma Shahriari

Hugh Dickenson had forty days. Not to live, to move out. The court order had been slipped under his door this last night, like an unwelcome pest. A stranger already inhabited his side of the bed, was already erasing his memory from the two story brownstone he and Emily had bought after Jack was born. Distant times now. His replacement had kids, wealth, and security. Hugh had nothing. He wasn't surprised. Emily had always carried out her decisions with stunning alacrity and determination. It was one of the things he'd really admired about her. It might have even been one of the reasons he'd loved her.

Grimacing, Hugh forced his mind to other matters. It didn't matter now. Nothing did. He was only going to concentrate on putting one foot in front of the other. He was in the desert, far from civilization and air conditioning. It was going to be a scorcher today; but for the moment, it was still relatively chilly. Dawn was still stretching and yawning, procrastinating on its way to work. The sun wanted to sleep for a few more minutes. Hugh didn't mind. It gave him more time to enjoy his surroundings.

Hugh was in hill territory, a no man's land that only outlaws bothered to travel through. Hugh liked it here, the sparseness, the rugged terrain. It was stubborn. Stumbling over scrub brush, loose stones and the occasional small animal, he hiked up to the peak of the nearest embankment. He was out of shape; by the time he reached the crest, he was wheezing with the effort. Emily had once told him he looked like George Clooney, but nowadays, he looked more like an Auschwitz victim. His lungs could barely stand the exertion of mounting this hill. He wondered how he was going to trek across all six of them. Hugh felt old. Saving him from his thoughts, the sun decided to rise, filling the area with honey golden light and a red misty haze.

"Red sky at night, sailors delight! Red sky in the morning, sailors take warning." Hugh muttered under his breath. Hugh never much liked sailing, in fact being around any big body of water petrified him. He wondered what reminded him of the phrase. Everything around him was tranquil and quiet. There was nothing to take warning of here. Other than the occasional rustle of brush or patter of small feet over stones, Hugh felt he could have been completely alone.

In the valley below Hugh's hill, there was a huge formation of rock, tumbled stones and debris which had formed a pile. Jack would have loved that. Jack would have loved everything here. It was perfect for climbing and running around. A heaven for Cowboys vs. Indians. Hugh forced himself to blink back sudden tears. Jack was so young, so courageous. Hugh had never been religious, but he wished he were. He would have a God to blame then, now he had nothing but the cold truth. His son was dead.

After months of hospitals, tests, and operations, his son had withered away into nothing more than a whisper between the bed sheets. His springy red hair, bronzed healthy skin and keen, intelligent eyes had faded until they too, were gone. Watching his son die had destroyed Hugh. It had destroyed his marriage too, but Hugh had stopped caring about that months ago. All he really wanted was Jack. Nothing else really mattered after that.

Hugh could feel the heat of the sun now. It was slowly warming his skin, waking him up and calming him down. Hugh didn't want to think about Jack, not now. He basked in the sunlight, drinking in the tranquility and quiet, forcing all other thought out of his brain. That was when he heard it for the first time.

He opened his eyes and looked around, intrigued. The sound was so soft that it was almost carried away by the wind. If it hadn't been for the flash of light, Hugh might have shrugged and gone on in his own direction. Down at the bottom of the valley, a light blinked. It was too far for Hugh to see clearly, but it seemed like a reasonable trek. Hugh was curious. He thought he was alone out here. He started down the other side of the hill, descending into the valley below.

As he gained ground, the sound grew, filling Hugh's ears. Soon, he could detect a lilting melody, slight variations forming notes and chords. Eventually, he could even recognize a reoccurring rhythm. Someone nearby was singing. What struck Hugh was that the song was so sad. It was as if someone had taken pure sorrow and given it a voice. He had heard his fair share of depressed or desperate tunes, but this was different. There was something timeless and haunting to this music. Hugh found tears were running steady rivulets down his face. The song continued, rising in volume.

Hugh realized he was on his knees, chest heaving as his body was wracked with sobs. Every repressed emotion he had about Jack, Emily, and his broken life attacked him at once, while he lay there, defenseless against his thoughts as the song swirled around inside Hugh's brain, building into a roar. He couldn't block it out, no matter how he tried. Hugh was sure he was losing his mind.

As suddenly as the music had started, it ceased. Hugh felt shaken. He struggled up from the ground and dusted off his pants, slightly embarrassed but far more bewildered. "Hugh." A voice behind him echoed. Hugh spun around, shocked. Behind him was a woman. She was no ordinary woman. There was an air to her frame, a terrible sadness to her smile. She was beautiful, but horrible. Her ebony hair seemed to shimmer and move with its own life as it swirled around her head in the wind. Her pale skin was barely darker than the blinding white dress which trailed in the dirt around her. It was her eyes which transfixed and petrified Hugh. They were a deep emerald green; Hugh was reminded of windswept seas and raging storms. Sadness clung to her, radiating from her in an almost tangible miasma. He could feel himself sinking down to his knees, weighted down by an inexpressible sorrow. Her eyes beckoned him, glistening with tears. A small smile adorned her vermillion lips. As Hugh was crushed under the weight upon his shoulders, he noticed the hem of her dress was caked in blood. "It is time," she said and started to sing.

Hugh Dickenson disappeared, never to be seen again.

A PLUCKED FLOWER
by Kamry Stewart

It was a long dreary day and I was in school doing my class work as usual. I finished all my work at that time so I read a book until my teacher Mrs. Coleman gave me another assignment to do. All of a sudden I was called to the front desk to go home. While I was packing to go home my dad walked upstairs with a puzzled look on his face. He started talking to my teacher while I was saying good-bye to my friends Sierra, Mikeila, and Iyana.

"Good-bye Kammy!" they said to me.

When I walked towards my dad I heard him say that I was going to be gone for at least a week. He grasped my hand tensile and I knew something was wrong.

"Have you eaten yet?" He asked me while my uncle was in the car.

"No, Sir. You picked me up before lunch", I said calmly

"Okay, what do you want to eat?"

"Jack- in the- Box", I said puzzled

"Okay."

We stopped at Jack- in the- Box by our apartments and went inside. I ordered the Ultimate Cheeseburger with curly fries and a soda. The burger was huge and greasy with a beefy, cheesy taste and smell and felt a little soft with fresh curly fries. After I ate we went to the house and I took a nap. When I woke up the sun was setting.

"Kamry!" My dad called

"Coming father", I said fumbling out of my bed. I was scared to go to my parents' room.

"Come sit on the bed in between me and you uncle." He said sadly like someone died. Then all of a sudden.... "BOOM!" I got the news. "Kamry the reason I waited to tell you was because it was hard for me." My dad said crying. I could see my uncle on the side of me crying. All of a sudden I felt tears falling down my face and I could smell and taste the salt. I knew I didn't want the news but my dad told me anyway.

"Kamry, your papa passed away last night in his sleep", he said

"He died a peaceful death and lived a great life", my uncle added, "At least he doesn't have to suffer."

"But...But why?" I said shocked and upset

"It was his time Kamry, God was ready for him", my dad and uncle said together

"We can sit here and cry for a few more minutes but I need you to pack. Then you can sleep in here tonight." My dad said.

While I was packing the thought came to my mind. That there was so much I didn't get to say to him. My first instinct was to call my friends but I didn't want to burden them so I sat alone in my dark room crying and thinking about all the things I wanted to say to him. What my facial expression would have been if I was down there at the nursing home visiting him? Then I just sat there and cried then I was finally sleeping. While I was sleeping I kept seeing him laying in the nursing bed sleep peacefully it was so terrible. When I woke up I saw that it was a dream I had tears out of my eyes so I went to the bathroom used the restroom and washed my hand and face and that's when I realized he is in a better place if he was still in the nursing home he would still be suffering and he isn't suffering anymore and I was better for a while.

GRANDPA TEACHER
by Savannah Tibbits

I keep in mind the white-haired man as the dial tone rings. He has known me longer than I have a memory for life. He has never aged; he has kept the same wrinkles, age spots, blue eyes, laughter, and strength. In his wood shop he towered above me, although he was always the gentlest teacher. He reminded me each visit, who I was and where I came from, and that if I believed either had changed, he would still be just as proud.

My grandfather always smells of cedar, as if he was recently out of working in his garage on his grandiose creations. I have very few memories of him without this smell, though I have not been able to create many memories with him. We have not spent much time together, although he has more respect from me than any other person in my family has received. The father of my mother has served each and every child in this family as a father, he has taught the strongest lessons of life and love; is the things that are important in life are the person you believe you are and the person you strive to become.

His pride in his heritage when he speaks, and his thick German eyebrows show his deep ancestry. He speaks of his family history, "My original forefather came from Germany in 1842" and although it isn't much of a life lesson, and he may have known little of this man, you can see the pride radiate from his face. He may wish that he had the same great accomplishments as his forefathers, but the family he created knows he has done so much more.

Calling him from this cold classroom, full of blue-screened computers and grey speckled desks, the environment creates the illusion of my grandfather being so distant. I feel as if I would like to reach through this gap in the world, the one in which his voice travels through, just to receive the tight, hard hug in which I receive from him each visit. When he answers, I become astounded by his voice. My memory has never saved the deep calm in his voice which radiates from his heart.

My grandfather grew up quickly, marrying my grandmother and creating a family at a mere 23, a marriage which would fall apart over time, but would give him the greatest opportunities and future for this family. He never quit, he always gave as much love as he could and labored hard for what he had. As a child, I received my mother's story of her poor childhood with a harsh mother and a father she rarely saw, but a father that was always there for them emotionally. He took my mother with her brother and sister each week to Luby's Cafeteria for lunch, her favorite lunches of her life. She always speaks of his love, his strength, and his passion for life.

In my family, we adopt others. My grandfather only has three biological children, but including who he counts as his own sons and daughters, he has seven, from 3 different marriages. Although he loves his children, he has an obvious joy for their children whom he has been blessed with, saying "I give, I don't receive... Grand-kids are so delightful. You can spoil them and then send them home." He gives so much attention to my cousins and I, so much love, I have never understood how he has never gotten tired. One day, though, I may understand.

"Love to me is very important, and what you share with your family... being with someone there has to be a common bond, a common understanding." Earl lives with his wife and two black cats, in a cookie-cutter neighborhood, in Katy, Texas. It is that welcoming home for the picture-perfect grandparent couple. My grandfather has worked hard for what he has and lives every day proud of his accomplishments, although life is trying to bring him down.

"I'd like to get over this Parkinson's disease," he tells me with solemnity, "live a little longer and enjoy my family." The grandfather I have always remembered for his strong and slightly-painful hugs, for his large pearly white smile, and the joy in his laughter on Thanksgiving, has all of our hearts cringing for not only his life, but for that face we always expect to give us that last bit of happiness. He gives us the love that sometimes only he is able to provide. "I'm 85, you know. Who ever thought I would make it past 2000? But life goes on and gets better all the time."

I have not spent as much time with my grandfather as I would want for myself. I have not given the love to him that I wish I could, or shown with all my heart how grateful I am for his strength and joy for my family. But, I think he knows. He knows how strong each and every soul in this family is drawn to him, how they yearn to be the one he is speaking to, and how he has changed each and every one of our lives with each memory he has created with us.

It is people like my grandpa, who not only give their whole mind to you as you speak, but their whole self in their response, who make you appreciate life the most. It is the teacher he has been, and teacher he will always be that makes him the core of our family. The rest of his life, and for the rest of the lives of the family who claims him as their own, that he will be the inspiration to show each other unceasing love, endlessly, for each child, mother, father, brother, sister, and neighbor alike. He is the strength to forgive others, to live happily, and to be thankful for all that we have been blessed with, each and every day.

ALL IS FLEETING, ALL WILL GO; WHAT IS GONE WILL THEN BE PLEASANT
by Yuliya Tkachenko

I am lying in my bed with my eyes closed. Outside is Saturday morning but on my mind it is another day somewhere else. My life looks like a total mess. I do not even have a normal bed in my room. How I can call this life normal? Walls in my room are painted in gray color and it does not make me any more optimistic. Seriously, whole apartment is gray; someone definitely has a lack of imagination.

Anyway, the worst thing now is a cultural difference, which I can talk about for hours, but my mom keeps telling me that all is fleeting and all will go.

A month ago I lived in one of the most romantic and beautiful cities, where I just got used to living. Oh, Rome! I just started speaking Italian and got a couple of friends. I made some plans for future summer like going to seaside in southern Italy. I learned Rome and already knew it better than other people, who lived there for their entire life.

I want to go back there. I want everything how it was. I want to feel like I'm back home wherever my home is.

Mom, can I put some Italian music on, please?

It was dark so I could see only night-lights and a piece of road ahead but not further than 15 meters. There were tall sycamores on both sides of the road. Those trees created some kind of tunnel the end of which I could not see. We were going on a straight road in the tunnel of sycamore heading south. We passed a first turn to Ostia, where is a sea and cute multicolor buildings. I knew that I will go there one day with my new friends.

Only fifteen minutes ago I could see sunset of magic colors. I never been in this city before and I do not have any idea how it can be. I was not tired but I was scared. There were signs of restaurants and hotels around, which I could barely read. I did not know the language neither Italian nor English. My destiny challenged me.

My mother kept telling me that all is fleeting and all will go, and it went.

Less than two months before that, I had a normal life. Oh, Kiev! I was studying in Ukrainian school and was doing well. I spoke my native language and had many friends. Everything seemed to be just how it was supposed. I had plans for the future but my family had other plans. So now, here I was, in Italy without knowing any Italian or having any friends.

I found my ipod and put on music, words of which I can at least understand.

My favorite coffee place was empty. Some music was on, I liked it but I did not paid attention to it. I had an hour of lunch break that I always spend here. I liked it here mostly because this place was always empty but also because of its open terrace and location. I loved downtown of Kiev it was busy and romantic at the same time.

I failed the last test on Ukrainian history. I did not want to study something I thought I will never need again. We were planning to leave a week ago but there were some issues with documents. I can not wait to leave this country.

Political and economical situation were messed, so there was no reason to stay here any longer. I loved people who live here, but meeting the same people every single day, going to mostly same places and talking about the same stuff was boring for me. I needed a change even though I did not want it. I knew I needed to move on.

I found a CD with Italian music and chose my favorite one. My heart trembled as soon as I heard it. There is only one disadvantage of leaving in downtown, which is noise of cars at night. Now I cannot hear anything but the music.

My new life is not that much impressive but it is just a beginning. I am the only one who can change it. I knew that all is fleeting and all will go. I knew that one other day I will wake up and have what I want and it can be even here, in Houston. I knew that everything what I am going through right now I will remember as a pleasant time of my life. Later I will not remember how hard it was just how I have forgotten my first move.

People are made like that; we remember mostly good things about our past. We forget our pain, despair and sadness. I will not remember any of that in a couple of month but now I have to recollect all of my strength and do something. I just have to remember that all is fleeting, all will go; what is gone will then be pleasant.

MEMORIES
by Yitzel Vazquez

I never thought this would happen. I was at my grandma's house watching TV with my other cousins. Our parents dropped us off there because we had no school and my grandma had to take care of us. We were all around the age of 6 or 7, my sister was also with me. I was lying on the floor watching Barney. My other cousins were running around, jumping on the couch, in the kitchen eating, etc. I looked at the window and realized it was really sunny, even though the curtain of the window was there, the light still shown through bringing much light into the room. At first I couldn't believe it; my dad had grabbed my mom and pushed her towards the window. Everyone got quiet. The only thing that was making a noise was the television. The first to get up was my grandma and then everyone else got up, including me. We ran to the window, pushed the curtain aside and saw my parents arguing.

My dad was saying "I called you at work and you weren't there!" Mom said "I was out!" He said "Where were you?" she said "We'll discuss this at home." My mom noticed we were all standing and looking at them through the window. I didn't realize I had tears running down my face, until my grandma told us to get away from the window and when I touched my face to wipe away the tears.

Ever since that moment we all saw my dad differently. I never thought this would happen, a few months later my parents got a divorce. My mom put restrictions on my dad where he had to be certain feet away from us unless someone we know was there to keep watch. Seeing my dad far away from me one afternoon was the hardest thing to deal with. Life can be really hard at times. I never thought this would happen. It was my sister Jailene. My brother Juan and I were outside one afternoon riding our bikes and playing. I was playing soccer with my brother; it was a really hot and sunny outside. When I saw him, he was on the sidewalk on the other side from where we were. He was looking at us telling us to come to him. I thought to myself, "I really want to go and hug him, but am I allowed to?Do I really want to go? What will happen?" All of these thoughts were running through my mind. My siblings looked at the direction I was looking and immediately dropped everything and ran inside the house to inform my mom; meanwhile I just stood there looking at him with tears running down my face. That's when I decided to run to where he was. As I crossed the street to meet him, I could hear behind me the leaves crunching and running by my side, also my siblings running after me. My dad had his arms wide open waiting for me to run into his arms. When I did he held me so tight it was hard to breathe and carried me in the air. I never thought this would happen. Once he set me on the ground.

He said "I've missed you so much Mija" there were tears in his eyes; I cried even more seeing my dad crying.

I said to him, "Papi don't cry! I've been okay, I miss you a lot too, and it's been really different not having you at home."

By the time that happened my brother and sister were already embracing our dad. Life can be really hard but this showed me that even though in life there are times were something bad happens something better is coming your way.

I turned around to see if my mom was looking, sure enough she was. Her facial expression reminded me of when someone passes away and you can see that their family is hurting; her face was showing sympathy and sadness, something I've never seen in my mom before. After we talked and said goodbye to our dad, we went back inside with our mom. Right when she closed the door she said "I'm going to take away the restrictions and let you all see your dad every weekend." We were all shocked because it had been two years with restrictions and now that she finally decided to put them down was a miracle.

My brother said, "Really you're going to let us see him without someone being there to watch us?"

My sister said "And you really going to let us see him every weekend?"

My mom said "Yes." I went up to her, hugged her, and said "Thank you Mom."

Now that I get to see my dad every weekend is good, even if I wanted them living together and become a family again. I know deep in my heart that God does things for a reason and only he knows why they are not together.

PROFILE OF A SARCASTIC GIRL
by Marianne Vina

It's around 8 o'clock at night. I take the phone off the stand, and then I walk upstairs, into my parent's room. The walls are like a peach kind of color, with a king sized bed, a love seat, a dresser, and two night tables around the room. The bathroom is across from the bed, where I am standing.

She is 13 about 5' 6", and is very sarcastic. She has a good smile, one that says I'm nice, but I'm also edgy. She wears blue jeans, a t-shirt most of the time. She has hair that is all shades of blonde, and has blue eyes, with glasses on them.

So then I dial the phone number 713-828-2090. The phone rings and rings until on about the 5th ring someone answers. Just like usually this is how I start my conversation with her: "Hello?"

She then answers saying "Hey."

Then I say "Hey. Can you talk?"

She then says "yeah."

So then what we do out of our regular talk is instead of me going on about some random thing I think up I say, "Hey Christiana I have the recorder right I want to test out if it works. I need to put you on the speaker phone, but I just want to test it out first before we begin."

So then she says "Yeah alright let's try."

So then I put her on the speaker phone, and we test the thing out. It was a silly kind of trial but it did work. So then we start the interview. I ask her some questions. Here are a few of them.

I say "Ok so where were you born?"

She replies "Neptune, New Jersey."

Then I ask another question "And in how many places have you lived."

She then replies "I've lived in 6 places."

I then say 6 just to confirm that's what she said.

So then I ask another "And can you tell us what those places are?"

She replies "Mmm. Let me see. There was New Jersey; umm after I went to New Jersey I went to Marin, Mississippi, and after that I went to some city in California. That's two. And after that I camp in some bunker in a random place in California, I went to Banger in Washington state, and after that I went to Port Orchard, and after that I went to Houston, which is here, and after that I went to Kemah, which is down by Galveston, and after that I went to Houston again. So technically that's seven not six."

She sounded somewhat happy when I asked her that, but also she sounded a bit annoyed. So then we continue the interview. I ask "Ok and how long have you, did you stay in each one of them?"

She replies "I have no idea." She sounds like one of those girls that just forgot something. It was a bit funny.

So I'm kind of a bit surprised so I say ok in a shocked kind of way. And I also laugh, because I know how she is, and that just didn't seem like her.

Then she remembers something and replies "Well actually four years in Washington state total, and then 6 years total in Texas."

So then I ask "Ok. And what is your full legal name?"

She then replies "Umm umm does that include my conformation name or no?"

I say no, because I feel it's not important to the interview.

So then we continue the interview.

She then replies to the question, saying "Well my full legal name is well when I was born was Christiana-Rose Eileen LaCross. But when I had my confirmation name it turned Christiana-Rose Eileen Cecilia LaCross. I put that on there anyway."

I then say ok. Then we start laughing like evil people in some kind of show.

I then say "Because your confirmation name was Cecilia. Right?"

She then says "Yes."

So then we continue with the interview I say "Ok. And what religion are you?" I say that in a kind of sarcastic way, because I already know the answer.

She then replies "Oh my God, Catholic."

I then say "As you can hear, well not a lot of churches do confirmation."

So then we continue, and I say "Ok next question. What are your parent's full legal names?"

She then replies "Are you a spy?"

I say no while laughing, because to her, I think, that I'm asking question so as to get information to some person.

She replies "Oh my gosh, some many questions."

I cough, so as to get some stuff out of my mouth.

She then we continue and she replies "Hmm ok my full dads legal name is Antony Joseph LaCross, and my mother's is Judith Lynn LaCross."

Then another question "What is your mother's maiden name?"

She replies "Habrolac."

Then I say "Next question is what your happiest memory is in the last 5 years?"

She replies "I can't remember."

Then I ask "What about in your life?"

She replies "I can't remember. I told you yesterday but I can't remember what it is now. Uhhh. Grrr. It's confusing."

I then say "So then..."

She interrupts, saying "Wait I'm thinking. I'm thinking."

She then replies "Give me a second. Alright. Uhh I know I know."

I say mmhmm, because it was taking a long time.

She then replies "No I don't know. Anyway wait no. Wait no. Wait. No. Umm. You're confusing me Marianne. Ok I'm confused."

I say then "Ok so then…"

She interrupts, saying "I know I know I know. Umm when my brother said he was coming home on Christmas Eve. And surprised me on Christmas Eve coming home from Abilene."

This continues on for about another 20 or thirty more minutes, I ask more questions, she answers some more. This is just a bit out of our conversation. She is my best friend, and I will always be by here, and the opposite is also the same. We love each other like sisters, and that's just it will always be.

UNTITLED
by Giavanni Walker

That strawberry cheesecake tasted so delicious. Every single scrumptious bite melted in my mouth like ice under the sun. I drifted off into a land of strawberry goodness. My mind focused on what seemed to be the best taste in the world and all of a sudden, everything was ruined. It was the doorbell. Not only was it the doorbell one time, but it was the sound of the doorbell repeatedly. That sound rang in my ears like the music from a horror movie. I reluctantly set down my cheesecake. My grandmother was resting peacefully and I didn't want that horrid sound from the doorbell to wake her. I ran with steps of disturbance and curiosity to find out who was ringing my doorbell so many times. My feet were hitting the floor one after another on the plush carpet in the living room. By the time I opened the front door, all I saw was a man running away.

"Hey!" I shouted. He started running towards me and I didn't know what to expect. I noticed his facial expression before I noticed anything else about him. All I knew was that he was a man. His facial expression told me that he was scared, worried, and anxious. He was jumping around and screaming like he was five years old and all he could say was "My aunt! My aunt!" I ran through my house to get my grandmother, but for some reason my house became an obstacle course because I couldn't force to get myself to her any faster with all the furniture hallways and turns I had to overcome. I woke her up, telling her what happened with the man and she jumped in a pair mix matched shoes and ran outside to investigate. I followed her because I wanted to know what was going on. My heart was beating so quickly that it felt like a hammer trying to burst through my skin.

My grandmother and I followed the man next door. This is when my heart stopped because the only person that lived next door in that house was Miss Louise. My mind went insane. She watched me grow up. She watched my big sisters grow up. She watched my mom grow up! There's no possible way anything could've happened to her. The craziest part about it is that I had just randomly given her a huge hug the day before. I know it sounds sort of weird, but something told me to give her a hug. I don't know what it could've been. I don't know why.

The man showed my grandmother something through the window of Miss Louise's house, but I couldn't see. I just heard my grandmother say, "She's on the floor in front of the front door. We have to find a way to open the garage."

Apparently, the man didn't have a key to the house. I knew they needed more help so I ran across the street to my boyfriend, Michael's house. I told him what was going on and he told his uncle, Terry. Michael and Terry followed me back to Miss Louise's house and helped the man pry the garage open.

All of us went inside the house and through the living room. That's when I realized that I shouldn't have walked any further. Miss Louise lay there, lifeless. Her lips were dark. Her eyes were wide open. Michael's uncle noticed that Miss Louise was trying to get outside because the lock on the front door was twisted halfway. I couldn't believe what I saw. I was 15 years old and I was in the same room as a dead body for the first time aside from funerals. It developed a feeling that felt so surreal. My thought began to get very conceptive and I regretted wanting to know the reason why I gave her a hug the day before. I wish I would've spent more time appreciating the hug than wondering why.

I saw the look on that man's face and he began to cry. My heart shattered into pieces and I ran out of the house with tears falling from my face. Michael followed me. Michael's uncle called paramedics while Michael and I sat on the sidewalk and had a long conversation about death and how everyone has to go through it. We talked about how we only have one life to live and how we should be careful of everything we say and do because once our lives end, there's no turning back. Michael gave me a long hug until paramedics came. They brought a stretcher into the house and put Miss Louise's body on a stretcher and took her away. Michael and I observed everything. The paramedics told us that she had a heart attack and that she had been dead for a few hours. Michael and I felt a sense of disbelief. My grandmother walked over to me.

"Are you alright?" she questioned sincerely.

"Yeah, I guess I'm fine. It's all just so overwhelming." Michael and I were still outside staring at the sunset.

I saw my grandmother go into the house and it wasn't long before I followed her. My mind was so filled that I couldn't focus on anything else except those pleading eyes of Miss Louise. However, I managed to remember that I eating strawberry cheesecake before that entire situation. I took a bite of the cheesecake to clear my mind a little, but this time I enjoyed it more because what happened that day made me realize that I should cherish every simple moment of life (even cheesecake) because no one's life lasts forever.

TAKE THE TIME
by Jasmine Washington

It used to be that I would wake daily to a warm "Good morning" from my grandmother. I would wake up to a dark freezing room, because a nightlight is just one more thing to run the light bill up. The room stayed cold because she kept about two or three fans on at night to support the blowing but not cold air conditioner. I woke because there were always little toes in my face, sweet and sticky breath being blown down my throat, and the smell of lightly golden buttered down and syrupy pancakes were being made. With a nose of a blood hound breakfast was detected. At the time I was old enough to do things on my own, so I would open my eyes and let my nose lead the way to the place it knew best, the kitchen; yet, every time my bare feet were unprepared for the prickly shock of cold tile floor they were about to feel. Rushing through the human icebox I would tenderly bump my grandmother's wide hips as if to politely say, "Hey"; on the way out I would give her a light kiss, her deeply structured cheek against my smoky colored lips.

If I had not gotten up so early, I would have been left with the portion that the smaller children were to have rather than my own portion. If I hadn't got up so early I would miss the opportunity to talk to my "Mo Mo", as referred to by the entire house. Although I know she cared for me it was always hard to get her time and attention, so when we did get her time we took advantage of it. We all often noticed the small things she did for us but at times it seemed that wasn't enough.

After stuffing my face with the delicious food that she prepared I would wake the whole house (at least everyone attending school) and began to get everyone ready. It took about an hour moving around six children including myself frantically here and there about the house. There were cries, screams, and the occasional re-wake. I had little help from the adults in the house but I was the oldest grandchild so I did what everyone called "deal with it". I brushed teeth, combed hair, dressed younger ones, and fought. By the time I was done wrestling one person to put their stinky little shoes on, it was someone else back in bed.

After all my hard work had been done, I would try to find my Mo Mo, hoping that she would be somewhere around so I could get a ride to school, but she wasn't. Getting everyone out the door and down the street to the school was another job but I got it done eventually.

Once the school day had begun it seemed to end quickly, being that I would daydream most of the day. Arriving home to granny, I would come through the door and she would ask, "How was school?" s tiredly, as if it pained her to say it. Angered by the fact that school started a week ago and she just asked about school I was angry. This had been the second time this week I saw her, besides the very first day of school when I woke to her hearty breakfast and kissed her deeply structured cheeks with my smoky colored lips. I wanted her attention bad. Willing to risk a lot, I thought long and hard about something to get her attention. In class I noticed the children who were on their best behavior were praised by the teacher; meaning that they got stickers, toys, and the teacher Ms. Day's attention. That night I acted like the children in the class, on my best behavior, the only difference was I was at home and after a week of discipline at school the rest of the frantic little toes seemed like angels. There were "yes ma'ams" and "no ma'am's" all over the place.

At night; Mo Mo came in and kissed everyone on the forehead. This simple kiss made me feel horrible about the upcoming plan.. By the next morning I became a little demon. The little toes, the adults in the house, and my teacher all noticed but only one said anything, Ms. Days.

"Jasmine, are you okay? You seem a little different today" she said worried.

"Heck yea," I said raising my eyebrows and rolling my eyes. I knew I just messed up. I had a lot of fright but little regret because I wanted attention and this was the only way to receive it. As the whole room got quiet tension built in my body, knowing I was about to get in trouble I closed my eyes tight and hope I got in the very least of trouble; wishing to only get a phone call home. But Ms. Days knew there was more to the story; I went from a sweet "yes ma'am", "no ma'am" girl, to a roll my eyes, pop my neck girl. She picked up the phone and began to talk then gave me "the look" and handed me the phone.

"Hello", I said. "What's wrong", I heard my Mo Mo's voice say. And I began in tears telling her how much I missed and needed her.

That day my grandmother told me some words I have held onto forever. She said, "Although it seems that I'm gone a lot I still love you and care. Whenever I am around I show you and tell you that I care, and the love that I have for you will never fade, not even when I'm dead and gone."

UNSPOKEN FEELINGS
by Brittney Winston

"Everything will be all right baby girl, you will always have me," my mom would tell me every time she looked at me.

My face hold a strong look of sorrow; with my cheeks cherry red, with my eyes hanging low, looking like balloons filled with water just ready to burst. I loved my mother to death, but in the back of my mind I knew that she couldn't fill the position of grandma. Many months had gone by since my grandma's funeral, but in my head it existed just yesterday; hundreds of people in this one small white church, hearing the pain in their voice as they screamed," Why her Lord, why her?"

It seemed impossible for me to have enough strength to go look at her body, but from a far it looked as if she wore a white suit. As I passed by, I tried to break from the smell of death. Throughout the funeral, thoughts roamed around in my mind. I felt as if I was being punished. After the funeral, people kept coming to me trying to console me, but little did they know my feelings stayed the same. The hold time I kept hearing the same ole phase.

"Sorry for your lost, I know she loved you very dearly, she was a great woman," a lady from the church said like everyone else.

"My granny still is a great woman", I replied, "Why everybody just won't leave me alone!"

I tried to run off, trying my best to hide from everyone, but before I could, my other grandma yanked me by my arm.

"I understand that you are very hurt, but that still don't give you the right to be disrespectful", my grandma said.

"But granny, they won't leave me alone."

"They just trying to show that are here for you", she replied.

"But Maw-Maw is still died".

"I understand that, but she is happy now, and it would make her even happier if you start being nice. You have to believe that everything will be alright."

"Yes M'am".

Five years later, at age ten, and in the 5th grade, things became out control. Being a child full of hostility and animosity made things very hard for me. My daily routine consisted of me go to school, come home, and locking myself in my room as I cried myself to sleep. There never seemed to be a day that I didn't have an altercation with someone, or better yet try to. I could remember all the times I visited my principal, Ms. Edwards. She used to smell like old perfume, with her hair down with curls at the bottom, nice suit, and red fingernail polish; I should know because her fingers consistently stayed in my face.

"You come in my office every day of the same ole thing, and I'm tired of it!" she exclaimed.

" Well, I'm tired of hearing the same ole speech from you, just call my parents like you always do so I can get out of here," I rudely replied.

"Just for that you are sitting in this office with me for the rest of the day," she replied back.

I just sat there, in that small office, and the smell of that perfume lingering the room, making me very nauseous. It soon got to a point where she didn't even look at me. After school, I never wanted to go home, because it stayed full of angry people bickering and screaming all the time. It seemed like we could never have a perfect day. Like me, my father didn't take my grandmother's death too well, so he started to drink. At one moment he is so happy, then the next moment he blowing up. I had a lot of fear towards my father that the time, because of the many fights he tired to hurt my oldest brother. Commotion seemed to always appear in the house. I just wanted to believe that a change could come for me and my family, but things stayed the same. Soon, the anger I had turned into depression. I didn't feel I had any one to talk to, so I would hold everything in. If you looked at me you would think that everything was all peachy, but deep inside I knew the really story. I remember the many times I would sit there and just start crying, most of the time I really didn't have a reason.

My depression started to get worse. I didn't believe in smiling, I always had my head down, gained weight, I wasn't very friendly, and just didn't see the point of living. Something in me kept telling me to believe, but that seemed very impossible, until that day we had the biggest altercation in the house ever, finally my mother said its time to get us some help. I was 15 years old, a sophomore in high school, when I went to my first consoling session. It was very weird for me to be there. My consoler was an older Caucasian man; he reminded me of Mr. Rogers from the show "Mr. Roger's Neighborhood". After many months with him, I learned to let things go, the fear I had father my father went away, and I learned how to express myself. He made me realize that I had nothing to deal with my grandma's death; that she did her purpose in life, and now it's time to do mine. I became a stronger person, lost weight, and nothing could take my joy away. I felt like a new person. No more did I lock myself in the room; I started to spend every moment I could with my family because I realized we all had our problem, but the love we shared was greater than all that. I remembered when my mom said I carry my grandma in me everywhere I go, but I started to feel that

I was starting to bring her out. I didn't want people to feel the way I felt by not having in one to talk to, so I tried to be there for them anyway possible. Till this day I think it was my grandma telling me to believe, because for every dark night, there is a day.

BECAUSE IT MATTERS
by Sierra Wood

There are some people who you meet and like immediately. Justin Whyte is one of those people. When he walks into a room he seems to evoke a sense of happiness in people, at least the ones who know him. Actually, he doesn't walk, he bounces. His bounce is like a strut that's so uniquely Justin it looks cool. He is at least 6, 2" with a grizzly like beard and glasses and may be the only grown man in the world who can make wearing a back pack look cool and still be respected. When I met him as a freshman in high school he surprised me by being so kind and I quickly took to him. Most debate mentors made me feel that I wasn't good enough to talk to them. They made it seem like I wasn't worth their presence but, Justin was completely different.. He seemed genuinely interested in me and my debate career as well as the rest of my team. This alone would have made me believe Justin was amazing but soon enough I found out more things about him that just made me like him more. All of those things kept adding up and made me more impressed by him, until one day I crowned Justin my "brother from another mother . . . and father". So, when I was assigned a profile narrative I knew the perfect subject that would embody someone who inspires me would be Justin Whyte.

****

On the day of the interview I was in a terrible mood. My seventh period AP class had just given me another point to add on my list of reasons to drop out of school. I was just trying to make it through the day when I received a text from Justin that read "I'm here". Immediately I felt better. I rushed to the office to wait for my favorite mentor and begin the interview. When Justin finally arrived in the office I led him to my advocacy room, again with Ms. Ayyadhury, who had just failed me the class before. As we walked to advocacy I started to see the effect Justin has on people, at least the ones he knows. All of the HAIS debaters who were roaming the halls stopped with smiles on their face as they joked with Justin, and asked him why he was there. I boasted that I was doing an interview and he needed to come along. Once we got in the room we started conversing like normal. All the while I was trying to figure out how to get to the juicy questions. The questions that would impress him or make him cry; I wanted the interview to be good! My real goal was to find out about Justin the man and not the debater because I only knew about him in the prospects of debate; my knowledge was rather lacking on the personal side. I started with his family.

****

Justin told me that the most important thing in his life is his children, Lucy and Henry, along with his wife of course. At the mention of their names he smiled and told me stories about Lucy talking and playing with Henry. I learned this summer at debate camp how good of a father Justin is and I asked him how he became that way. He answered that it was his father, "I think it was just his attitude towards every single thing that we wanted to do . . .He would tell us we could be anything that we wanted to be, it didn't matter if we wanted to be the president or a garbage man as long as we were doing what we wanted to do. If I could be half as good as he was with us I think we'd be alright." As the interview went on I wondered how anyone could ever be a better father than Justin. He told me about how Henry, his oldest child, was hospitalized as a baby and required open heart surgery. This struck a chord in my heart because my dad was still recovering from his quadruple bypass. I could not imagine an infant going through the surgery. Justin's face darkens a bit and I hear his voice change from joking debate mentor and friend to a concerned and upset father as he relayed the story of Henrys surgery to me. Throughout this conversation nothing surprised me more than what Justin says next. "And that is the reason I got back into debate." A sense of curiosity makes a home in my brain and I could only stutter out a confused "How?" This is when Justin puts his hands together as if to say "this is going to be a long story". He then began telling me the story of how doctors at a world renowned hospital gave his son the wrong medicine and made careless mistakes that could have had dire consequences if they had not been solved. How were they solved? Justin went super dad on Texas Children's Hospital. He used his debate skills to communicate his problems throughout the chain of command until he got all the way up to the C.O.O of Texas Children's. Justin said that without debate he would not have been able to communicate his problems so well or understand exactly what the doctors were explaining to him about Henrys surgery and the mistakes that they made. While Justin told me how important debate skills are, I realized that everything he said would somehow connect back to debate. Later he told me that my hopes to find out about Justin the man not the debater would never be met. It's impossible because Justin cannot separate the two. This makes me realize that no matter what I will always be a debater as well; the activity becomes a part of you that can never be let go. That realization brought Justin to his next point, his mission in life.

****

"What is one thing that you want people to remember about you?" I asked Justin.

"That I wanted to give debate back." Justin replied simply. Justin Whyte has helped give debate back to hundreds of debaters through The Houston Urban Debate League and gives up spending time with his family on a daily basis for debate and teenagers just like me. The last thing that Justin told me before the interview ended was "it matters and what that it is I don't really know but doing what you want to do matters. Making a difference for other people maters . . . All too often that gets pushed to the back. I feel incredibly lucky to do something that I love. Debate matters and helping kids learn the activity so that it helps them in the future matters." I walked out of that interview prepared to work hard again and do my work because Justin gave me a reason to. When kids ask me why I work so hard to get into a good college, or to win a tournament I simply remember what Justin told me and say "because it matters."

A COLD ROOM
by Sierra Wood

"C'mon Mama, it's your turn" I heard my mom say and within two seconds I was out of the waiting room and power-walking through the ICU to room 427. As I entered through room it got colder and all the little hairs on the nape of my neck saluted the change in climate. Even if I were blind I would have known I was walking into a hospital room, there are no other places in the world that can be that silent and so loud at the same time. The beeping of machines connected to my father were chirping in my ear the entire time I visited him, they kept me on my toes, they scared me. I looked down at my father and my emotions swirled, I was happy to see him, worried about his current state, and relieved that he was still alive. When I grabbed my Daddy's hand he knew it was me, he squeezed my hand back and that alone decided that yes I was happy to see him.

I stood beside him holding his hand and smiling while I examined what damage I could see. The first thing everyone noticed was his swollen lips. It looked like he went in for a bypass and ended up getting botched Botox. He had a tube in his throat that was breathing for him and a strap on his chin so he wouldn't swallow his tongue. My poor Daddy looked like a dog in the middle of the summer. The next thing I noticed were the chords running through him and machines and monitors and all sorts of technology I wasn't familiar with. The beeping kept my heart beating faster, it was the drums and my heart was the dancer. Wes explained to my delusional father that he had a bunch of things connected to him so that he wouldn't try and pull them out in his morphine induced confusion. Occasionally my Dad would look around at us and ask questions with his eyes, he couldn't talk with that tube down his throat, so we explained his dilemma as calmly as possible. Mostly we told him we loved him, kissed his hand and got choked up.

Next my Aunt Laurie came to visit, there are only two visitors allowed at a time in ICU so Wes had to leave. My Aunt Laurie and I looked at his scar together when she came in. Stretching from his chest to his belly my dad had a brand new battle scar. It looked like they cut him half which essentially they did. That scar will always be there to remind him to eat right and never smoke again, unless of course he enjoyed having a quadruple bypass. We stood there and held my Dads hands and looked at him for what seemed like hours but, at eight when the nurses kicked us out it still wasn't long enough. My Dad heard the nurses telling us to leave and immediately his expression changed. His blue eyes became a little darer and his eyebrows furrowed in anger; he didn't want to be alone. His hand gripped me tighter; they're rough from all the hard work he's done over the years. Those callused hands have picked me up over the years and comforted me in times of need. So, when he grabbed my hand tighter asking for comfort, asking me to pick him up I couldn't help but tear up.

"Daddy, they're telling me I have to leave. You need to get some rest." I said to him while I caressed his forearm.

He shook his head no in anger.

I quietly kissed his hand, "I love you Daddy, go to sleep, everything's going to be okay, I'll see you tomorrow."

I looked into my Daddy's blue eyes and smiled, he winked at me in return, and that wink was about all I could handle. I hurriedly walked out into the hallway away from my Daddy and tried not to cry.

My Aunt came out into the hall with me and hugged me until I couldn't take it anymore. I cried for my Daddy, I cried out his heart attacks, I cried out his diabetes. I cried for my mom, I cried out her stress, I cried out her worries. I cried for myself, I cried out my fears, I cried out my anxiety. Then, my Aunt and I walked back into the waiting room. My mom stood there but she still had stress, she still had worries. My Dad was in a room behind me, he still had diabetes but no more heart attacks. And, no matter how much I don't want to admit it I still had fears and I still had anxiety but at least, I still have my Daddy.

JOURNEY TO INSPIRATION
by JaNiecé York

It was a Saturday night and the moon crescent was seen from up above. As I made my way towards a white door I opened up to his world. He was sitting there on the couch watching TV, and eating his dinner, smelling the aromas of food lingering closer to my nose causing me to lose my task. Hearing the cricket's chirp and the annoying noises of knifes' and blades rattling from the movie he was watching. I asked myself, "What is inspiration?", and that's when it hit me.

Grey eyes, a smile that will lighten up any bad day, tall, hardworking, personality to make anyone laugh, and a loving man who endures his families' happiness. My inspiration of life is my father. So thrilled to do this interview, I asked questions proudly awaiting the most interesting remarks and comments. From childhood to present day or the love he has for his family and friends. To me, a great man deserves great honor this is why he is my inspiration.

There were many intriguing things about my father, well especially throughout his child years. He was a normal child so as I seen him but my looks were despising. Having toys to my dad was a privilege he looked at it as a way for him to stay in good well beings; it was his opportunity to stay out of trouble from the neighborhood kids. He knew that life was up to him to make his own decisions he knew what was best for him. Making the paths in his life did caused him to be the man he is now my father he played with toys such as "boxes of toy soldiers, cowboys and Indians" to occupy his time, but his past changed my perspective "being young is your chance to find yourself and that is what I did. Most of my mistakes in life was when I did things to prove a point, growing up was all about showing that you weren't a coward and so I did many things out of stupidity. Yes I do regret things but it's all out of learning from your mistakes. I think of how I could have done things differently but then I think WHY, I still question myself. You do things now and I laugh because it's and resemblance of myself and I may say something but you yourself have to learn to do things because you want to not because I ask you to. That's when I realized that I was digging my own hole in life, and on my own path and my life took a turn when I was forced to move to California. My dad said, "I lived in Pacoima, California and I attended San Fernando Senior High. I was misbehaving and my mom made me stay with my dad", that's when I knew that it was up to me to pick my own destiny, "I remember being in a bet, and having to mess with a bull in a patch not too far from my house and it chased me in my neighbors yard and just when I thought I was about to get hit my moms; friend in the house next door grabbed me just in time". Commonly a child has pets it could be a cat, dog, or a hamster but my father had two rabbits, "I use to put them on a leash and take them for walks I treated them as if they were my dogs, people looked at me as if I was crazy but I thought of it as a joke". His life is full of humor he had many stories to tell me to take me away from many troublesome times too.

As a boy my dad had many struggles as a child. Being a single boy he had to grow up in the streets, causing him to fight because the neighborhood kids would pick on him everyday. It was his choice to stay out of gangs, "I was a leader not a follower" I remembered as a child before going to bed I would sit in his lap, give him a kiss on the cheek, and those words would echo from his mouth, but mostly "You are willing to do anything that you are willing to run after" those words will forever stick to my heart. Having conflicts and troubles with his parents being separated he recalls an incident where he was so upset till he threw rocks at every window at his high school and went to jail. Learning that in life things happen but the way you handle them is up to you. Revealing that all you can do is take life one day at a time and everything will fall in its place. Then I asked the one question that impacted me the most. How would you like to be remembered? Responded by saying "I like to be remembered by all the good things I did in life and how good I was to my family".

When ending my interview I learned a lot about my father's personality but also the values of life. "Yesterday is the past, tomorrow is the future, but today is a gift that why it is called a present", he continued by saying that "life will go on no matter if you're not ready to go on with it" which stated that he conquered life because he didn't let things get the best of him, this makes him the successful man he is today. That's why he's my inspiration to continue my journey to my future.

PROMOTING RELIGIOUS TOLERANCE AND UNDERSTANDING AMONG THE YOUTH
by Roberto Daniel Conlon

Religious intolerance has claimed the lives of many throughout our history and it continues to do so. It has also separated us by stereotypical prejudice. All religions and denominations have been chastised or looked down upon at some point. Many people who are ignorant of other religions will usually believe negative stereotypes against the religion that their religion is in conflict with. A few examples of religious intolerance are: believing that all Roman Catholic priests are pedophiles and sexual predators and that all Muslims are terrorists. Obviously, this is not completely true. Yes, there has been a history of pedophilia among the clergy in the Roman Catholic Church, but these clergymen do not represent the Catholic Church. There have been Muslim terrorists, but most terrorists are not Muslim. Only few Muslim religious radicals have gone and performed Jihad. After the September 11th Terrorist Attacks many innocent Muslims were persecuted and non-Muslims became fearful of the growing religion.

Religious tolerance begins in the home and at the school. I would propose that religious tolerance be inculcated at a very early age. This could be introduced through children and young adults being exposed to diverse religious beliefs. For example in this country all public schools and many private schools are secular. I would recommend that members of a religious community visit the schools and expose the students to their faith by not seeking conversion, but by promoting education. Although, the religious holidays at any institution are based on the Christian calendar and their days of religious observance, students from many religions celebrate their individual religious holidays. Education regarding minority religious holidays will promote understanding and tolerance. Students will finally understand the significance of Rosh Hashanah and Yom Kippur, Diwali, and Eid Al-Fitr and Eid Al-Adha. Students will now have a basis for an understanding of tolerance.

Exposing young people to faiths other than the one that they practice (or not) will at least give the students on opportunity to learn and lose their fear. This communication opens the door for dialogue at the school and hopefully in their homes. I firmly believe that knowledge, communication, and dialogue are the key to religious tolerance. Acceptance of our diverse views and belief systems pave the way for tolerance and respect.

UNTITLED
by Brittany Gilbert

Pain is undying
Pain is a feeling I didn't know had a game to it
So I closed my eyes and they played a lullaby so I could sleep to it
Ridicule and betrayal is how I feel when it comes to it
I take this pain, her pain, and his pain and multiply it
What they feel, Is what I feel
I wish that I could look Pain in the eye and pray that God give it mercy
I am her, I am she
I am one who is free to be as God made me
Be who my Grandmother prayed for me to be
Pain is sweat that I released
So that I may cool off only for it to come and heat me up again
We let down instead of pick up
So when I fall I expect pain
Because, I knew it had a game
So that meant
Someone had to push me into the ocean where I
I slipped and fell and I was in shock
But did he care or did she care
ENOUGH
To come and save, me I know I felt myself giving up to easily
I will swim to pain and come to you creep up behind to just to say
I am not nor' will I ever be beneath you
Pain is a game that I pushed under a vocabulary word called shame
Because, you want me to be embarrassed by you
Now I see who can be truthful and say, I apologize because I caused
your pain

HELLO GOODBYE
by Rynique Lucas

I'm mad without reason

In the light

I darken the area

In a heat wave I freeze

In the snow I burn

I tarnish the pure with my bitter anger

I'm an extra puzzle piece

In the moonlight I come alive

I then begin my evil workings

I'm a fifth degree hurricane

In my path of destruction

are parts of myself

I begin to lie, cry, even die

I lose sight, sanity, and all thoughts of humanity

I crush and kill hopes, dreams, and spirit

In my absence life is restored

plants grow green

and pain is an imaginary thing

So now I ask "Why do I exist?"

I live though not alive

so what if I die

By Nicole Owen

JUST GIVE UP
by Rynique Lucas

As you get closer

I run away

you call my name

I pick up the pace

until I'm far away.

You try to get through

I fight it

you pry gently

I build more walls

until you finally quit.

stop trying

never do it again

Don't hold my hand

I don't deserve it.

NO MORE
by Rynique Lucas

I disintegrate slowly in your shadow,

but you never see.

Its great how amazing

you turned out to be.

Every day it seems to get worse,

one more scar,

that I say doesn't hurt.

Just a second is all it takes

to end the suffering,

no more pain.

I will fall and forever lie

in that spot 'til the end of time.

Today is the day,

I have reached the end,

the day I will say my last words.

I'm sorry it has to end this way,

but before I go and never awake,

I will say your name,

and see your face.

THE MEETING
by Akhirah Muhammad

"Help! Someone please help me!" The screams stopped me from my monthly routine. The shrieks got closer and louder and then all together, just stopped. I worried about these cries I heard, so I laid my knife down and slid the bucket to the side. I walked out into the alley behind the meat market, not knowing what I would find. I walked into a kidnapping in progress and began wishing I had kept the knife.

"Hey, let her go!" I said to the two men trying to whisk a little girl away. She couldn't be more than 9 years old. I wrestled with the two men for what seemed like forever until they finally gave up and drove away. Her lifeless body lay on the ground. I wondered if she was still alive and how far they had gotten with her, but then she jerked upright with an ear piercing yell.

"Stay away from me! Please just leave me alone," she cried. I could see the fear in her eyes as she tried to get away from me. I walked closer trying to reassure her. "Hey, I'm not going to hurt you. You're safe now; you can trust me, I promise me." Coming from my mouth, this was shocking seeing as my occupation wasn't kidnapping little girls but it wasn't far from it. She seemed to believe me and took my hand so she could get up.

"I'm going to call an ambulance, please do not run off anywhere." I told her. I had no idea what they had knocked her out with and if it could affect her. I wanted to make sure she was fine. "Hi, this little girl was almost just kidnapped behind the meat market. I stopped it and she's fine, but can you send an ambulance out here to check her out." I sounded calm but in reality, I knew that if an ambulance came out here for a little girl, then so would the cops and this, I could not risk. I had to move my work to another spot before the cops showed up. "Sir, an ambulance is on the way. Please stand by."

As I started walking back towards the meat market, I could hear her foot steps behind me. "Stay here. An ambulance is on the way and they'll call your parents." I could not have her follow me. What if she was spooked by the blood and thought I was a monster of some sort. "Where are you going? Shouldn't you wait with me for the ambulance, just in case the cops show up?" I could see this wasn't going to be easy.

"Look, I have some work to complete. And no, I do not have to wait with you. Just scream if something else happens and beat on the door when the ambulance gets here." I have to move my work and fast, so walk again towards the door with a faster pace."

THE CONFESSIONS
by Akhirah Muhammad

I knew I only had about 5 minutes, before I would have company, as I walked to the knife and bucket. I rinsed the knife in the sink. All the blood spread onto my hands and into the sink turning pink and then disappearing down the drain. I placed the knife with the rest of my knife collection. Grabbed the bucket of body pieces and walked to the basement.

It seemed so light when only hours it seemed heavy in my arms. The howls came back to my mind and sent a sudden shiver down my spine. I now had millions of questions. One for certain was: How can I take lives and turn around just as easily and save one? How could I find pleasure in these ladies shrieks, begging, and pain, but find it horrid to kidnap or harm a child. I guess I'm not that big of a monster after all.

When I came back up stairs the little girl was standing there waiting for me. I was horrified not because she was in here but because she was standing in blood. A pool of it was cased under her feet. This could be a major problem especially if the police asked for all her belongings at the hospital. My heart raced as if I were being chased by lions.

"Didn't I say to wait outside," I screamed at her. I did not mean for it to come out that way but it did, I was furious.

"I'm sorry I just got bored waiting. My mom says I have a short attention span," She said sincerely. This little girl just would not go away. "So you got a name Ms. Short attention span," I asked as nicely as possible

"Katie Johnson, but my mom calls me Kate. What's your name?" She's a very inquisitive little girl but I guess that's a fair question. "The name's Jack Davis. Let's get that animal blood off your shoes before the ambulance gets here." Again the blood fell on my hands and into the sink as a pink color surrounds the sink and goes down the drain, washing away who I really am.

"Why was there so much blood," she asked being inquisitive again. It seemed as if she knew but wanted to make sure she was right. I guess she knows you can blood more than one way. "I'm a meat cleaver. What that means is I cut up animals so they can be out in markets so that people like you can eat." I led her back outside and by then the ambulance was on its way up the alley.

"Did you call about the little girl." One of the paramedics asked as he stepped out of the struck.

"Yeah that was me and this is the little girl. The guys that were trying to take her knocked her out with something. I just wanted to be sure she was fine." I really I was being honest. It is not like I went looking for the medics to come to my place of business.

I watched them drive away but little did I know this little girl would be the cause of my world being flipped upside down.

TIMED WRITING
By Angus Niziol

Stumbling into the hallway the host nonchalantly commanded me in the imperative objective to run forward into the cellar to grab the round challises that contained the sweet nectar that us teens have been craving once the holiday began, these challises, also known as "soda cans" were the height of the objective at the party.

The party, it was a cold Canadian evening when we had been given the invitation to the great mansion that my companion, Evan, has resided in. With no stalling we had gotten our coats and instantly ran forward in our adventure to his grand palace.

After arriving and exhausting our current supply of very underwhelming "sodas". We were ordered to find or search for more in the cellar, stumbling and turning over every cabinet, desk and shelve. We were soon fully about to abandon our mission, until however, at the last moment we had discovered them and ever sooner began running.

Hurling and throwing all of our new found treasure into our shirts and about to run back to the crowd, we had realized our mistake. As the last of the "cans" were taken, there was one missing, hurling toward the indefinite fate of crashing into the ever so fragile glass pane known as a "TV" as the screen cracked and shattered, we had known we were forsaken.

To this date we still hold the lie about not knowing what happened to the TV that night, unknown of how or why to tell him.

SCRIPT OF BIOGRAPHY
By Angus Niziol

[Narration]: As the cold and bitter winds of the blizzard blew through the flat and seemingly endless streets of Regina, Saskatchewan, we had finally begun to ponder the consequences of our actions. It was a bitter cold afternoon in the dead of the Canadian winter, one could assume only a crazy person would go for a walk to the park at this time of the year, either that, or hormone driven twelve year olds, and hormone driven we were, with the afternoon sun gleaming against the snow you could see two distinct humanoid figures, all black and walking with a great amount of strain on their bodies, you just barely make out that they were having a conversation.

"I can't believe you of all people would want to drag both of us out on a mile long walk in meter deep snow, all for what? A snow fort, I honestly can't comprehend your logic behind wanting to build a snow for in the minus forty weather with a blizzard in progress." My cousin told me.

"Hey! When you live in Houston any opportunity you see snow you got to make the most of it, besides I had thought you were used to this stuff, or are you just not manly to survive out here?" I said hysterically.

"Oh you think I'm not manly enough?!?" He said.

"You better think again, were building this snow fort and I guarantee that you will wimp out before I do." He said proudly.

My reverse psychology had been presented well enough to keep my cousin from forfeiting his "manliness", regardless however, as the snow continued to downfall up towards our chests we gradually began to change our minds as our journey soon grinded to a stop. "I hope you know at this pace we won't reach the park till tomorrow right? Are you sure you don't want to just go back, it should be about supper, and I don't know about you but an hour out in this blizzard sure makes me hungry." He said anxiously.

"Man, that sounds great but we have to be close by now, we should just get to the park then we can trek on back, sound good?" I said with doubt.

"I can't believe this," He retorted.

As our courage and stupidity began to dwindle we began to find some sort of alternative way to get back to the house without retracing our steps, no such option was found, we would have to take that hour long walk right back to the house were we could dump our failure and shame onto the dinner plate.

"Yeah you are right, this was a bad idea." I said trying not to sound guilty.

"I told you, over and over again, you didn't listen and now look were we are, almost trapped in the snow." He said discouragingly.

"Wait, Wait, Wait, what is that over there? Is that who I think it is" I said in disbelief. "It can't be... IT'S ERIC!!!!" He said ecstatically.

As we had discovered our cousins' car we ran with great joy thrusting our bodies through the car door to our ever so loving heat. We let off so much relief as our cousin was nonchalantly shaking his head in disgust while listening to his I-pod.

"It sure is great that we found you; it might have been an hour or two before we got back." I said gratefully.

"Yeah, this moron over here decided to drag me over to the park in an attempt to build a snow fort, all of this for a dang snow fort." He said sarcastically.

"It doesn't matter, both you guys are imbeciles, they made us come out here and look for you guys so you would come back and we could eat our supper, you guys owe me absolutely big time you have no idea." Eric had said. "Yeah, yeah, yeah." We both said in alliteration. "Just get us home." I said relieved.

IS WAR NECESSARY?
By Neelam Damani

My mouth is dry.
Shawls and prayers drape my shoulders
A dirty plastic bag in my hand with bits of colored paper
I stand, arched.

Hours arch over me through windows and shattered glass and bits of
steel.
Taking steep steps into a rotting room,
I stand there, alone. With my mouth dry.
Explosions of bright garlands
lie alongside the open grenades,
lie there weak and helpless.

Through broken glass in the broken frame,
I look up at the portrait of the bearded man,
laughing at the ruins of a rich man's wife.
His reddish-brown tweed coat
and golden spectacles
laugh at this woman fighting a dragon
   A woman
        frightened of bombs
      frightened of the bloodbath that they have brought
        frightened for her husband, her father, her mother.

Into one hundred pieces

of shattered bits

    here was once a radio, a stove, a stool, a bed?

Now, all gone.

Except a pink swing on which I now sit

with my dirty plastic bag and bits of colored paper.

Falling apart before the dragon has come.

Worn, but waiting for that hour of prayer,

Ignoring the sounds of tanks, explosions, and machine-gun fire

    c R a c k L i n G

        inside my head.

Waiting for that hour, I bow to the ground.

(Found poem inspired by a newspaper article in The New York Times)

THE SILENT COMPANION
By Neelam Damani

The clock struck nine.
After weeks of practice looking in mirrors,
And standing like a statue,
She felt ugly as an ogre.
Looks were important and she didn't want to quarrel.
Her tears fell like diamonds,
Each more precious than the last,
Gathering in the creases of her table napkin.
She wiped them softly, carefully, gently
Lest they disappear into the dark night.

The prediction still seemed dangerous,
Like a birdsong getting loud and desolate.

She peeked out of her bedroom window and saw the hordes
Gathered in the castle courtyard.
A tiny man with bushy eyebrows.
A nun. A choirmaster. A maid. A king.
The music hummed from their lips
Like the smooth curve of a porcelain cup,
Drawing her with ropes invisible out of her bedroom door.

She licked her lips.
Petrified. Terrified. Wishing it would soon be all over.
She was a pretty girl,
With a heart-shaped face.

"The daughter of the wind," they'd said.
They curtsied and bowed
As she walked down the steps.
Their hearts racing
  But hers, sinking
    Sinking through the floor as she reached the last step.
But ready like a statue,
Ready to be their savior.

As she waited for the ray of light
To kiss the castle gates,
She heard a soft whisper, like dew falling
Like the wind calling out to her,
  "You're not alone, Azra. You're not alone."

The gates opened that very moment
And the crowds separated like clouds after a rainstorm
Giving way to her.
She leaned for a moment on her golden sword,
Seeing what she had missed all this time:
  Faces soaked, hearts uplifted by prayer.
  By hope.
  By love.
  For her, who was destined to go on.

Raising her head, she looked deep into their hearts.
And took the first step
          then another
               then another
And without looking back, she marched on,
With her head held high.

TOKEN... BLACK GUY...
By Jeremy Jjemba

Multicultural,

Multilingual,

I am able to switch from, Oli' otya Ssebo, to hello Sir.

From hakunah matata, to no worries.

From yes ma'am, to no madam, and from y'all, to you all,

From writing books in good English,

to speaking fluent Luganda,

to ordering room service in Kiswahili.

To flying first class, my pilot is Dutch and my attendant is French,

I land and depart on the same hour.

No matter the weather.

 I am international.

"American I am, none can deny, American but hyphenated."

As American to Ugandans, as Ugandan to Americans, my voice of
accents, my charming dark face. With a strong image like I am Idi Amin.

 Viewed by some as exotic, by some as inferior, I am different I mean.

Different from you!

It is the same everywhere I go. I am who they stare at, as they wonder
where I come from.

Eyes! Keep falling on my face.

 As I came looking for my grain, back in December, some looked at me,
as you would a stranger, picking me apart: some shouted. "You might

speak fluent Luganda and you might have been born in Uganda but you
are not Ugandan like us!"

African! Ugandan! American! The picture is yours to paint.

I dine with extraordinary figures

 A son of ordinary figures, a token of luck,

Same with one head, one tail, flipping back and forth between the

fringes of both worlds by masking discomfort of loneliness with a royal

customary bright smile across my bright dark face

Eradicating the slanders that with a pen in my hand, I'm acting white!

DISCOVERING AFRICA
By Jeremy Jjemba

Imagine a valley with an antique sky

Night, moonlight and sparkling stars

The stars form the skylines that make up the land of the Zulus

And the Maasai People,

The thin dessert sand makes up the beautiful form of the Kalahari

The home of the Basarwa People,

Africa, like a mother You birthed us,

Your treasures bring the world a splendid spark

Over Your wide untouched land

Over Your undiscovered sunsets and shadows

Over Your desert mines of Kush

Over Your shadows of historic pyramids

Africa,

You lack nothing except glorification

Africa,

My mind ponders to Your innumerable and boundless wonders.

Africa, like a mother You birthed us.

My words alone cannot express the beauty and the amazement that

Mamma Africa brings to the world, my words alone cannot exaggerate

the beauty of this place.

THE PEN AND THE PAPER
By Jeremy Jjemba

One morning,

The paper said to the pen:

"We are married!"

"As in husband and wife?" asked the pen.

"Yes," said the paper.

Then, the paper asked the pen:

"What kind of words will you write on me?"

"I will write whatever you like!"

"Agreed," said the paper!

So off they went writing about whatever they liked:

As I sat here alone

Writing miserable, idealistic and wishful love poems.

PARANOID STYLE OF THE ROSENBERG TRIAL
By Peter Kurtz

In November of 1964, Richard Hofstadter published an essay called "The Paranoid Style in American Politics." This essay exposed the strategic tactics used in American politics to heighten public nationalism and conformity towards a conservative ideology. During the 1950's, this "paranoid style" dominated American politics at the height of the Cold War, and subsequently condemned the Rosenbergs to a sentence of death. This paper reopens certain aspects of the Rosenberg Trial in an attempt to expose the paranoid tactics used during the Rosenberg case.

Richard Hofstadter's essay identifies three major elements that spawn the paranoid style of American politics. The paranoid style is best defined as the creation of a national paranoia through complex conspiracies that threaten society's way of life in which there exist a natural struggle between good versus evil for the advancement a nation's political agenda. These three elements of conspiracy, national security, and good versus evil, serve as the platform for the paranoid style. In the Rosenberg Trial, Judge Irving R. Kaufman and the prosecuting attorney (Irving Saypol & Edward Kuntz) utilized all three of these elements to heighten national security and set an example out of any whom dared treasonous espionage.

The Rosenberg Trial began on March 6th, 1951. The federal government had charged Morton Sobell, Julius Rosenberg, and Ethel Rosenberg of the treasonous actions of delivering information,

333

documents, sketches and other materials to Russia, which posed a vital threat to the national security of the United States. The prosecution of the trial immediately began to formulate an image of an interwoven web of conspiracy that produced a monumental threat to the United States. The prosecution asserted that Julius Rosenberg worked as the "center of a wheel...reaching out like tentacles of an octopus" in a masterminded conspiracy that funneled information through a hierarchical spy network that led to Stalin himself.[1] They provided the court with a diagram that simplified the Rosenberg conspiracy, indicating that the Rosenbergs had recruited a number of spies including David Greenglass and Sobell, to funnel information and provide it to a Soviet Spy named Aleksandr Feklisov. Aleksandr Feklisov in turn provided the information to a man named Yakovlev, whom fed the information to Zarubin, and ultimately Stalin.[2] The prosecution presented David Greenglass' testimony as proof that the Rosenbergs had recruited David Greenglass (the Rosenberg's brother-in-law), and several others (including Morton Sobell), to retrieve information directly from the Manhattan Project in Los Alamos, New Mexico. David Greenglass also provided some sketches of highly explosive lens molds, and a descriptive account of secret sign that he had reportedly used to provide a Soviet Spy named Harry Gold with the information.[3] Greenglass claimed that Julius Rosenberg had cut a Jell-O box into two pieces and had given one piece to Harry Gold and one to himself. At the meeting, Greenglass and Gold supposedly matched the two pieces together to serve as the secret sign.

---

[1] "The Summation of Irving Saypol for the Prosecution." Professor Doug Linder's online "Famous Trial" archive at http://www.law.umkc.edu/faculty/projects/ftrials/ftrials.htm. Nov. 27, 2003.
[2] See enclosed diagram of Soviet Spy Ring.
[3] See enclosed diagram of David Greenglass' sketches.

Harry Gold testified that he had received a piece of paper and a piece of a Jell-O box from Yakovlev with instructions to meet a David Greenglass and to say, "I come from Julius."[4]

The prosecution furthered their argument of a conspiracy against Rosenberg through the testimonies of Elizabeth Bentley and Max Elitcher. A friend of Morton Sobell and Julius Rosenberg, Max Elitcher testified that he witnessed Sobell pass secret information to Julius Rosenberg during a trip to Catherine Slip in New York. Although he denied having any involvement, he admitted that Julius Rosenberg had tried to recruit him as a Soviet Spy.[5] Elizabeth Bentley, known as the "Red Spy Queen", testified that she had purportedly talked with Julius Rosenberg over the phone to provide information to a Soviet Spy named Jacob Golos, until Golos' death in 1943. Bentley testified that she had lived with Golos and worked as a Soviet Spy until she voluntarily turned herself into the FBI in 1945. She had made herself a celebrity by publishing an autobiography entitled, *Inside the Russian Spy Organization.*[6] Upon cross-examination, she contradicted herself by stating that she did not live with Mr. Golos, after previously stating that her and Mr. Golos had lived together in "what was a communist conception of marriage."[7] This contradiction seemed to have no impact upon the case. Accompanied by Greenglass' sketches, these witnesses provided ample evidence for the prosecution to draw a believable picture

---

[4] "Testimony of Harry Gold, Witness for the Prosecution." Doug Linder's Archive. http://www.law.umkc.edu/faculty/projects/ftrials/ftrials.htm. Nov. 27, 2003.

[5] "Max Elitcher Biography." Ibid.
[6] "Elizabeth Bentley, Biography." Ibid.
[7] "Elizabeth Bentley, Witness for the Prosecution." ibid.

of a complex conspiracy against the United States perpetrated by Julius Rosenberg.

In their case, the prosecution emphasized the precariousness of the Rosenberg's actions in their conspiracy. They had Walter Koski, an employee of the Atomic Energy Commission as a physical chemist with expertise in the area of high-explosive lenses, testify about the importance of the information provided by David Greenglass' sketches.[8] He testified that Greenglass' drawings contained top-secret information that portrayed the principle idea behind explosive lens molds, and that Greenglass could have gained access to this information.[9]

The contemporary atmosphere of the 1950's also supported a national paranoia of Communism and Atomic war. Just four years prior, the Chinese revolution occurred, and the world found Communism spreading like wildfire. The United States had developed the Atomic bomb in 1945, and witnessed Soviet Russia's development of the Atomic bomb by Sept. 23, 1949 with Truman's statement of the Soviet's capabilities. The United States felt a desperate need to stop the spread of Communism, and protect their national security by weeding out treasonous individuals. This threat of national security is easily portrayed through Judge Kaufman's statement upon sentencing the Rosenbergs:

I believe your conduct in putting into the hands of the Russians the A-bomb years before our best scientists predicted Russia would perfect the bomb has already caused, in my opinion, the Communist aggression in Korea, with the resultant casualties exceeding 50,000 and who knows but that millions more innocent people may pay the price of your

---

[8] "Walter Koski, Witness for the Prosecution." ibid.

[9] ibid.

treason. Indeed, by your betrayal you undoubtedly have altered the course of history to the disadvantage of our country.[10]

This statement also reflects why the Rosenbergs were easily portrayed as the "evil" of an American nation. They threatened "millions of innocent people" and undoubtedly produced a "disadvantage" to the United States, causing the "aggression" of at least one war. i.e. The Korean War.

The prosecution went a step further in their summation of the trial by explaining that the Rosenbergs were not evil simply because they were Communists, but because Communism taught an "ideology which teaches worship and devotion to the Soviet Union over our own government."[11] No one could support Democracy and Communism at the same time because Communism demanded full loyalty. This full loyalty to Communism converted individuals into an evil state of mind, which had consumed the Rosenbergs, and made them a threat to national security by fulfilling their ideological duty to Soviet Russia through an interwoven web of conspiracy.

The question about whether the Rosenbergs were guilty or not, is irrelevant. Louis Nizer states that this question "can only result in a wrong answer. The question should be "Do you think there was sufficient evidence warranting the jury, which sized up the witnesses, to decide that the Rosenbergs were guilty?""[12] When combining the radical anticommunist sentiment of the 1950's, with the already powerful paranoid style of American politics, the prosecution found the Trial of the Rosenbergs easy to wield. The Rosenbergs were not on trial, but what they symbolized, and / or the paranoia they created, was the center

---

[10]"Judge Kaufman's statement upon sentencing the Rosenbergs." Ibid.
[11] "The Summation of Irving Saypol for the Prosecution." Ibid.
[12] Louis Nizer. The Implosion Conspiracy. Doubleday & Company. Garden City, New York. 1973. Page 9.

focus of the prosecution. President Eisenhower stated; "The executions [of the Rosenbergs] were necessary to refute the known convictions of Communist leaders all over the world that free governments…are notoriously weak and fearful and that consequently subservient and other kinds of activity can be conducted against them with no real fear of dire punishment."[13] This explains why Morton Sobell received only 30 years imprisonment for claiming the 5th amendment versus the death sentence. He never admitted that he was a Communist. Klaus Fuchs, the real Soviet Spy that funneled atomic information to Russia, only received nine years imprisonment. David Greenglass received only fifteen years, and his wife gained immunity even though she admitted her direct involvement within the conspiracy plot. But Ruth Greenglass wanted money which represented Capitalism, not Communism.

Both Julius and Ethel Rosenberg adamantly denied having involvement with any of the federal charges placed against them. However, they did admit that they believed in Communism, and formerly socialized with other Communists. That was all the prosecution needed to wield the paranoid style of conspiracy, national security, and a fight between "good" and "evil", into an effective piece of political propaganda that condemned the Rosenbergs to a sentence of death.

---

[13] "The Rosenberg Trial."
www.geocities.com/Athens/Acropolis/6660/Essay45.htm Nov. 26, 2003.

I AM
By Chad Meyer

I am

oblivious

    to

        caste . . .

Many of us who are strong
were born of weak circumstance,
While
the weak have taken their seat
in lofty places,
    how lowly shall they f

        a

        l

       l

And **I shall,**
    Rise up
        among them
Quickly . . . .

LIGHT RAY
By Ralph Polley

"I had a feeling once about Mathematics - that I saw it all. Depth beyond depth was revealed to me - the Byss and Abyss. I saw - as one might see the transit of Venus or even the Lord Mayor's Show - a quantity passing through infinity and changing its sign from plus to minus. I saw exactly why it happened and why the tergiversation was inevitable - but it was after dinner and I let it go." – Winston Churchill

I remember one afternoon, when I was about 19. I was sitting on a couch in a small basement apartment in Albany, N.Y., trying to imagine the pathway of a ray of light. It seemed to me that the universe, though very large (very, very large) must in some sense be finite. I imagined that, if you chose a particular point though which the light ray had passed, that ray, if unhindered, would eventually pass through that same point again. Like a satellite orbiting the earth passes through a point again and again. I did not think the path was curved, but rather that straight lines in some sense eventually "come back". But then, as I watched the pictures in my mind, I realized the light ray would be passing through the point each time from a different direction. And, what is more, it would pass through that point from every possible direction before once again passing through it in the direction it first did so. I then realized that this meant that *there was only one path through the universe*. Next I realized that this path must necessarily skip between points that are, from our point of view, unconnected. That is, before

340

returning to the original point in the original direction, the unhindered ray would pass through every point *in every order*. And, when it passed near to us through seemingly unconnected points, it was what we normally call very, very far away in space and time. Somehow, all this implied to me that every point is right next to (whatever that means) every other point. In my mind I say the universe collapse to a single point.

This was, to me, only a charming fantasy until many years later, when I read about the Michelson-Morley experiment that attempted to measure the speed of the earth with respect to the ether. The experiment failed of course; there is no ether. But as a result of the experiment, George FitzGerald deduced that distances were foreshortened from the point of view of an object that was moving very quickly. That is, a distance that would appear to me to be a million miles, would look shorter to a person traveling at, say, 200,000 m/s. If d_0 is the distance as it appears to me and d_1 is the foreshortened distance, then the exact formula for calculating that foreshortened distance, is $d_1 = d_0 \sqrt{1 - \dfrac{v^2}{c^2}}$. (We can take the speed of light to be about 300,000 kilometers per second.)

To make this clearer, let's consider two observers, Burt and Ernie. Imagine that Burt is floating in space; there are no objects nearby and Burt feels himself to be still. Burt sees a star that is, form his point of view, 1,000,000,000 kilometers away. Just then, Ernie comes speeding by, traveling in the direction of the star at 299,000 kilometers per second (very fast - $99\dfrac{2}{3}$ % of the speed of light). Now, for the purposes of the formula above, $d_0 = 1,000,000,000$ and $v = 299,000$ kilometers per second. From Ernie's point of view, the distance to the star is found by

$$d_1 = 1,000,000,000 \sqrt{1 - \frac{299,000^2}{300,000^2}} \approx 81,581,588.34 \text{ kilometers.}$$

This is less than 10% of the distance as it appears to Burt.

Now consider what happens if Ernie speeds up to the speed of light. The distance to the star becomes

$$d_1 = 1,000,000,000 \sqrt{1 - \frac{300,000^2}{300,000^2}} = 0. \text{ No matter how great a}$$

distance is considered, Ernie, from his own point of view will arrive there instantly. For Ernie, there is no distance; the universe has no size. Ernie has no size either.

Shortly afterward, Hendrick Lorentz discovered that the mass of an object is similarly affected. If Ernie's mass when floating next to Burt is 1 kilogram, then his mass, m, as he flies by Burt at 299,000 kilometers per second is $m = \dfrac{1 \ kilo}{\sqrt{1 - \dfrac{299,000^2}{300,000^2}}} \approx 12.26$ kilograms. Ernie is more

than 12 times more massive.

If Ernie increases his speed until he approaches the speed of light, the second term inside the radical in the denominator approaches one, the denominator approaches zero, and Ernie's mass grows without limit. If Ernie flies by at the speed of light, he (and the whole universe from his point of view) has no size and he has infinite mass.

As in my vision, the universe has collapsed to a single point, the speeding object has merged with it and become both infinitely small and infinitely massive.

Afterward: I understand that I have not sufficiently studied the concepts presented here to say that this is true. It is likely that I have badly misapplied the equations involved. I only offer this essay as a possible example of the confluence of intuition and science.

PAULINE
By Robbi Russey-Goldstein

"When will we be there Mom?"

"Just about twenty more miles before we pass the Border Patrol and then ten more minutes past that."

"It's so far out here, I can't see anything."

"I know, it's very dark. Perhaps you could occupy yourself looking for the Marfa Lights."

"But I thought Paw-Paw said that was crock of shhhh--."

Laughing, "Yeah he did."

"So why would I even bother? Can't you just drive faster?"

"Calm down and play me some good songs from your IPod."

The drive is always long going out to the ranch, especially when you only plan to be there a few days, but seeing family was always worth it. This trip, especially, turned out to be one of those unforgettable experiences.

They past the Border Patrol, and as promised the entrance to the ranch was only ten minutes after that. Grandmamma had placed bright colored plastic poinsettias on either side of the entrance, so you wouldn't miss it in the dark. Driving late at night was always an adventure, seeing that you had to watch out for animals on the road. Although it created stressful driving conditions, they arrived safely, just the same.

"Finally," Steven sighed, when they pulled up to the gate of the main house.

Denise honked the horn just once as they exited the car. Dusting off the recent "car food" crumbs from their jeans; each grabbed their garbage and bags, and walked towards the house as Grandmamma came out to the screened porch.

Denise yelled from the car, "Hey Mom, we're here and I'm ready for my cocktail. Are we staying in the back house or the game room this time?" Waiting for a response and shivering, "Brrrrr, it's cold out here."

"Good to see you too! I changed the sheets in the guest house, so you guys go there. I got a few new cats recently too, so you shouldn't have any problems with mice crawling through the walls at this point. Dinner's ready, so snap it up." She greeted Steven, giving him a hug and a laugh, because of his rolling eyes, as he muttered, "Mice. . . . Great," under his breath.

They dropped their things on a king-sized bed in the guest house, went into kitchen of the main house through the screened in porch, and grabbed a cold beer and Gatorade out of the outdoor refrigerator. The house had the smell of hot oil and jalapenos, which Grandmamma used to make the salsa she sold on the weekend at the flea market. Dinner was a mixture of vermicelli, beans, and meat, served on tostadas with grated cheese, onions, and tomatoes.

Paw-paw had aged and although he did the work of a thirty-five year old man, he paid for it at night when he finally sat down to rest. However, he got up happily to make a cocktail for visitors.

"Whatcha havin'?" he said as he crossed the room to greet the kids.

"I'll have a hug, a kiss, and a vodka soda with lime please."

"Coming right up. How was the drive? Did you see any trouble when you passed the by the Border Patrol?"

"Nah, smooth sailing, but my ass hurts."

"This should help," he said as he handed her a drink, along with a smile and a wink before he went back to his comfortable chair to watch whatever game was on.

Grandmamma was Paw-paw's second wife. His first wife, Pauline, had died a few years earlier. She'd been in a wheelchair and on a breathing machine because of lung cancer, caused by heavy smoking her whole life.

The "men" watched sports for a bit, while Grandmamma and Denise caught up, cleaned up, and finished their drinks. After a beer and a vodka soda, Denise was ready for bed and went back out to the back house to clean up and get ready. The next day was a big day for Steven, so they needed to go to bed early. He was planning on joining Paw-paw at the neighboring Ranch to deal with some cattle and the local veterinarian. So it was time to hit the hay.

"Let's go, Steven. Come brush your teeth."

"Coming Mom," he replied, a little too exhausted to argue.

The back house was just one room, attached to a spacious bath and laundry room, but the appliances were small and they had a history of issues with the shower leaking. None of this really mattered, because it was the ranch after all, and who would complain about a shower, when you were surrounded by such an amazing view and wildlife? There was a small television with a VHS player attached, so after settling in, Steven popped in "The Lion King" to fall asleep to.

Falling asleep wasn't a difficult chore this night. It had been a long day and both of them were exhausted from the ride.

Long after the television had been turned off and not knowing what time it was, Denise was awaked by the feeling of someone sitting on the bed next to her. Steven was asleep on the other side of the bed, so she just brushed it off, thinking she was dreaming. She'd left her dog home on this trip, but the sensation reminded her of Harley putting his legs up beside her on the bed, attempting to wake her for his early morning walk. But he wasn't there. Having spent these seconds reaching for consciousness, another sensation overcame her. It felt, not only like pressure sitting on the side of the bed, but now, she felt pressure on her whole being, as if a child had laid down atop of her, wanting comfort and attention. She held her breath until the pressure was gone. Breathing out heavily, she remained completely still, trying to figure out if she were awake or asleep and just dreaming. This frightened her and she remained frozen. Near her, she heard a loud snoring. This was no ordinary snore, this was a snore you hear recorded into cartoons where the blanket rises and falls to the breath. Steven had never made this kind of sound before, so pronounced and loud, as if it weren't real. Denise reached around with her right arm and touched Steven. The snoring stopped, but the weight she'd felt before returned. This time only for a split second before the side of the bed tilted down again, and suddenly the room was still and quiet. The rest of the night passed peacefully, and although stressed from the experience, Denise decided it was her imagination and was able to sleep.

The next morning in the kitchen, she decided to address the subject of last night with her mother. Grandmamma had a history of episodes in her life where she felt a little clairvoyant, like a sixth sense, so Denise wasn't afraid to broach the subject to her.

"Hey Mom, something weird happened last night out in the little house."

"Yeah?"

"It felt as if someone else was in there, but I know nobody was."

"What do you mean it 'felt like' someone was in there?"

"Well, if felt like someone sat down on me when I was sleeping, and then there was this noise."

"I don't know."

"Was the room ever used for anyone other than guests; maybe a ranch hand or something?"

"Not that I'm aware of, but I have to admit I've gotten an odd feeling a few times when I was out there at night doing the laundry--like you said, It felt like someone was there."

A shiver ran down Denise's spine as she considered the idea of a ghost being in the room where she was sleeping. Not really wanting to know more at this time, she dropped the issue and just passed it off as a fluke, or possibly a dream and knowing that she would be sleeping there again the next night, and possibly many more nights in the years to follow, was reason enough to get over any fear that the situation might have been planted in her mind.

Paw-paw and Steven left for the ranch shortly afterwards, and the day began.

Later that night after the men returned from ranching and dinner was finished off and cleaned up Denise decided (in weak moment) to ask the question to Paw-Paw.

"Has that back house been used for anything other than family and friends in the past?"

"Hell, that room has only been used for grandkids in the past twenty years."

"And before that?"

"Well, before that, Pauline used to sleep out there in order to not wake up the whole house with her snoring. Why do you ask?"

Denise stood frozen, unable to breathe for just a moment, processing the details of the previous night of restless sleep. She began to open her mouth to reply when Grandmamma and Steven walked through the kitchen door, and Denise, unable to wait another second said, "Steven, what do you think about sleeping next to the fireplace tonight out in the game room?"

"I don't care where we sleep Mom, but will I be able to watch a movie out there tonight?"

Grandmamma responded, "Of course, the TV and VCR work just fine out there too." She looked around the room at Paw-paw, who had his nose deep in the newspaper and back to Denise, without saying another word. She just seemed to know.

Turns out, the only place to sleep from that day forward was the game room, on the dusty sofas, with a fire going that needed to be stoked all night, but it was better than the alternative.

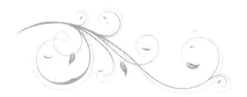

TABLE 43
By Robbi Russey-Goldstein

The table was ready at six o'clock sharp. Each of the eight guests found an invitation in their cabins when they arrived on the ship. They were asked to be prompt because there would be another seating for dinner at eight. They were assigned to table number 43.

As guests entered the dining room, they were treated to an elaborate buffet display. The color, curve and content of the tables gave the impression there could possibly be royalty on board. The ice carvings represented the glamour of old Hollywood, with an Oscar standing high in the middle. Attendants lined the entryway, waiting to serve the invited guests. The table linens and decorations additionally reflected the style and excitement of old Hollywood. The guests, arriving on time, made their way to the tables.

Evie and Teresa were the first to arrive. Together, the two grandmothers waited eagerly to see who else would show up. Evie had a small frame, but a large voice that sounded as if she had been a smoker for most of her life, but there was no evidence of cigarettes about her. Her hair was white and cut into a short bob and she wore oversized, thick glasses, which made her blue eyes appear larger than they were. Teresa was nearly the opposite of Evie. She was plump, dark headed, brown eyed and taller of the two. They had been friends for quite some time and sported heavy Boston accents. Both had buried husbands and babysat grandchildren, but now was their time to explore the world and have an adventure.

The youngest of the couples at the table were new parents, Sarah and Brad. Their first child was born that spring, just months after winning the Grand Prize in a raffle drawing that put them on this celebrity cruise. Sarah was a thin, blonde girl in her twenties and her husband Brad was tall and handsome, with curly brown hair (which was thinning). This was their first cruise and their first trip overseas.

Two seats remained empty that week, which led to conversational speculation about who was missing, but the elderly and very handsome couple, Margaret and George attended dinner each night as assigned. The two were very quiet and dined in silence on the first night while the other four engaged in getting to know one another, telling stories of their nights in London, which is where their adventures began, or so they thought.

Brad and Sarah were given tickets to "Les Miserables" at the Palace Theater, then dinner afterwards at Wheeler's. While there, they met a couple that would be joining them on the cruise, but this was no ordinary couple, this was a celebrity couple, Beverly Garland and her husband. All of the older guests at the table were impressed with the story because they remembered seeing Beverly Garland in the movie "Topper" and most recently she was the step-mother on the television series "My Three Sons."

Evie and Teresa reported that Esther Williams was supposed to be on board as well.

Margaret seemed impressed with the stories, but didn't add her own.

It wasn't until dessert that Sarah actually looked over and took notice of George's hands. His thumbs seemed all mangled and out of joint. He had managed to get through dinner without anyone noticing and as quickly as Sarah looked away, he picked up his napkin and held his hands under the table. Brad noticed too and was afraid of Sarah letting the curiosity get the best of her, so he prepared his foot to gently kick her under the table, but then she only asked, "What brings the two of you on this cruise?" Margaret and George looked at one another as if wondering, "Who is going to answer?" but after a moment of silence, Margaret jumped in.

"We are celebrating our 50th wedding anniversary, and our children gave us this cruise as a gift."

"Wow" said the rest of the table in unison. Brad and Sarah looked at one another, each thinking, "I hope we last that long." Sarah asked the obvious next question, "How many children do you have?" To which George responded in a proud and fatherly tone,

"Eight."

The table was in awe. This made it official; Margaret and George had won the "wow" factor and the utmost respect at the table from the first night on.

As the week progressed, stories of celebrity sightings got more interesting. Esther Williams was indeed on board. When Brad and Sarah arrived at their designated boat for the disaster drill, Ms. Williams' named was called over and over, until someone finally answered, "She'll just swim to shore." to which the crowd roared with laughter. Margaret and George ran into Fred MacMurry, who played the father in the series "My Three Sons" and starred in many old Hollywood films and was best known for his role in "Double Indemnity."

As the week progressed and table number forty-three became increasingly relaxed and they were all enjoying a good time. After many fits of laughter, Sarah decided to ask George and Margaret another personal question. She had hoped that they would mention some detail of why his hands were all mangled, but it just never seemed to come up.

On the fourth night together with this group, Sarah just couldn't wait any longer and blurted out (before Brad could load his "under the table" weapon) "George, may I ask about your hands?"

He responded, "What about them?" The table sat silent, unable to detect sarcasm in his tone, but then, he chuckled first and they all sighed and relaxed in relief.

"Well, this happened to me during the war. I didn't want to fight in the war, and was already overseas in Panama when things went sour. Margaret and I had just been married, when that thing broke out, so we decided to live up in the mountains where we thought we wouldn't be bothered."

The table remained completely silent as he went on.

"Eventually, after years of living in peace, in a grass hut village on the mountain, somebody turned me in. As an American, they imprisoned and tortured me, leaving me hanging by my thumbs behind my back for hours each day, trying to get me to tell them were other American soldiers were hiding. Obviously, I couldn't tell them anything, but there were other American soldiers there and they didn't speak either. To me, I wasn't one of them, but to the Panamanians, I was.

Wide eyed, Sarah continued, "For how long did they do this to you?

"I suffered four months of this daily torture and interrogation, the Americans eventually came in and got most of us out. I was a lucky one, I survived."

It was Brad who asked the next question, "What happened to you Margaret?"

"Well, I was pregnant with our third child when they took George, but the ladies in the village where I was hiding helped me with that. All three of my children at that time had been born on the ground inside a grass hut, up in the mountains."

Teresa jumped in, "You should write a book. I know I would love to read that story. What an incredible story." Evie nodded in agreement.

Margaret laughed at this moment, saying, "He did write a book. We have boxes and boxes of copies at home, but we ran out of money and they were never bound."

"Can we all have one?" Brad asked, with great anticipation..

"I'll be happy to mail you an unbound copy when we get home."

"That would be amazing. Please, please, please send us a copy." begged Sarah.

For the rest of the week, table forty-three engaged in relaxed conversation. George and Margaret shared more stories about their children and grandchildren. Sarah and Brad hypothesized about the size and scope of their own projected family, and Teresa and Evie just drank and laughed and cracked inside jokes at one another, to which everyone laughed because they were such a jolly twosome.

Soon the cruise was over, but the relationships built around table forty-three were not.

Months later the book came in the mail. George kept his word and sent everyone a copy of it unbound. Sarah sent a heartfelt Thank You note back to him.

The next winter, Brad was scheduled on a business trip to Boston, so Sarah planned to go with him in order to visit Teresa and Evie, which turned out to be just as entertaining and interesting as their days on the cruise.

After several years went by, Teresa sent a letter that Evie had gotten sick and peacefully passed away with her family surrounding her. Sarah realized when this happened, that no one had heard another word from George and Martha, so she wrote them another letter, asking how they were and announcing the birth of her newest of three sons.

A few weeks went by when a letter arrived in the mail from one of George and Martha's daughters. It read;

Dear Sarah,

Your letter arrived at my parent's house a couple of weeks ago, and I am sorry that I am just getting around to responding. My family and I are aware that you met our parents on the Celebrity Cruise we sent them on for their 50th Wedding Anniversary. They told many hilarious stories about the two of you, as well as the other two ladies at the dinner table you shared. As you probably know, our family is huge, so I feel compelled to congratulate you on your growing family and it is with great joy that I send blessings your way. However, it is with great sadness that I report the following events Mom and Dad were on their way to our family reunion last September. It was the 23rd year that we managed to plan our reunion when everyone would be available. This is a miracle in itself considering the obstacles. Dad called us before they left the house, to be sure we knew when to expect them, so when they didn't arrive in a reasonable amount of time, we began to worry and called 911. They didn't immediately know of any accidents on the roads and they assured us that the weather was not a hindrance. This answer did not soothe our nerves one bit, so we set out on the road ourselves. After about thirty minutes of nail-biting, we happened upon an ambulance and fire truck attending to our parent's car, which was pressed up against a tree off the side of the road and another car against it. Our parents were both killed on impact. I'm sure you can imagine the shock we must have all felt. The driver of the car that hit them was a drunk driver, who was also killed on impact. He had crossed the median and ran head on into their car. This past year has obviously been a very hard time for us all, but when we receive letters like yours, telling us how our parents touched your lives, we are filled with pride. Considering the beautiful, long-life together, that they shared with all of us (including the two of you), in addition to what they survived when we were so young, we can sincerely say they lived a great life. Thank you for your kind letter and sharing some moments of your lives with our parents. Our family wishes the best for yours.

Sincerely,

Caroline.

Sarah realized that Caroline was right, they had all shared moments of their lives with one another, precious moments worth remembering and celebrating. The lessons she learned from the experience were numerous. Mostly, to live life to the fullest, because you never know if you'll ever have another chance to enjoy the world around you. Margaret and George did not die in vain; they died with love and left their stories for others to tell. Table forty-three had strengthened the bonds of those around it, and left each one with memories of hilarious shenanigans, fits of laughter and stories of inspiration and great courage. She wondered who the others were that had received such a life enriching invitation to dine at six, at Table 43.

Made in the USA
Charleston, SC
17 May 2012